Fighting Words

INDIVIDUALS, COMMUNITIES, AND LIBERTIES OF SPEECH

Kent Greenawalt

PRINCETON UNIVERSITY PRESS

PRINCETON, NEW JERSEY

Copyright © 1995 by Princeton University Press
Published by Princeton University Press, 41 William Street,
Princeton, New Jersey 08540
In the United Kingdom: Princeton University Press,
Chichester, West Sussex

Library of Congress Cataloging-in-Publication Data

Greenawalt, Kent, 1936–
Fighting words : individuals, communities, and
liberties of speech / Kent Greenawalt
p. cm.
Includes bibliographical references and index.
ISBN 0-691-03638-1 (alk. paper)
1. Freedom of speech—United States. 2. Freedom of speech.
I. Title.
KF4772.G738 1995
342.73′0853—dc20 94-42501
[347.302853] CIP

This book has been composed in Adobe Sabon

Princeton University Press books are printed
on acid-free paper and meet the guidelines
for permanence and durability of the Committee
on Production Guidelines for Book Longevity
of the Council on Library Resources

Printed in the United States of America

1 3 5 7 9 10 8 6 4 2

To
Bill and Peggy
Ann and Bill
Kim and Bonnie
—A Community of Family

———————————

CONTENTS

PREFACE

THIS BOOK builds on four lectures about freedom of speech: "Insults and Epithets: Are They Protected Speech?" an Edward J. Bloustein Lecture at Rutgers School of Law, published in 42 Rutgers Law Review 287 (1990); "O'er the Land of the Free: Flag Burning as Speech," a Melville B. Nimmer Memorial Lecture at the University of California, Los Angeles, Law School, published in 37 University of California at Los Angeles Law Review 925 (1990); "Free Speech in the United States and Canada," presented at a conference at Duke University on constitutional law in Canada and the United States, published in 55 Law and Contemporary Problems 5 (1992); and "First Amendment Liberties: Individuals and Communities," a University Lecture at Columbia University and then a Frank B. Strong Lecture at Ohio State University Law School, previously unpublished.

Each lecture was self-contained. "Insults and Epithets" dealt with the perplexing problem of abusive speech. "O'er the Land of the Free" concentrated heavily on a single controversial decision of the United States Supreme Court upholding a constitutional right to burn the American flag. The discussion of free speech in the United States and Canada in the third lecture was heavily descriptive, providing an overview of how the two countries deal with similar problems. The final talk, "First Amendment Liberties," considered how the broader debate in political philosophy between communitarians and liberals might bear on sound adjudication under the First Amendment, including the major problem of free exercise of religion.

Although the lectures diverged substantially in focus, their content overlapped. "Hate speech" figured significantly in three of them. The theme of individuals and communities figured in the background of the first three lectures, receiving only occasional explicit mention, but was emphasized in the final lecture. Certain crucial subjects, including obscenity and sexual harassment, were not covered in depth in any of the lectures.

When Malcolm DeBevoise and Princeton University Press invited me to turn the lectures into this book, we agreed that something more than a simple reprinting would be desirable. Aided by the penetrating and perceptive comments of Frederick Schauer and Steven H. Shiffrin, two distinguished free speech scholars, we decided that I should eliminate unnecessary overlap, expand the content of some lectures, add material on obscenity, workplace harassment, and campus speech codes, and draw connections between the lectures.

In the book that has emerged, approximately half the material is now being published for the first time. With the conclusion, there are eight chapters. The first chapter is introductory, explaining the major themes of the book and sketching some fundamental ideas of free speech theory. The second chapter presents the basic approaches to free speech in the United States and Canada. I have added some ideas about how differences between the countries and their constitutional systems help to explain variations in judicial approaches and results. Material from my original lecture on Canada and the United States that directly concerns the specific topics of the following five chapters has been reserved for those chapters. This material provides a comparative dimension for some, though not all, of the subjects of the book. Chapter 3 discusses flag burning. Chapter 4 addresses abusive speech, particularly hate speech directed along lines of race, gender, religion, and ethnicity. Chapter 5 treats two narrower issues about abusive speech: campus speech codes and harassment in the workplace. Chapter 6 considers the legal status of obscenity. Chapter 7 tackles fundamental questions about how far courts resolving issues of free speech (and the free exercise of religion) should consider individuals or communities.

Differences in texture from the original lectures remain. Some chapters pay close attention to details of legal doctrine and argument, others address wider themes, portraying principles of constitutional law and suggesting how they might develop, but not providing extensive analysis of particular judicial opinions. The variations among chapters show that the book remains partly a collection of closely related lectures, not the unified manuscript I would write from scratch. Nevertheless, these variations have a positive virtue; they remind the reader how various stages and levels of analysis are important. Broad theory is not a substitute for careful understanding of particular legal problems and doctrines; and narrow doctrinal approaches risk sterility if they are not informed by broader understandings.

Many people have helped with the ideas in this book. The faculty and students of Rutgers, the University of California, Los Angeles, and Ohio State raised interesting and challenging questions after the lectures there. The highpoint of the Columbia lecture, before a general university audience, was my failure to grasp a question put by my son Sasha; but conversations at home with him, Robert, and Andrei aided in clarifying my thoughts. The lecture at Duke was part of a conference of Canadian and American judges and lawyers, including most members of the Canadian Supreme Court. That occasion did much to spark my interest in free speech jurisprudence "north of the border." I presented the lecture on individuals and communities to faculty groups at Fordham and the University of Virginia, and the flag burning lecture to a similar group at New York University (where I was visiting). I discussed a number of the lectures at faculty lunches at Columbia. In early 1994, I gave two chapters for a workshop at McGill University. On each occasion, I received highly insightful criticism. I also benefitted greatly from conversations in a Seminar on Free Expression and Communitarian Values I taught at Columbia this past spring. Mark Barenberg, Vincent Blasi, Stephen Macedo, Elaine Pagels, and Peter Strauss read parts of the manuscript and offered detailed and very valuable comments.

I have already mentioned the readers' reports of Frederick Schauer and Steven Shriffin. They were indispensable to my conception of how the pieces of analysis might fit together, and have helped greatly to shape this book.

For two of the lectures, Michael Dowdle provided excellent research assistance and criticism (during the year I spent at New York University Law School). Shauna Van Praagh, then an Associate-in-Law at Columbia, made me aware of recent Canadian decisions, educated me about important features of Canadian law and practice, and provided perceptive criticisms of a draft of that lecture. Diane Virzera and Kenneth Ward, through their research efforts, helped me to understand feminist thought and civic republicanism for the lecture on individuals and communities. Laura Brill read part of the manuscript, making clarifying editorial suggestions and correcting many of the notes. Galina Krasilovsky very carefully reviewed the text, quotations, and citation form; she caught numerous errors and proposed alterations that made the text clearer and more readable. She also drafted the index.

Alessandra Bocco of Princeton University Press made considerable improvements in the manuscript with her copyediting, which was done quickly and in a way that was fully respectful of my aims with the manuscript. In many places she came up with a more felicitous phrasing or raised questions that compelled me to be clearer. I also have her to thank for my title. Without Malcolm DeBevoise's strong initial encouragement, I would not have undertaken this book.

Sally Wrigley, my secretary, has, as always, managed a succession of drafts with humor and spirit; she has been aided, at times, by members of the Columbia Law School Faculty Secretariat under Rasma Mednis.

My summers have been largely free for work, thanks to the generosity of Columbia Law School alumni (1989–1994); The Mildred and George Drapkin Faculty Research Fund (1990); The Stephen Friedman Fund (1991); and the Class of 1932 Law Research/Writing Fund (1993). I am grateful to The University Center for Human Values at Princeton for providing a very congenial setting for my final review of the book.

Citation form in this book is an amalgam of legal and academic styles. Full citations are given the first time any source appears in a chapter. When an article is cited for the full article, citation is generally to the first page alone.

Fighting Words

———————————————

Chapter One

INTRODUCTION: FREE SPEECH THEMES

THE CENTRAL SUBJECT of this book is freedom of speech, including freedom of the press. I address this subject in light of related themes: (1) the underlying reasons for having free speech; (2) the kinds of communication to which these reasons apply; (3) the significance of constitutional texts for the determination of free speech cases and the development of judicial doctrines; (4) the importance of a country's legal traditions and broader culture; (5) the degree of deference courts do (and should) give legislatures and executives when they face free speech problems; and (6) the extent to which legislatures and courts should focus on justice toward individuals or the health of communities.

No one doubts that freedom of speech and of the press is a cornerstone of liberal democracy. No one doubts that Canada and the United States are liberal democracies. Observing how these countries treat freedom of speech tells us much about relationships between citizens and government, relationships among citizens, and relationships between branches of government.

REASONS FOR FREE SPEECH

Freedom of speech and of the press rests on the belief that special reasons exist for liberty of expression.[1] Justifications strong enough for the government to restrict other activities may not be sufficient to restrict speech. The special reasons for free speech connect powerfully to underlying premises of liberal democracy. Some reasons are consequential, looking to positive effects of liberty; others are nonconsequential, claiming that independent of consequences restriction denies a right or constitutes an injustice.

The most familiar consequentialist justification for free speech, found in John Milton's *Areopagitica*, John Stuart Mill's *On Liberty*, and the eloquent Supreme Court opinions of Oliver Wendell Holmes and Louis Brandeis, is that liberty of expression contributes to the discovery of truth. In essence, the claim is that if people are exposed over a period of time to various assertions, they are likely to sort out which are more nearly true. Accompanying this cautious optimism about the human capacity to discern what is true is a strong skepticism that governments deciding which assertions to suppress will do a good job of protecting truth.

The truth discovery justification has attracted its share of challenges in recent decades, but none of the attacks undermines its basic premises. Even if many of the presently fashionable doubts about the "objectivity of truth" are well grounded, it does not follow that every claim is as good as every other. Within some compass, factual statements about depletion of the ozone layer and soldiers raping women in Bosnia are more and less accurate. What about assertions of value? Even if extreme relativism about values were warranted, discourse could nevertheless assess the coherence of claims about value and help clarify what cultures and individuals do value.

The worry that pervasive inequality in a "free" marketplace of ideas impairs the emergence of truth is more troubling than skepticism about truth itself. This worry is central for proposals to equalize opportunities for communication, but it hardly supports outright suppression of speech by the government.

The most serious concern about the truth discovery justification for speech is that people believe whatever views are already dominant or fit their irrational needs. Here two comments are in order. First, the question is not whether free individuals are paradigms of rationality while sifting claims of truth; the question is whether truth will prosper better in freedom than under government dictation. Individuals may be untrustworthy in their evaluations; but governments deciding what people may hear and see may be even more suspect. Second, any serious consideration of how individual propensities for delusion compare with government tendencies to abuse a power to suppress speech must address different domains: people may evaluate propositions of mathematics with more detachment than proposals for health care. Any claim that the government is more to be trusted than a regime of free discussion must explain why that is likely for the domain in question. All in all, the truth discovery reason remains an important justification for freedom of speech, although we need to recognize that many factors besides government suppression may deflect people's understanding.

One kind of truth that speech can reveal is abuse of authority, especially government authority. This particular justification for free expression had special significance for the founding generation. When the wrongs of those in power are publicly exposed by the press, as in the Watergate scandal, others can respond accordingly. Officials who are aware that their behavior may be exposed to public scrutiny will be less inclined to yield to the temptations of corruption.

Freedom of speech can contribute to the accommodation of interests. The resolution of many social problems requires not the discovery of "true principles" but the adjustment of competing interests and desires. Free communication allows people to indicate their wishes, and thus makes appropriate decisions more likely; it also teaches a tolerance of differences. Since failures of accommodation and tolerance often generate conflict, liberty of speech (despite its divisive side) can help achieve social stability.

Freedom of thought and expression promote individual autonomy, involving considered freedom of choice. At least in liberal democracies, autonomy is regarded as intrinsically valuable as well as the basis for people developing a lifestyle that is more fulfilling than they could achieve by simply conforming to standards set by others. Communication is a prerequisite for autonomy. It is also a crucial way for people to relate to each other, an indispensable outlet for emotional feelings, and a vital aspect of the growth of one's character and ideas.

Arguments from liberal democracy figure importantly in modern defenses of free speech. These arguments largely involve the reasons I have already discussed as they apply to political discourse and decisions, and to the participation of people in the political process. Liberal democracy rests finally on the choices of citizens; they and their representatives can grasp significant truths and understand how interests may be accommodated if speech is free. The government's own view of truth is especially to be distrusted in the political domain, because officials want to stay in office and promote their own political agendas.

Certain nonconsequentialist reasons that relate to liberal democratic conceptions of government also support free speech. One important idea is that the government should have limited powers and that most speech lies within a private domain. Much speech is within a private domain because it concerns matters, such as aesthetics and religion, that are, to oversimplify, not the government's business. Other speech, say about racial inequality, relates to dangers that are a proper concern of the government; but, even here, the speech may seem "private" because it is too remote from harms that might justify government interference. A second idea is that, regardless of whether free speech actually *promotes* autonomy and rational decision, granting liberty of speech may itself *constitute* a recognition of people, both speakers and listeners, as autonomous and rational. A third idea is that free speech for all may constitute public recognition that people have dignity and are equal.

Neither the nonconsequentialist nor consequentialist justifications yield clear principles by which one can easily decide when suppression of speech is unacceptable. These perspectives provide a set of considerations regarding the government's relations to citizens that indicate which kinds of interferences with speech are most troubling. The perspectives also provide reasons that count, sometimes forcefully, in favor of freedom.

KINDS OF COMMUNICATIONS REACHED BY REASONS FOR FREE SPEECH

What communications do the reasons for free speech cover?[2] Liberal democracies have a great need for free discourse about public affairs, but the reasons for liberty of speech are much broader, extending to all subjects of human concern. They clearly cover general statements of fact, such as "rapid inflation causes social instability," and particular statements of fact, such as "Serbians shelled Sarajevo yesterday." They also cover general and particular assertions of value: "love is the greatest good" and "you should not lie to your friend about your grades."[3] The reasons for free speech also cover stories, works of art, and outbursts of feeling whose aim is to express and illuminate by means other than explicit statements of fact or value.

The reasons for free speech hardly apply to some sorts of communication. Consider two people agreeing to commit a crime. Their words of agreement dominantly represent commitments to action, not assertions of facts or values or expressions of feeling. Their words *change* the normative environment the two people inhabit, creating new obligations and claims. The communications are what I call *situation-altering*; they are much more "action" than "expression." It should come as little surprise that the punishment of ordinary criminal conspiracies has rarely been thought to raise problems of free speech. Orders or commands, offers of agreement, and invitations, such as "just try to hit me," are similar to agreements in their situation-altering character. These also change the normative environment. So do what I call *manipulative threats* and *offers*. Suppose Gertrude tells Claude, "I will give you two thousand dollars if you hire my sister"; or, "I will tell everyone about your time in prison if you do not hire her." Gertrude's comment in either instance sets in play consequences that would not otherwise occur; they are situation-altering.

Hovering between situation-altering utterances and ordinary assertions of fact and value are what I call *weak imperatives*. These weak imperatives are requests and encouragements that do not sharply alter the listener's normative environment, as does a command. If Gertrude says to her distant acquaintance, "Please hire Joseph," or "Beat him up," her immediate aim is to produce action, but she has not created new rights or new obligations, or new consequences of Claude's behavior. Weak imperatives often indicate feelings and reflect beliefs about values and facts, and they cannot always be disentangled from expressions about these matters. Weak imperatives are covered by the reasons for free speech to a greater degree than situation-altering utterances, but they may be prohibited more often than assertions of fact and value.

The chapters that follow raise substantial questions about how particular communications fit into this rough categorization. I discuss how courts have responded to problems and offer some arguments for variant approaches.

CONSTITUTIONAL TEXTS

In the United States and Canada, as well as within most other liberal democracies and under some international treaties, constitutional documents provide protection of free speech and free press. A constitution binds all branches of the government, and courts typically review compliance by the legislative and executive branches. Since courts must construe constitutional language to decide if a provision has been violated, the language itself can matter. The constitutional text may affect both the subsidiary doctrines with which courts approach specific cases and the results of those cases, a significant point when one looks at decisions of the Supreme Courts of the United States and Canada.

LEGAL TRADITIONS AND BROADER CULTURES

The ways in which courts, and legislatures, approach free speech problems are influenced by legal traditions and broader cultures. Does a country have a tradition of an independent and active judiciary? Are constitutional rights long established or relatively novel? How have subjects like libel, now understood to raise free speech concerns, been treated in the past? These aspects of legal tradition may influence present approaches as much as the specific language of constitutions.

Wider cultural characteristics are also important. Is the country one in which cultural history is accorded great significance? Is the practicing philosophy of the country highly individualistic or does it emphasize the place of persons within communities? Variations along these lines may help to explain why the Canadian constitutional language differs as it does from that of the United States Constitution, and why the Canadian Supreme Court has reached different conclusions about some vital issues.

Judicial Deference to Political Branches and Subdivisions

A crucial aspect of most constitutional cases is how much deference a court should give to the legislative or executive branches. The constitution limits what those branches are supposed to do, but when a case arises that challenges legislative or executive action, judges must decide how much weight to accord the judgment of members of that branch that they have behaved within constitutional boundaries. In favor of judicial deference is the notion that the will of the majority, best represented by legislative or executive decision, should be fulfilled unless it clearly violates the constitution. An argument against deference is that a constitution limiting governmental powers establishes that principles of public government are not simply democratic in the sense of allowing final determinations by the majority. Limits on what legislatures and executives may do should be given full effect. That argument is bolstered by the claim that courts are much better able to assess constitutionality than the political branches. In actuality, the degree to which an action of another branch reflects a judgment about constitutionality varies greatly. A legislature may deliberate carefully about that issue, or be cavalier. As often happens in search and seizure cases, if what is challenged is the behavior of an individual police officer that is not supported by legislative or executive regulation, the officer's judgment about constitutionality hardly represents the public. Two subissues about deference, thus, are how much attention a court should give to the actual degree of deliberation of another branch and how far the representative quality of the institution or person whose action is challenged should matter.

In federal systems, including both the United States and Canada, questions of deference are complicated by the relationship between central and provincial (or state) governments. Courts must ask themselves how far limits in a federal constitution should be interpreted to restrict the latitude of regional governments.

Within any country practices of deference are, of course, only one aspect of legal tradition, but they are crucial enough to warrant this separate mention. Insofar as my analysis of cases leads to recommendations about what courts should do, I am implicitly making judgments about the appropriate degree of deference.

Individuals and Communities

One major theme of the book, the primary subject of chapter 7, is how free speech principles concern individuals and communities. Any country's dominant culture will place more or less emphasis on individuals or communities, and this will affect the kind of latitude the political branches and courts will afford to speech. I go beyond descriptive generalizations, and ask, concentrating on the United States, how individuals and communities should be regarded in adjudication of particular free speech cases.

Much of chapter 7 is taken up with showing the complexity of the apparently straightforward dichotomy between individuals and communities, but a few preliminary observations may help. The typical target of those who emphasize community is a supposedly liberal notion that individuals are abstract units who in their essential being are separate from the communities to which they belong. When the critique of this liberal abstract individualism is carried to adjudication, the claim is that the Supreme Court has reflected this vision in its decisions of cases and development of doctrine.

Some complexities of analysis arise because leading liberal theorists do not actually adopt the view often ascribed to them. Liberal theory is rich enough to recognize the centrality of communities for human life; thus, genuine disagreements between thoughtful liberals and communitarians are much more subtle than any simple-minded account would propose. When thoughtful versions of competing points of view are applied to constitutional issues, differences are less stark than some rigid division of communitarian and individualist theories might suggest. Of course, courts, and perhaps much of the public, may conceivably have swallowed an "abstract individualism" that few political philosophers defend, in which case some "individualist" decisions might be challenged both by communitarians and by liberals who have a sense of community.

On the communitarian side, some very different approaches lie in uneasy relation to each other. At least four lines of division emerge: between conservative and radical communitarians; between those who emphasize the national community and those who emphasize local communities; between those who focus on the political community and those who focus on other communities; and between those who value communities for their own sake and those who value their nurturing of individuals. A conservative is likely to look at past practices as defining the communities worth defending; a radical has a more constructive ideal of community that involves critical judgment toward past practices. Someone who emphasizes the national community may look with favor on restrictions of smaller communities that will be objectionable to someone who thinks the vital communities are local. Some communitarians hold up an ideal of an overarching political community; others emphasize the importance of communities that are not congruent with units of government. Finally, some communitarians talk as if communities have intrinsic value of their own; others emphasize their necessity for the flourishing of individuals. These differences play out in various approaches to free speech issues.

A final, difficult distinction is between true communitarianism and other reasons to sustain actions of the political branches. Imagine a Supreme Court justice who is a conservative, national, political communitarian. Such a justice is likely to regard the actions of Congress as a reflection of the national community and an indication of what is best for that community. Imagine another justice who believes in abstract individualism, or who has no reflective opinion on whether an individualist or communitarian philosophy is sound, but who believes, based on original constitutional intent, that judges should give great deference to the political branches. These two justices might vote similarly in almost all cases, but I consider only the former to be a true communitarian.

These abstractions are developed in the chapters that follow, and especially in the penultimate chapter, where they take on more complexity. That chapter, as well as the entire book, illustrate the difficulties of deciding just how much attention should be paid by courts to individuals and communities in free speech cases.

Chapter Two

GENERAL PRINCIPLES OF FREE SPEECH ADJUDICATION IN THE UNITED STATES AND CANADA

CANADA and the United States are neighbors with much in common, including liberal democratic governments with a commitment to freedom of speech. Yet their constitutional and judicial histories, the language of their free speech clauses in context, their free speech doctrines, and, for some issues, the results of cases differ significantly. These differences reflect yet deeper aspects of culture.

This chapter compares judicial approaches to free speech in the two countries. I concentrate primarily on the kinds of speech mainly engaged in by extreme dissenters and outsiders. This speech is itself a major concern of constitutional protection, and it has proved the source of central constitutional doctrines.[1] I begin with brief comments about constitutional language and general approaches, and then discuss subversive speech and other speech that encourages criminal acts, symbolic speech, and public demonstrations. (Chapters 4 and 6 deal with "hate speech" and obscenity or pornography, two areas in which the Canadian Supreme Court has moved in a direction that varies from that of its American counterpart.)

Canada and the United States stand at different stages in the development of constitutional doctrines of free speech. American principles are based on the two hundred-year-old Bill of Rights, whose enactment closely followed the original Constitution. Significant free speech adjudication began at the end of World War I, and doctrines have grown over the last seventy-five years. Judges have paid little attention to documents and judicial rulings of other countries. This comparative inattention was once justified, and is now at least explicable (though no longer justified), because the United States has led in the active judicial protection of constitutional rights.

Canada's constitutional history is quite different. The Canadian Charter of Rights and Freedoms drastically altered the constitutional landscape in 1982, although some minimal judicial elaboration of ideals of free expression preceded it. Its adoption gave the Canadian Supreme Court authority to declare laws of the national and provincial legislatures invalid because they infringe individual rights. In exercising this review, the Court has drawn extensively from the legal materials of other countries, including the United States, and of the international legal order. The Court has regarded itself, to a degree so far uncharacteristic in the United States, as giving meaning to liberties that transcend national boundaries. Related to this difference between the two supreme courts is a remarkable and gross asymmetry in scholarly understanding of what is happening in each system. Canadian free speech scholars are acutely aware of what the U.S. Supreme Court does. Most American scholars have at best a dim idea of Canadian free speech law. Because of this asymmetry I have made more effort to provide citations for basic Canadian doctrines than for familiar American ones.

Constitutional Language and General Approaches

Two critical inquiries in free speech cases are what counts as speech and what constitutes interference with speech. Another central inquiry is how stringently courts will review government actions that interfere with speech. In respect to these three inquiries, judicial approaches may be expansive or modest; and they may be "conceptual" or "balancing." An expansive approach understands speech broadly, including virtually all written and oral communication, fine arts and music, demonstrations, and symbolic acts such as flag burning. It treats indirect threats to speech as well as focused interferences as raising constitutional questions. A modest approach constrains the limits of constitutional speech more closely, perhaps not including private communications about private subjects, demonstrations, and physical acts such as flag burning, and perhaps assuming that government practices that are not aimed against expression raise no constitutional issue. An expansive approach to review treats impairment of speech with skepticism and requires a heavy burden to justify it; a modest approach permits impairment under fairly relaxed standards of review, with courts giving much more deference to the political branches.

A court that uses a balancing approach to decision openly weighs crucial factors; a "conceptual" approach employs categorical analysis. An inquiry as to whether a regulation or practice is sustained by a compelling interest relies on a kind of balancing. Courts look at all the arguments underlying regulation to see if they show that the government's interest is very powerful. A rule that defamation of public officials is constitutionally protected unless the writer knows the statement is false or recklessly disregards possible falsity, is categorical.[2] A court, or jury, looks to see whether the facts of the case fall in the protected or unprotected category. Of course, conceptual approaches themselves reflect some implicit underlying balance of rights and interests. Many applicable standards explicitly employ a combination of conceptual and balancing approaches. For instance, if "content distinctions" can be upheld only upon an extremely strong showing of government need, "content distinction" operates as an important category that triggers highly stringent balancing review.

Constitutional language and traditions concerning judicial review of legislative and executive action largely determine the approaches a country's judges now take. The text of the United States Constitution offers the courts little guidance. The First Amendment says, "Congress shall make no law . . . abridging the freedom of speech, or of the press." The "the" preceding "freedom of speech" *might* have been taken to mean that all that was protected was whatever freedom of speech then existed at common law, but courts have declined that limiting perspective. Despite the specific language about "Congress," the clause has been understood to cover any abridgement of free speech by any officer of the federal government. The Fourteenth Amendment, with its requirements that states not deprive persons of due process of law or abridge the privileges or immunities of citizens, has been held to make the First Amendment applicable against the states.[3] Since the U.S. Constitution does not provide grounds for government justification of violations of individual rights,[4] a court's formal determination that free speech has been "abridged" is also a formal decision that a government action was impermissible.

The Canadian Charter of Rights and Freedoms differs strikingly. Section 2 provides that everyone has the fundamental freedoms of "thought, belief, opinion and expression, including freedom of the press and other media of communication."[5] The Charter applies directly to both the national and provincial governments. Under Section 1 of the Charter, fundamental freedoms are subject "to such reasonable limits prescribed by law as can be demonstrably justified in a free and democratic society." According to Section 33(1), Parliament or a provincial legislature may, by making an express declaration that its action complies with Section 1, adopt legislation that operates notwithstanding the protections of Section 2. A Canadian court may thus decide that an act limits freedom of expression under Section 2, but is nonetheless legally valid because it satisfies the standard of Section 1 or has been shielded by an express legislative declaration under Section 33(1). The latter possibility means that the effectiveness of Section 2 as a judicially enforceable restriction depends on the hesitancy of legislatures to rely on the power of override given by Section 33.

These differences in constitutional language might be expected to yield variances in judicial approach.[6] The basic American constitutional standard of "abridging the freedom of speech" seems to call for conceptual categorization to do much of the work of constitutional decision, although courts may need some explicit balancing to avoid unacceptable results. In discerning the fundamental freedoms of Section 2, Canadian courts might rely even more exclusively on conceptual approaches, because they can use the open standard of Section 1 for problems that they think call for explicit balancing.[7]

Since Section 1 permits government justification of action that infringes Section 2 freedoms, Canadian courts can find a violation of Section 2's freedoms more easily than an American court would find a violation of the First Amendment. But one would expect the flexibility that Section 1 introduces to lead Canadian courts to invalidate fewer laws and practices as unconstitutional than do American courts. This is partly because the Section 1 justification of exceptions appears by its language to grant more latitude to the political branches of government than does the language of the First Amendment. It is also because the tendency of many balancing tests (though not the compelling interest test) is to induce deference to legislative or executive wisdom. A court that is "balancing" considerations that were before the legislature may be more hesitant to conclude that the legislature made a mistake than a court inquiring whether the legislature ran afoul of some conceptual barrier.[8]

Another reason we might expect Canadian courts to be less "activist" than American ones evolves from a long tradition of treating legislative judgments (at least ones that respect division of powers) as finally authoritative. That tradition may be one explanation why the language of the Charter is less absolute than it could be. The tradition may also substantially affect how courts approach the constitutional language they interpret. The Charter's novel principle of direct judicial invalidation based on individual rights[9] could not be expected to alter drastically and swiftly long habits of deference to the political branches. Underpinning variations I have mentioned thus far may be a yet deeper cultural distinction. Among political societies, the United States is perhaps the most individualist. In Canadian society respect for groups, itself reflected in other parts of the Charter, and for the whole community, plays a more dominant role.

KINDS OF SPEECH PROTECTED

Although both the Canadian and American Supreme Courts perceive similar values underlying free speech issues,[10] their cases reveal variations along lines one might expect. Both courts have accepted broad rationales for freedom of speech and an accompanying expansive view of the speech that raises constitutional questions. In the United States, nonpolitical speech, as well as speech related to public affairs, is protected. Commercial communication for profit enjoys a degree of protection, but less than that given other expression. Music and art count as speech. Forms of expression that indicate emotional intensity or capture attention are protected even if less offensive words or methods could convey the same substance.[11] The law of defamation is largely constitutionalized, and other private law doctrines impinging on expression receive constitutional scrutiny. Controversially, the Supreme Court continues to say that obscene expression is unprotected. Drawing the line between what is obscene and what is not remains a perplexing inquiry that is addressed in chapter 6.

In pre-Charter days, when freedom of speech was invoked mainly in connection with division of powers issues regarding the relative authority of the national and provincial governments, Canadian opinions suggested that free speech was limited to expression about political affairs; but the advent of the Charter has led to coverage roughly similar to that of the United States. One exception that is important, but less so than it appears at first glance, concerns the common law of defamation and other common law bases of liability. According to present interpretation, court-created common law rules enforcing private rights do not present Charter issues.[12] An American's initial reaction is skepticism that all such actions of the judiciary can continue to be thought of as beyond the scope of Section 2. If a provincial court held that criticism well within the range of ordinary political comment (e.g., "the Prime Minister has been an inept and irresponsible leader") constituted defamation, would the Supreme Court conclude that no fundamental freedom had been violated?

In comprehending the present status of common law and Charter rights, however, one needs to recognize a critical distinction between common law in the United States and Canada. In the United States, common law is generally state law; if state common law doctrines do not infringe the federal Constitution or federal statutes, they are not a matter of federal concern and they are unreviewable by the Supreme Court. In Canada, Supreme Court powers are different. The Supreme Court is the court of last resort in a unitary system and may revise common law decisions of any lower court. Whether in some theoretical sense parts of the common law might be viewed as "federal law" or "provincial law," the Supreme Court can overturn what it regards as a bad common law judgment. Thus, in my example of a comment about the Prime Minister, the Supreme Court could cast the common law of defamation in light of Charter values, protecting the political remark without declaring that the Charter had actually been violated.

This reality reduces the practical significance of a rule that common law doctrines applied between private parties do not directly infringe

Charter rights. Nonetheless, the present rule is somewhat anomalous in that (1) rules of private law under the Québec Civil Code do raise Charter issues whereas analogous common law rules in other provinces do not, and (2) within a "common law" province, a judicial doctrine that has not raised a Charter issue becomes a Charter issue if the doctrine is enacted in identical form by a legislature.

BASIC AMERICAN DOCTRINES

Attempting any brief summary of American doctrines for reviewing regulation of speech is difficult, because the law is complex and shifts subtly as new cases are decided. There are specific standards governing the punishment or civil recovery for particular kinds of speech. One is the standard I have already mentioned for when public officials may recover for defamation; the defendant must have acted with knowledge of falsity or in reckless disregard of falsity.[13] In the next section, I shall discuss another such standard, the *Brandenburg* test for public advocacy of illegal acts.

More generally, American law entertains a strong presumption against prior restraints. Only the very strongest reasons can justify the government's censoring of speech before it is made. This principle precluded government interference with the publication of highly classified material about the Vietnam conflict in the "Pentagon Papers case,"[14] and it has made restrictions on pretrial publication of events virtually impossible[15] in criminal cases.[16] Some military information in wartime may be censored, however, and relations between the military and press during the conflict in the Persian Gulf tested the appropriate boundaries of that exception.

In the last two decades, a principle of "no content regulation" has emerged as a central doctrine of First Amendment law. The fundamental idea is that some messages should not be favored over others. Certain differences in content are permissible bases of distinction; a message directly urging someone to commit a crime may be treated differently from a message urging someone to obey the law. But, in general, differences in viewpoint are not a permissible basis for distinction. Differences among categories in speech (e.g., political as opposed to sexual) are also treated with suspicion.

When the government interferes with speech in a manner that would normally be impermissible, its action will be sustained only if it is necessary to serve a compelling justification and is narrowly drawn to achieve that end.[17] In free speech cases in which they use the "compelling interest" test, judges rarely sustain what the government has done.

Within the boundaries of speech enjoying some protection, certain very limited categories of speech are considered to have lower value; most notable are commercial advertising and sexually explicit speech that falls short of being obscene. Regulation of these types of speech is subject to less stringent standards of review.

Less stringent standards also apply when government regulation serves a purpose that is independent of the substance of what is communicated. Thus, the government may restrict the size of billboards or limit the volume on sound trucks, without showing that it has a compelling interest.

Canadian constitutional doctrine, up to the present, is less complicated than that of the United States. There is an expansive approach toward determining freedom of speech. Any restriction of protected speech constitutes a limitation under Section 2. The critical inquiry in almost all troublesome cases is the test of possible justification under Section 1. The Court must first assure itself that the restriction is a "limit prescribed by law," not an unauthorized or unconstrained act. If that threshold is met, the government must have an objective that is of "pressing and substantial concern in a free and democratic society," and the impugned measure must meet a test of proportionality that has three parts: the law must be rationally connected to the objective, it must impair freedom of expression as little as possible, and its effects must be proportional to the objective. I shall say more about the features of Section 1 review as I describe particular cases. In time, Canadian courts may develop various subsidiary doctrines similar in character if not in substance to those in the United States; but the contextualized standard under Section 1 makes such doctrinal proliferation unnecessary.

SUBVERSIVE ADVOCACY AND CRIMINAL SOLICITATION, AND OTHER CRIME-RELATED SPEECH

A central aspect of American development of freedom of speech has involved subversive advocacy, extreme dissent. The famous language of "clear and present danger" was first used in Justice Oliver Wendell Holmes's 1919 opinion for the Supreme Court in *Schenck v. United States*, which upheld a conviction under the Espionage Act.[18] He said, "The question in every case is whether the words used are used in such circumstances and are of such a nature as to create a clear and present danger that they will bring about the substantive evils that Congress has a right to prevent."[19] For most of the Supreme Court Justices who then accepted this language, and perhaps for Holmes himself, the formula was not very protective of speech. In a case decided by the Court within a week of *Schenck*, a man was punished for helping to publish twelve articles of small circulation that were favorable to Germany and that called those who resisted the draft "technically ... wrong," though more "sinned against than sinning."[20] Thousands of people were convicted and sent to jail during World War I for comment no stronger than this.

In subsequent cases, Justices Holmes and Louis Brandeis, in dissent, developed "clear and present danger" into a doctrine that would significantly protect speech. They said that if speech promoting subversion was to be punished, the danger had to be great and its occurrence proximately close. These opinions failed to make clear whether the test required *actual* present danger or only an *aim* to produce a harm quickly. Additionally, the question of whether the test applied to speech that explicitly urged the commission of a particular crime remained unanswered.

During the 1930s and 1940s "clear and present danger" emerged as the critical test for subversive advocacy and as the standard for a wide range of free speech problems.[21] Its "reformulation" by a plurality in *Dennis v. United States*,[22] a post-war prosecution of leaders of the American Communist Party, represented a severe setback for free speech. Under this standard, a court was to ask if "the gravity of the 'evil,' discounted by its improbability, justifies such invasion of free speech as is necessary to avoid the danger." This language allowed speech to be punished if it posed some threat of a very great danger in a rather distant future. As other Justices pointed out, American courts were hardly in a position to estimate how likely it was that domestic Communist speech would contribute to a violent revolution many years hence. Justice Felix Frankfurter, concurring in the result, urged a "candid and informed weighing of the competing interests" in free speech and national security. But any potential this "ad hoc" balancing approach might have had to provide serious judicial scrutiny was surrendered by a later part of the opinion, which said that Congress's judgment in adjusting the interests should be set aside "only if there is no reasonable basis for it."[23]

In the 1960s the Court announced what remains the standard for subversive speech. Overturning the conviction under a criminal syndicalism statute of a speaker at a Ku Klux Klan rally, the Court *per curiam* said a state may not "forbid or proscribe advocacy of the use of force or of law violation except where such advocacy is directed to inciting or producing imminent lawless action and is likely to produce such action."[24] According to this *Brandenburg* test, imminent lawless action must be the speaker's objective *and* be actually likely to happen. In a 1973 decision overturning a demonstrator's conviction for disorderly conduct, the Court indicated that "imminent" meant likely to occur within a very short span of time.[25] The defendant had remarked to his fellow demonstrators, "We'll take the fucking street later."[26] Presumably he must have meant later in that day. According to the Court, even if his words implied illegal action at a later time, his conviction had to be overturned in the absence of evidence that he intended to produce "imminent disorder."[27] No doubt, the word "imminent" contains some degree of flexibility, but the Court has adopted a very stringent standard for punishment of speech likely to encourage criminal action.

The extent of applicability of the *Brandenburg* test remains unclear. The Court's cases have involved public political advocacy. Does the test set a general constitutional limit on punishment for urging criminal acts? If a sister writes her brother urging that he steal money from their parents, is that protected speech if the theft is not to happen for a few weeks or the brother is unlikely to do what the sister asks? American cases have not generally assumed that such ordinary criminal solicitation presents a serious First Amendment problem. Because directly urging someone else in private to commit a garden-variety crime does not significantly implicate the values of free speech, *Brandenbrug* should not be thought to cover such situations; but no case contains a developed or satisfactory explanation of the distinction between public advocacy and private solicitation of crimes.[28]

What has free speech to do with the many other communications that commonly occur as aspects of criminal activities? Words exchanged by people constitute agreements to commit crimes; words are used among participants to plan and carry out crimes; words commit harms by threat or deception. Many crimes in the standard catalogue almost invariably involve verbal utterances, and other types of crime often do. I indicated in chapter 1 that an utterance lies outside freedom of expression if it directly alters the social environment, "does" something rather than tell something or recommend something. I gave as examples words of agreement that commit people to action and threats that introduce a new danger into victims' lives. It is fair to say that American courts have not yet felt a need to explain why typical utterances connected to crime lie outside the First Amendment.[29]

Direct issues about subversive or revolutionary speech have not been considered by the Canadian Supreme Court since the advent of the Charter. In *Boucher v. The King*,[30] a 1951 case that interpreted a broadly worded prohibition on seditious libel, the Court held that a Jehovah's Witness's attack on various groups was not within the statute's scope. The case is often cited as an application of free speech principles operating prior to the Charter. The decision supports narrow construction of provisions dealing with dangerous speech, but itself sheds little light on the bounds of Section 2 of the Charter.

Language in recent Supreme Court cases suggests very broad Charter coverage of "criminal language," indeed coverage so broad that it makes one wonder if the Justices have faced up to the full implications of what they have said. The most important opinions were in a triumvirate of prostitution cases.[31] The defendants, among other claims, raised a Section 2 challenge to the Criminal Code prohibition against communicating in a public place for the purpose of engaging in prostitution or obtaining a prostitute's services. All six Justices deciding the cases agreed that public solicitation for prostitution was covered by freedom of expression under Section 2. Four Justices nevertheless sustained the Code provision as a permissible limitation under Section 1.

On the coverage of Section 2(b), Justice Wilson's dissent was most important, because three members of the majority indicated agreement with her reasoning.[32] She stated that the government's purpose is to restrict the content of expression by singling out meanings that are not to be conveyed, rather than dealing directly with a variety of harmful consequences.[33] "Whether the citizen is negotiating for the purchase of a Van Gogh or a sexual encounter, Section 2(b) of the Charter protects that person's freedom to communicate with his or her vendor."[34] Since prostitution per se is not illegal in Canada, it was not certain what Justice Wilson would have thought about solicitation to commit an independently criminal act, each instance of which might be regarded as involving a harmful consequence. On this point, Justice Lamer was much clearer. He said that Section 2(b) "protects all content of expression irrespective of the meaning or message sought to be conveyed."[35] He identified provisions in the criminal code whose *actus reus* may consist wholly or partially of speech, including counselling a party to commit a crime and uttering threats. He suggested that whenever the law makes it criminal to convey a message through a traditional form of expression like speaking or writing, that should be viewed as a restriction on freedom of expression. Direct acts of violence and direct attacks on the physical integrity and liberty of another are unprotected. In *Regina v. Keegstra*, which I shall discuss in detail in chapter 4, Chief Justice Dickson, writing for the majority, indicated that threats of violence fall within the scope of Section 2(b), because they are classified according to the content of their meaning. Only direct acts of violence are uncovered.[36]

Since the Supreme Court has yet to address many difficult questions about the boundaries of freedom of speech, one cannot reach confident conclusions about how it will ultimately resolve them. But if one tries to piece together comments in opinions subscribed to by majorities, the following *seems* to be the present law in Canada. Speaking and writing are covered by Section 2(b), even when they are intimately related to independent criminal activities. In this respect, no distinctions are drawn between informing, urging, and offering and threatening, distinctions I believe are crucial.[37] If an offer of services is covered by Section 2, as the prostitution cases indicate, so also would be acceptance of an offer. Thus, agreement between two people to commit a crime would also be covered by Section 2(b).

What would be the practical consequences of this expansive view of freedom of speech? Of course, Section 1, which permits reasonable limits on expression, will allow almost all criminal punishment of such speech to stand. But application of Section 1 typically involves a serious test of the significance of the government's objective and of the need to suppress expression. Even if a criminal prohibition is otherwise constitutionally permissible, the government objective might conceivably not be weighty enough to survive Section 1 review, or punishment of agreements and offers to commit the crime might not really be needed. If the courts engage in the genuine review Section 1 is said to require, they will end up saying that in respect to some criminal laws that are properly enacted, the government cannot punish agreements, offers, counseling, and perhaps even participation that involves only utterances, such as telling another participant what acts to perform.[38]

I doubt that the courts will do this. For standard sorts of crimes, even minor ones whose enactment may have been unwise, I think courts will find the speech values in these communicative activities too weak to warrant more than perfunctory review under Section 1. Should that course be followed, an unfortunate effect of the Supreme Court's present direction might be a softening of the stringency of Section 1 review when more serious speech is involved.[39] If American courts have yet to explain the constitutional status of most criminal speech, perhaps the Canadian Supreme Court has reached too quickly for an overly expansive generalization that fails to recognize the significance of differences in the nature of utterances.

Symbolic Speech

Symbolic speech, very roughly, is expression that takes the form of action that is not a common means of expression. Since all language is symbolic, saying just where ordinary speech ends and symbolic speech begins is somewhat artificial. And it is not clear that "symbolic speech" should be a constitutionally significant category. What may be more important is whether the state's *reason* for impinging on activity relates to its expressive quality. I shall return briefly to that question later.

A student wears a black armband in school to protest a war, a registrant burns his draft card, a protester burns an American flag, a homeless person stands naked in front of City Hall to make a statement about the inadequacy of public efforts to deal with homelessness. These are all forms of symbolic speech. The dominant aim of the actor is to communicate a message, and his action is understood in that way by observers. Although it might be said that every action "expresses something" about the actor and is understood by others to do so, not every action raises a free speech problem. There must be a deliberate attempt to communicate a message.

In dealing with symbolic speech, the U.S. Supreme Court has drawn a sharp distinction. One standard of review is used when a regulation is not directed at communication; another standard is used when regulation is directed at communication. The idea of a regulation "directed at communication" is a kind of fraternal twin of the idea of content discrimination. A regulation that is aimed at communication almost always is directed against undesired content.

Regulation is *not* addressed to communication when a law forbids acts for reasons having nothing to do with the fact that some subcategory of the acts is communicative. Public nudity is forbidden for reasons unrelated to some people's appearing naked in public to communicate messages. One possible approach to such cases is that the constitutional guarantee of free speech has no bearing; if people happen to violate laws, their communicative motivation would give them no standing to be treated differently from others who violate the laws. Another possible approach is to say that the communicative aim does give the acts a special position. When it decided a major case on the subject, the U.S. Supreme Court equivocated.

In *United States v. O'Brien*,[40] a young man was prosecuted for destroying his draft card. Exercising extraordinary restraint about determining Congressional purpose, the Court said that Congress had reasons for people to keep draft cards that did not relate to expression. Everyone who knew anything about the statute adopted by Congress understood that members of Congress were upset about the symbolism of draft card burning and wanted to stop the burning of cards in protest. But the Court declined to investigate motivation and it accepted as plausible bases for the statute thin claims by the government that registrants needed to have their cards for administrative reasons. So, despite the contrary reality, the Court treated the case as one in which the purpose of legislation had nothing to do with expression. Chief Justice Warren's opinion then said,

> We cannot accept the view that an apparently limitless variety of conduct can be labeled 'speech' whenever the person engaging in the conduct intends thereby to express an idea. However, even on the assumption that the alleged communicative element in O'Brien's conduct is sufficient to bring into play the First Amendment, it does not necessarily follow that the destruction of a registration certificate is constitutionally protected activity.[41]

The opinion then proceeded to announce what has come to be called the *O'Brien* test, under which a government regulation otherwise within constitutional power is sufficiently justified:

> if it furthers an important or substantial governmental interest; if the governmental interest is unrelated to the suppression of free expression; and if the incidental restriction on alleged First Amendment freedoms is no greater than is essential to the furtherance of that interest.[42]

In demanding that the government's interest be substantial and that the restriction on expression be no greater than is essential to further the interest, the *O'Brien* test sounds fairly stringent; but the Court comfortably sustained O'Brien's conviction. The *O'Brien* test has now been applied to various areas besides symbolic speech. Some lower courts have used the test more actively than the Supreme Court to vindicate challenges to government practices, but judges employing the test usually end up approving the government's restrictive action. The *O'Brien* approach, minus its equivocation, does represent a position that some significant review is called for when expressive action runs afoul of regulation not aimed at expression, but the review has generally proved fairly relaxed.

A 1990 religious freedom case raises the question as to whether the Court will long continue to indulge even the form of *O'Brien*. The apparently settled principle under the Free Exercise Clause of the First Amendment, based on a handful of Supreme Court cases, was that when a person violated an "ordinary" law because of religious conscience, a court asked whether the government had a compelling interest that could not be satisfied if an exemption were given.[43] In one well known case, the California Supreme Court had held that a prohibition on the use of peyote could not be applied against members of the Native American Church who ingested peyote during worship services.[44] In *Employment Division v. Smith*,[45] the Supreme Court announced not only that such results were wrong, but that the whole compelling interest approach to this subject was misguided. If a state law is otherwise constitutional, the state needs to meet no further burden to apply the law against persons acting from religious conscience. This result surprised and appalled most scholars of the religion clauses, not to mention persons in religious groups who pay attention to the Court's work. Outrage over the decision proved sufficient to lead Congress to pass legislation reestablishing the compelling interest test for such cases.[46] What should be noted here is the possible relevance of the *Smith* case for the *O'Brien* test.

Prior to *Smith*, a person violating a "neutral" law from religious conscience benefitted from stricter, more favorable review than a person violating a neutral law in order to express an idea. That is, the compelling interest free exercise test was more advantageous for a defendant than the *O'Brien* test. And this made sense. A person who acts from religious conscience may feel there is no alternative; a person expressing an idea wants to do so effectively, but does not ordinarily feel some inner compulsion to use a particular means. Especially given the United States's long history of regarding religious conscience as an overriding obligation, the approach to the two grounds for violation seemed appropriate.

After *Smith* (and prior to Congress's action), the person acting from religious conscience was treated like an ordinary violator for constitutional purposes, no better, no worse. Should persons deciding to express themselves by a violation be treated better than religious objectors? I am skeptical. No doubt, reasons relating to the nature and function of speech can be adduced as to why the *O'Brien* test, as applied to these situations, should not suffer the judicial fate of the free exercise compelling interest test. Moreover, courts are not always coherent in their approaches to related problems. Still, a constitutional position favoring free speech challenges over free exercise challenges is somewhat anomalous. Thus far, only Justice Scalia, the author of the Court's opinion in *Employment Division v. Smith*, has urged a similar approach for free speech claims,[47] but the Court's reasoning in *Smith* casts some shadow over the long-term vitality of the usual employment of the *O'Brien* standard.

When regulation is directed at expression, review is much more stringent than under *O'Brien*. In *Tinker v. Des Moines School District*,[48] school authorities forbade students from wearing black armbands to protest the Vietnam War. The school's interest was precisely in discouraging this form of constant communication about the controversial topic; it lacked any other reason to forbid wearing black armbands. Had a similar regulation by a city of its citizens been involved, the law would clearly have been unconstitutional. Given the state's concern for the school setting and disciplined education, the Supreme Court said that students had a right to express themselves if they did so without " 'materially and substantially interfer[ing] with the requirements of appropriate discipline in the operation of the school' and without colliding with the rights of others."

Two recent flag burning cases are examples of the difficulty a government faces if its law is viewed as directed at communication. In *Texas v. Johnson*,[49] in 1989, the Court had little problem concluding that the state's asserted reasons for prohibiting flag desecration—to avoid violence and preserve the flag as a symbol of nationhood and national unity—failed to meet "the most exacting scrutiny" as constitutional justifications for prohibiting acts of flag burning. The following year, the federal Flag Protection Act suffered a similar fate.[50]

What is doctrinally interesting about the flag cases is not the application of stringent review once it was determined that the statutes were directed at communication, but the intricacies of deciding what counts as being directed at communication. Chapter 3 explores this problem.

The Canadian Supreme Court has not resolved a "symbolic speech" case under the Charter, but the approach it would take is suggested by the opinions in the hate speech case that we shall examine in Chapter 4.[51] If the government is aiming at the content of messages, as the United States Supreme Court decided was occurring in the two flag destruction statutes, then the protection of Section 2(b) would apply, and the standards under Section 1 would determine if restriction was permissible. According to Chief Justice Dickson, if the individual is engaging in expression, very broadly defined, and the government's purpose is *not* to restrict expression (what the U.S. Supreme Court said was true in *O'Brien*), Section 2(b) does not apply unless the accused can show that his "activity supports rather than undermines the principles and values upon which freedom of expression is based."[52] Thus, someone who appeared in public without clothing to communicate a message would have to convince a court that this promoted rather than interfered with open discussion and consideration. If he prevailed on that issue, he would then face the Section 1 standards. What Justice McLachlin said is rather similar, that when the government's aim is to accomplish a goal unrelated to expression, a complainant who argues for initial coverage under Section 2(b) must show that his or her expression implicates one of the values of free expression.

PUBLIC DEMONSTRATIONS

I shall say relatively little about a complex area of First Amendment law and its Charter analogue: regulation of public demonstrations. The key features of American law are these. In its streets and parks, the state must permit some demonstrations.[53] It cannot close off these traditionally public forums from those who choose to express themselves by demonstrating. It may, however, engage in reasonable time, place, and manner restrictions.[54] There is considerable latitude about where and when demonstrations must be allowed, but restrictions are subject to significant judicial review. The courts' inquiries now include whether alternative channels of communication are available, and whether a regulation is narrowly tailored to serve the government's interest; but the government need not show that the regulation of the time, place, and manner of demonstrations is the least intrusive possible.[55] If restrictions reflect viewpoint discrimination, favoring some perspectives over others, they will be held invalid, absent highly compelling reasons.[56] And if the restrictions confer unfettered discretion on executive officials, they will also be held invalid, largely because wide discretion allows executive officials to engage in viewpoint discrimination. If demonstrations threaten some danger of a violent response, the essential responsibility of the government is to do all it can to protect the demonstrators and stop the violent bystanders,[57] but in extreme circumstances, it can demand that demonstrators stop.[58]

These basic principles apply not only to areas that are traditional sites of public expression, but also to areas the government decides to open up to such expression.[59] In other areas that are not traditional forums and have not been opened up, the government may preclude demonstrations altogether or allow them on a much more limited basis; but the constitutional restrictions against viewpoint discrimination and excessive discretion apply. In striking down a law that generally forbade demonstrations near public schools, but permitted demonstrations related to school labor disputes, the Supreme Court held that content discrimination favoring discussion of some *subjects* over others is also unconstitutional,[60] unless the content distinction drawn bears a reasonable relation to use of that space.[61]

We can roughly see principles operating here close to those that control symbolic speech. If the concern of the government is not to suppress particular messages, but to control impediments to traffic or similar nuisances, it has considerable leeway, so long as it does not close off traditional forums. But any action taken that restricts, or authorizes restriction of, a demonstration *because* the message is controversial or unpopular is presumptively unconstitutional. When the state aims at the communication, it is unlikely to succeed. It is just this unifying principle that makes it doubtful whether symbolic speech is itself a significant category. The state's reasons for restraining speech often play a much more prominent role than whether an activity, looked at by itself, counts as straightforward speech (such as posting election signs on utility poles),[62] as "speech plus action" in demonstrations, or as symbolic speech.

In some decisions the Supreme Court has suggested that time, place, and manner review is essentially the same as the O'Brien test.[63] From the perspective of state purposes, this coalescence makes sense, but there are disparate factors to be considered. Street demonstrations are a unique and important form of communication; they cannot be closed off completely, and regulation that sharply limits them should be carefully reviewed. This would suggest that time, place, and manner review of street demonstrations should be more stringent than O'Brien. On the other hand, some forms of symbolic speech represent the way in which people truly want to express themselves, and may be part of the substance of the communication.[64] That consideration suggests that such symbolic speech should receive more protection than some matters covered by time, place, and manner.

In Canada, some pre-Charter cases suggested that demonstrations are collective action rather than a form of speech and that public authorities may have the same power to regulate public property as private individuals have to control use of their property;[65] but it is now clearly established that demonstrations are expression within Section 2(b) and that regulation of public property is constrained.[66] In a recent case involving distribution of pamphlets and discussion by a political organization at an airport, *Regina v. Committee for the Commonwealth of Canada*,[67] all Justices agreed with the basic ideas that some public spaces must be open for public expression and that government regulation of state-owned spaces are subject to review. The opinions indicated agreement with the U.S. Supreme Court that streets and parks are open to expression; but they rejected any rigid "public forum" approach as insensitively focusing on only one relevant factor.[68] The Justices differed on the right approach to determining whether expression in a public place is covered by Section 2(b), and to some degree also on the specific elements of analysis under Section 1. All the Justices agreed, however, that a bar on distributing political pamphlets and undertaking political advocacy in airports violated Section 2(b) and was not saved under Section 1. A majority found that the government policy was not "prescribed by law" as Section 1 requires[69] and a majority also found that it failed other Section 1 standards. Insofar as the case is a guide to how ordinary demonstrations will be treated, it suggests fairly robust protection.

This chapter has revealed both strong similarities and significant differences between the free speech law of the United States and that of Canada. Chapters 4 and 6 will provide a much richer look at how the Canadian Supreme Court goes about evaluating government arguments that it has satisfied the requirements of Section 1 of the Charter and thus may impinge on freedom of speech under Section 2. These chapters will show both that the Canadian court is less absolutist in its view of free speech than the American Supreme Court has been, and that its outlook is somewhat more centered on communities.

Chapter Three

FLAG BURNING

THIS CHAPTER considers highly controversial behavior that lies on the edges of speech: flag burning. Here I closely examine one U.S. Supreme Court case and treat more briefly its immediate successor. The opinions in these cases reflect major free speech doctrines in the United States, and illustrate complexities in their application, complexities obscured by the sort of summary of the law that chapter 2 provides. I address the soundness of the Supreme Court's decisions in 1989 and 1990 that state and federal laws against flag destruction are unconstitutional under general First Amendment principles, and I inquire whether some exception from ordinary principles is called for, to be achieved by a constitutional amendment if necessary. The analysis draws out broader aspects of the law of symbolic speech.

In the most important case, *Texas v. Johnson,*[1] the Supreme Court held, five to four, that Gregory Johnson's conviction under a Texas statute punishing flag desecration violated the First Amendment. Johnson and other demonstrators during the 1984 Republican National Convention had protested Republican policies and dramatized the dangers of nuclear war. Johnson set on fire a stolen American flag. He was convicted under a penal section entitled "Desecration of Venerated Object," which forbade intentionally or knowingly desecrating a state or national flag.[2] To "desecrate" meant to "deface, damage, or otherwise physically mistreat in a way that the actor knows will seriously offend one or more persons likely to observe or discover his action."[3]

Judged by attention and notoriety, *Johnson* was a case of the first magnitude. Newspapers widely reported the opinions under leading headlines, and the result upset many people. Politicians and columnists spoke their minds. President Bush expressed dismay at what the Court had done, and, echoing his 1988 campaign themes, appealed to the values of the flag. He spurred a serious effort to amend the Constitution that generated weeks of Congressional debate and gained great momentum. A revision of the federal statutory law on flag destruction, which proponents claimed could withstand constitutional challenge, deflected temporarily strenuous efforts to amend the Constitution.

Despite these trappings of importance, the case is trivial by other measures. Not many people want to burn flags. The decision does not affect lives in the manner of *Brown v. Board of Education*[4] and *Roe v. Wade.*[5]

The case lacks great doctrinal significance because it represents an application of existing First Amendment doctrines. It does not protect some fundamental liberty of action. If our country did not permit its flag to be desecrated, it would not be much less free and democratic.

The relative triviality of *Texas v. Johnson* is striking when the case is juxtaposed to the swift course of world events in 1989 and the years following. The thirst for political liberties has proved a powerful striving of the human spirit, not just a shallow desire of a dominant bourgeois class in capitalist societies. When one thinks of movements and issues in Eastern Europe, China, and South Africa, the question of a right to burn the flag of one's country does not seem compelling. But this comparative triviality shows something good and strong about American democracy. Only a country whose fundamental institutions are solid and accepted has the luxury to worry about such a minor matter. A critic might respond that many serious issues face American democracy; obsession about flag burning pandered to an uninformed public and reflected cowardice about confronting hard problems. The critic would be right. Still, wide agreement exists on broadly liberal premises about the boundaries of speech and protest. That people worry so much about this narrow form of political expression, rather than the substance of messages of political dissent, suggests a firm understanding supporting broad latitude for dissent.

FIRST AMENDMENT PRINCIPLES

First Amendment analysis of flag burning cases proceeds in three stages. First, is flag burning a free speech issue at all? Second, if so, what is the standard for judging the constitutionality of the state's effort to make it criminal? Third, what is the outcome under that standard?

Why Free Speech Is Involved

Do people convicted for flag burning have a claim that they were engaged in speech? One conceivable position, suggested in chapter 2, would be that only writing and speaking, as well as perhaps art and music, count as expression under the First Amendment. All other (or ordinary) acts would fall outside the protection of the free speech and free press clauses. It is easy to see why the Court has long rejected this position. As Melville Nimmer pointed out, speaking and writing themselves are communications by symbols;[6] if the significance of an ordinary act is to express an idea, the act should be treated similarly.

Oversimplifying to a modest degree, the Court indicates that the issue of coverage turns on the communicative nature of Johnson's act.[7] It refers

to an earlier flag case[8] that asks whether "[a]n intent to convey a particu-
larized message was present, and . . . [whether] the likelihood was great
that the message would be understood by those who viewed it."[9] As Nimmer explained, it is not enough that conduct convey some meaning to
observers;[10] under such a standard every act seen by others would qualify
for First Amendment protection, since every act reveals some implicit
meaning to others. It also is not enough that an actor have a subjective
aim to communicate.

The unworkability of using a subjective criterion alone is evident when
one reflects on prosecutions for public nudity. A college student who
streaks across campus on a dare may have no message he is trying to
communicate consciously. A person who sits naked in cold weather in
front of City Hall in protest of treatment of the homeless has an obvious
message. So do nude dancers, as all the Justices recognized in *Barnes v.
Glen Theater, Inc.*[11] What of bathers who are nude on a relatively se-
cluded part of a public beach in the summer? Some simply enjoy bathing
and sunning nude. A few may find the sensation unpleasant, but wish to
upset prudish restrictions. Most enjoy bathing nude, and, disapproving
of the restrictions they are violating, also take appearing nude as a kind
of implicit statement against the restrictions. Let us suppose that on a
particular day all the bathers expect to be seen by each other and by a few
members of the larger public. None have signs around their necks or next
to their towels explaining why they are nude. An observer cannot know
why any one person is nude. We can quickly understand why any serious
constitutional test for whether a person can be convicted should not turn
on a particular person's subjective motivation, discoverable only after the
fact and difficult then to determine with any confidence.

This illustration suggests a possible further limit to conduct protected
by the First Amendment—that communication be the conduct's dominant aim. It may be that those who break laws of which they do not
approve wish in part to communicate their disapproval, and are so understood by others; but it is doubtful that such ordinary lawbreaking
should qualify for serious First Amendment scrutiny.

In any event, such subtleties are not a problem in *Johnson*. If acts other
than utterances of language count as speech, Johnson's acts clearly did.
He was in a political demonstration, and burning the flag was an intense
symbol of rejection of American policy and nationalism. In context, the
general drift of Johnson's message was comprehensible to observers.
Chief Justice Rehnquist's dissent flirts with rejection of this conclusion.
He says that "flag burning is the equivalent of an inarticulate grunt or
roar that, it seems fair to say, is most likely to be indulged in not to
express any particular idea, but to antagonize others."[12] If ordinary actions, or even verbal utterance, were performed *solely* or *dominantly* to

antagonize, perhaps the actor should enjoy no protection under the First Amendment; that is a problem I consider in chapters 4 and 5. But plainly much more was involved for Johnson. His burning of a revered symbol antagonized, but it also communicated a strong message. The initial threshold of constitutional protection was crossed easily by Johnson.

The Constitutional Level of Scrutiny

The second stage of analysis is determining the constitutional level of scrutiny. This was the important stage in *Johnson*, and it was the possibility of a different answer at this stage that guided those who adopted the federal statute passed after the case was decided. The critical question for the second stage is whether application of a law will be governed by the formulation in *United States v. O'Brien*[13] or by some more demanding standard.

As chapter 2 indicates, O'Brien was convicted for publicly burning his draft card. Congress had recently enacted a provision forbidding destruction of draft cards. Before that, the law had punished failures to observe selective service regulations, which had required registrants to keep their draft cards. Burning one's draft card was already punishable by up to five years in prison under the combination of regulations and statute. The new statute prescribed the same penalty. Few doubted that the overriding aim of Congress was to restrict public burning of draft cards by protesters against the Vietnam War. Refusing to look beyond language to underlying purpose, however, the Court treated the statute as not directed at communication, and elaborated its test for such circumstances, a test quoted in chapter 2. To paraphrase, a regulation must further an important or substantial governmental interest that is unrelated to the suppression of free expression, and it must not restrict free speech more than is necessary. As I have suggested, the Court seemed to set a fairly stringent balancing test that goes well beyond the "rational basis" review that applies to any statute. As Vincent Blasi has noted, exactly how stringent the *O'Brien* test turns out to be depends

> on what meaning is ascribed to two extremely open-textured criteria. First, what determines whether a governmental interest invoked to justify the regulation of speech qualifies as "important or substantial"? Do most interests routinely served by general legislation meet this test or does the special value of the freedom of speech mean that proposed restrictions must serve interests of unusual significance, say interests that are highly tangible, immediately threatened, and considered by most persons to be of high priority? Second, what makes an interest "unrelated to the suppression of free expression"? Does "unrelated" mean simply that one could desire to promote the interest

by legislation while remaining indifferent to the predictable impact of the legislation on speech activities? Or does "unrelated" mean something stronger: that any impact on free expression of legislation promoting the interest is speculative, say, or contingent, or marginal?[14]

In Supreme Court practice, the *O'Brien* test has so far not provided significant protection. Neither in *O'Brien* itself nor in any later case has the Court actually held that a defendant's communicative activity was protected against application of a law not directed at communication. Chapter 6 sketches the casualness with which a plurality finds an important purpose in the nude dancing case, although the "low value" of that expression may have been influential. Everyone recognized that Johnson's prospects would have been poor indeed had the Court used only the *O'Brien* test. Thus, the inquiry whether the Texas provision was directed at communication was of major importance, as was the similar inquiry about the federal statute passed to undo the effect of the *Johnson* decision.

Some of what the Supreme Court says in *Johnson* on this subject is a bit confusing. An initial effort at categorization can help dispel the confusion. One way in which a law may be *directed at communication* is in distinguishing between good messages and bad ones. This is what is known as viewpoint discrimination. Since the government should not be in the business of preferring some messages to others, most viewpoint discrimination rightly has been seen as highly threatening to free speech values and is considered to be invalid when lacking an extremely strong justification.[15] Another way in which a law might be said to be directed at communication is by penalizing communicative acts that have harmful consequences, with harm judged independently of acceptance or rejection of the message. A law forbidding communications that are highly likely to cause deep emotional upset or to trigger violent responses is of this sort. We may call this harmful reaction regulation. A third way in which a law conceivably might be said to be directed at communication is when it protects the communicative value of something. We may call this symbol protection. It is incorrect to suppose that such a law inevitably must be aimed at acts which are themselves communicative. Suppose a country's flag is one solid color, bright red. To protect the symbolic force of that color, the government forbids any other human use of bright red except in the flag. No walls or cars may be painted bright red, no clothes may be dyed bright red. The law aims to protect the communicative force of a symbol, but it is not aimed particularly at communicative acts.

Viewpoint discrimination, harmful reaction regulation, and symbol protection are the three critical categories for *Johnson* and for appraisal of the succeeding federal law. Laws may be directed at communication in at least two other ways as well. Statutes may treat certain subject matters differently from others; they may restrict communications about sex to an extent greater than communications about politics or religion. Finally, laws may restrict particular methods of communication, such as sound-trucks, billboards, or demonstrations, more than other methods. Subject matter regulation is not at issue for flag burning. Method restriction is involved, but it is not of independent importance because the basic reasons for restriction lie in the messages that are communicated (not some separate harm or inconvenience that the method involves).

In considering viewpoint discrimination, harmful reaction regulation, and symbol protection, we need to be sensitive to possible relationships between what the law does on its surface and what else is really going on. One connection involves high correlations. Thus, harmful reactions, such as violence, may correlate strongly with the communication of particular (unpopular) viewpoints. The second connection involves underlying motivations. Regulation that is on its face designed to forestall harmful reactions may be motivated by an aim to attack unpalatable views. With these categories and relationships in mind, we are ready to face the opinions.

The Texas statute under which Johnson was convicted prohibited flag desecration, defined as damage or mistreatment of the flag "in a way that the actor knows will seriously offend" someone "likely to observe or discover his action."[16] Since burning has been a recommended way to dispose of worn out flags, not every burning of the flag is offensive. In form, the statute was regulation to prevent harmful reaction, the offense to observers. But, what is it that makes flag burning offensive? Almost always it is that the people burning the flag are intentionally showing some kind of disrespect for it. That need not be so. We can imagine someone lighting a campfire with a flag that happens to be near at hand, and the Court itself mentions a tired person dragging a flag through the mud.[17] Either act might cause offense, and the actor might know that, yet he would have no message to communicate. But these are rare instances.

The Court recognizes in a footnote that the statute *could* apply to someone lacking a communicative purpose.[18] Why does it not conclude that the statute was aimed at something other than communication? The answer lies in its understanding that the intentional showing of disrespect caused offense in *Johnson* and would cause offense in almost all instances. The Court differs with Chief Justice Rehnquist about the ground of offense. Although the Court says it is the message that caused offense, Rehnquist says it is not the message but the use of the symbol of the flag. Each is half right. Rehnquist is correct that people would not be offended, or would be much less offended, were the message of hostility to government communicated in some other way. But suppose demonstrators were visibly supporting the government by performing a skit in which the "good guys" stop a "bad" flag burner. This burning probably would not cause nearly as much offense to the people who were upset by what Johnson did. The intense negative reaction flowed from a combination of the message and its being communicated by flag burning. One might, indeed, fairly view the flag burning itself as *part* of the message, a radical rejection of conventional norms of behavior. In this light, no sharp separation of message and method of communication is warranted.[19]

Assuming that the basis for people's offense is the message communicated, the Court does not immediately conclude that strict scrutiny of the statute is required. It asks instead whether the state has an interest behind its prohibition on flag burning that is unrelated to the suppression of expression.[20] If the state had such an interest, it would apparently succeed in achieving the more relaxed scrutiny of the *O'Brien* standard.

One asserted state interest was the prevention of violence. The Court points out that "offense" is often not followed by violence and that First Amendment decisions closely circumscribe when speech may be punished because of a likely violent reaction. Much controversial speech causes offense, and states cannot forbid all offensive speech because violence may occasionally result. This is standard First Amendment doctrine, and the Court rightly eliminates prevention of violence as a basis for the Texas statute.

The Court seems to assume, however, that if the statute had applied only when violence was highly likely, it would not have been directed at expression. That assumption involves a serious confusion, one that obscures what is at issue when offense is caused. Someone who reacts violently to a communication initially feels offense and anger. The content of the message triggers violence, just as it triggers offense. If the state's genuine wish is to prevent violence or offense, it can say it does not really care about the content of the communication; it wants only to prevent an independent harm, physical harm or emotional upset. Without quite resolving the point, the *Johnson* Court expresses doubt that "a desire to prevent a violent audience reaction is 'related to expression' in the same way that a desire to prevent an audience from being offended is 'related to expression.'"[21] But plainly the relations are similar. What differs is that preventing violence is usually a more important state interest than preventing offense and that it is less likely to be a cover for suppressing unpopular messages.

We need to recognize that the relations to expression are similar, because we should be open to the possibility that deep offense alone may sometimes be the basis for restriction on speech. Consider the accompanying subsection of the Texas statute that forbade desecration of a place of worship or burial.[22] Usually when places of worship and burial are desecrated, it is not by the owners. But this provision is not formulated as a protection of property; it is formulated to protect symbols and sites. And we can imagine a case in which the actual owner of a place of worship or burial chooses for some reason to desecrate it. Such acts can cause deep offense to worshippers or family members. There are specific victims in a way that is not true when someone burns a flag.

One reason libel is actionable is because it offends. And what about fighting words? The drift of modern Supreme Court opinions, as chapter 4 suggests, is that only the prospect of immediate violence is a basis for forbidding the use of harsh personal insults and general epithets. But suppose five white males shout racial and sexual epithets at a lone black woman in the park. Should this be protected speech because a violent response is highly unlikely in the circumstances? I believe deep offense should sometimes warrant restrictions on speech, but probably only when there are immediate, identifiable victims.

Having disposed of violence prevention as a possible basis for the statute, the *Johnson* Court turns to another asserted state justification, that of preserving the flag as a symbol of nationhood and national unity. The Court says that this interest of the state is related to expression. It suggests that the state's concern is that flag desecration will cause people to stop believing that the flag stands for nationhood and national unity or that we enjoy unity as a nation. "These concerns blossom only when a person's treatment of the flag communicates some message."[23] Since Johnson's "political expression was restricted" because he expressed dissatisfaction with the country's policies, the "State's asserted interest in preserving the special symbolic character of the flag" must be subjected to the " 'most exacting scrutiny.' "[24]

The Court's analysis on this point flows smoothly, too smoothly. It treats application of the Texas law like application of a law that forbids displaying within fifty feet of an embassy signs that tend to bring that foreign government into "public odium" or "public disrepute." Such a law, struck down in *Boos v. Barry*,[25] was a straightforward regulation of content; it was viewpoint discrimination. Displaying near the Israeli embassy a sign praising Israel or neutral toward it was not criminal; displaying a highly critical sign was criminal. But was viewpoint discrimination really involved in the Texas statute? Suppose people constantly dragged flags through the mud and used them to light campfires. The strength of the flag as a symbol might well diminish if people continually treated it shabbily. And its strength as a symbol could be damaged even if people mistreated it in demonstrations in favor of nationhood and national unity. Thus, the threat to the flag as a symbol of nationhood and national unity arises not only from mistreatment that casts doubt on whether the flag represents national unity, on whether national unity exists, or on whether national unity of the sort we have is desirable. It is just this point that leads Justice Stevens to say in dissent that "[t]he content of respondent's message has no relevance whatsoever to the case."[26] Nevertheless, the most offensive instances of shabby treatment are probably those that in some way attack the government, national unity, or the idea of the flag; and this type of attack was an aspect of Johnson's causing offense. Further, most people who wish to treat the flag shabbily knowing that what they do will offend others are people with just such anti-establishment messages. In effect, the Texas law impinges much more heavily on people with these messages than on others. The *Johnson* Court oversimplifies by assuming that an effort to preserve the flag as a symbol of national unity *must* be directed at communications against that idea; but its conclusion that the interest of Texas is aimed against such communications is sound. As a consequence, it rightly employs the compelling interest test rather than a less strict standard of review.

Application of the Standard to Johnson

In the third stage of First Amendment analysis, the Court has little difficulty determining that Texas has failed to meet "the most exacting scrutiny."[27] The government may not prohibit the expression of an idea simply because it is disagreeable. Nor may the government preclude messages from being expressed in the particular ways chosen by those who want to express the ideas. People normally are free to choose how they will express themselves. The government may not restrict symbols to be used for a limited set of messages. The Court closes with the thought that its

> decision is a reaffirmation of the principles of freedom and inclusiveness that the flag best reflects, and of the conviction that our toleration of criticism such as Johnson's is a sign and source of our strength. . . . It is the Nation's resilience, not its rigidity, that Texas sees reflected in the flag—and it is that resilience that we reassert today.[28]

The Federal Statute and the Court's Response

In the aftermath of *Johnson*, most political discussion focused not on *whether* the decision should be undone but on *how* to undo it. Our political leaders have learned the lesson that being cast as unpatriotic is not healthy for political life, and their confidence in the public's understanding of true patriotism is not excessive. Republican leaders wanted a constitutional amendment and claimed that only an amendment could succeed in altering what the Supreme Court had done. Many Democrats, encouraged by constitutional scholars such as Dick Howard, Rex Lee, and Laurence Tribe, argued that statutory reform could turn the result around.[29] Since the *Johnson* decision was five to four, turning the result around amounted to shifting one vote. The *Johnson* opinions held out tidbits of hope in this respect.

The Flag Protection Act of 1989 provided that anyone who "knowingly mutilates, defaces, physically defiles, burns, maintains on the floor or ground, or tramples upon" a United States flag is guilty of a crime.[30] The Act excepted actions to dispose of worn or soiled flags. Congress defeated efforts to amend the bill to cover only public acts; the law reached acts committed in private as well as in public. The inspiration underlying the statute was plain enough. The definition of the crime was removed as far as possible from focusing on communicative acts. The objective was to have this statute treated like the draft card statute in *O'Brien*. If the law was treated as not directed at communication, the *O'Brien* test would apply to communicative flag burning. Convictions would then be upheld.

From the perspective of a realist jurisprudence that does not place much stock in coherent doctrine, the drafters had grounds for optimism. The *Johnson* Court says that "[t]he Texas law is thus not aimed at protecting the physical integrity of the flag in all circumstances, but is designed instead to protect it only against impairments that would cause serious offense to others."[31] The Court then refers in a footnote to Justice Blackmun's dissenting opinion in *Smith v. Goguen*,[32] a 1974 case involving conviction of a young man who affixed a flag to the seat of his pants.[33] Justice Blackmun then thought that the conviction was permissible because the opinion of the Massachusetts Supreme Judicial Court indicated that punishment was not for any communicative element but for interfering with the physical integrity of the flag.[34] The new federal law, focusing on physical integrity, was evidently tailored to pick up the vote of Justice Blackmun.[35] Furthermore, the vote of Justice Kennedy with the majority in *Johnson* came as something of a surprise, and he expressed regret that constitutional principles compelled the result they did. Finally, some Justice, appalled at the future prospect of a constitutional amendment, might have been inclined to forestall that eventuality by finding application of the new statute acceptable. Thus, proponents of the statutory route for shifting the result in *Johnson* had a reasonable hope that their efforts would be crowned with success.

What of doctrinal coherence? The Court might have distinguished

Johnson because the federal government has a legitimate interest in the flag's physical integrity per se or because the government's aim to preserve the flag as a national symbol was different somehow from the similar purpose that Texas asserted.

The government's interest in preserving the physical integrity of the flag may be put as some kind of property interest or as a sovereignty interest. In his *Johnson* dissent, Chief Justice Rehnquist drew on a case giving exclusive use of the word "Olympic" to the United States Olympic Committee.[36] He suggested that the government may have a similar limited property right in the flag. Later he mentioned an opinion by Justice Fortas urging that private ownership of a flag is subject to special burdens and responsibilities.[37] However, those who burn flags are not trying to take a "free ride" on the work of others as are those who use the word "Olympic" for their own endeavors. And the only conceivable property interest the government has in privately owned flags is to protect the flag as a symbol. The House of Representatives pressed the sovereignty interest before district courts considering dismissal of prosecutions of people who burned flags in protest against passage of the new Act.[38] These courts rightly recognized that any sovereignty claim in flags comes down to a claim to protect the flag as a symbol. The property and sovereignty arguments dissolve into an argument that the government should be able to preserve the flag's symbolic power.

The Senate emphasized in litigation that the federal law's aim to preserve the flag as a symbol differed from that urged by Texas. The idea was to preserve the flag as an embodiment of diverse views and not as a representative of any one view.

This argument fell on deaf ears as far as the members of the *Johnson* majority were concerned. Justice Brennan's opinion for the Court in *United States v. Eichman*[39] treated the federal law as aimed at communications hostile to national unity and the existing government. On that premise, decision against the statute became easy. Matters would have been more difficult if the Court had accepted the idea that the statute was not aimed at communicative acts or was aimed at a species of communicative acts that were not categorized in terms of the content of their messages. Justice Stevens in dissent emphasized that the statute plainly forbids flag burning on behalf of a wide variety of messages, not only flag burning hostile to the government or national unity. Some of the Court's language suggests that a statute is aimed at communication if it aims to suppress all messages conveyed by flag burning, even apart from the strong correlation of flag burning and messages hostile to the government or country. Such a statute would be aimed at communication, and it would restrict flag burning as a mode of communication, but it would not involve content discrimination in the sense of viewpoint discrimination. The argument for "exacting scrutiny" of statutes disfavoring a mode of communication is less obvious than the argument for such scrutiny of viewpoint discrimination; however, strict scrutiny probably remains appropriate if the government has no reason for disfavoring a method of communication other than the disturbing effects of the communications.

The most complex questions are raised if one perceives the statute as protecting the flag as a symbol, without being directed at communicative acts in particular. Is the aim to protect the flag as a symbol an impermissible or highly suspect objective for penal legislation in and of itself?[40] This question is a critical one for provisions directed against flag misuse as well as flag destruction, for provisions meant to guard against trivialization of the flag as well as symbolic rejection. Let us suppose that most of the acts a legislature is worried about are not hostile expressive acts at all; it fears that various uses or misuses of the flag will dilute its force. Recall the example of a law forbidding people to use the bright red color for any purpose, the aim being to preserve the symbolic force of that color in the flag. One may argue that the government can have a flag, that it can promote reverence for the flag, and that its aim to do that by laws limiting use are a permissible means. On the other hand, special protection for a communicative symbol with particular content, however vague, may itself amount to a kind of viewpoint discrimination. As Professor Nimmer put it, the flag symbolizes the nation and to "preserve respect for a symbol *qua* symbol is to preserve respect for the meaning expressed by the symbol."[41]

The argument to this effect is strong enough to distinguish this case from one in which the government's interest in preventing behavior has nothing to do with communication. The Court said in *O'Brien* that the government's interest in preserving draft cards was unrelated to expression. That could not be said about the government's interest in preserving flags. At a minimum, the aim is to preserve the powerful expressive force of the flag. Thus, the *O'Brien* test does not seem apt (or, alternatively, the government fails to satisfy the *O'Brien* requirement that its interest be "unrelated to the suppression of free expression"). But "most exacting scrutiny" may not be right either. The aim to keep intact expressive symbols people have come to care about, and that the government regards as a positive force, is not the same as an aim to suppress messages because of their content. If the only challengeable aspect of the new federal law had been its attempt to preserve the flag as a symbol, perhaps some test more rigorous than what *O'Brien* has come to mean, but less rigorous than most exacting scrutiny, would have made sense.

The Possibility of an Exception

I have concluded that both *Johnson* and *Eichman* were more complicated cases than the majority indicated, but that an application of standard First Amendment principles did support the Court's results. I now turn away from standard doctrines to ask whether something very special about the flag calls for an extraordinary approach. One could employ an argument for exceptional treatment to attack the result in *Johnson*, to support a different outcome under the federal law, or to support a constitutional amendment permitting flag legislation.

I discuss the issue in terms of making an exception to ordinary First Amendment principles. What that would amount to more specifically is subjecting flag legislation to less than "most exacting scrutiny," even though by ordinary standards, it falls within a category for which such scrutiny is appropriate. The special nature of the flag *might* instead be the basis for an argument that the government's protective interest is so compelling that properly drafted legislation satisfies "most exacting scrutiny." On this account, ordinary First Amendment approaches would be employed; what would be extraordinary would be satisfaction of the test of strict scrutiny absent violence or some other immediate or indisputable harm.

Much in the *Johnson* opinions shows that the powerful symbolic quality of the flag makes the case special. Justice Kennedy, then the most recent appointee, wrote a concurring opinion, explaining that "the law and the Constitution," as he saw it, "compel the result."[42] He agreed with the dissenters "that the flag holds a lonely place of honor in an age when absolutes are distrusted and simple truths are burdened by unneeded apologetics."[43] He talked of Johnson's statements as "repellent . . . to the Republic itself" and of the enormity of Johnson's offense.[44] But he did not believe the Constitution gives the right to rule as the dissenters urged, "however painful this judgment is to announce."[45] Justice Kennedy's opinion reminds one of the cry of the recently appointed Justice Blackmun in *Furman v. Georgia*[46] that however much he disapproved of capital punishment, the Constitution did not authorize him to declare that it was generally unconstitutional.

Chief Justice Rehnquist's opinion, for himself and Justices White and O'Connor, is largely an amalgam of history and poetry about the flag and a series of citations to past cases indicating that none have decided that flag desecration statutes are unconstitutional. An arresting reference in the first part of the opinion is to a statement by Representative Charles Wiggins during the Vietnam War: "The public act of desecration of our flag tends to undermine the morale of American troops. That this finding is true can be attested by many Members [of Congress] who have received correspondence from servicemen expressing their shock and disgust of such conduct."[47]

Pinning down the theory of the Rehnquist opinion is not easy. The Chief Justice suggests that Congress can recognize a kind of property interest in the flag, that flag burning, like fighting words, is not an "essential part of any exposition of ideas," that state cases have held that public burning of the flag is inherently inflammatory, and that Johnson could have expressed his ideas by other means.[48] Rehnquist simply disregards Supreme Court cases whose holdings undermine most of these arguments as applied to *Johnson*.[49] In his final paragraph, the Chief Justice writes that "[u]ncritical extension of constitutional protection to the burning of the flag risks the frustration of the very purpose for which organized governments are instituted."[50]

Although Justice Stevens challenges some of the majority's reasoning, perhaps the heart of his position is that "[e]ven if flag burning could be considered just another species of symbolic speech under the logical application of the rules that the Court has developed in its interpretation of the First Amendment in other contexts, this case has an intangible dimension that makes those rules inapplicable."[51] Stevens notes that the flag represents more than our nationhood; it represents the ideas that characterize the society.[52] He worries that sanctioning public desecration will tarnish the value of the flag, and urges that such tarnish is not justified by the trivial burden on expression of forbidding physical mistreatment of the flag.[53] He closes with the claim that if the ideas of liberty and equality are worth fighting for, "the flag that uniquely symbolizes their power" is worthy of protection.[54] The Court itself talks of "the flag's deservedly cherished place in our community" and suggests that its decision will strengthen that place by reasserting the flag's resilience.[55]

All the opinions share a feature that speaks volumes about the flag's importance and the expected audience for the opinions. No opinion cites a single law review article or other scholarly work. It is almost as if all the Justices intuitively felt that cluttering their opinions with neat doctrinal distinctions and ample references to authority would detract from the majestic simplicity of the flag and the majestic simplicity of freedom of speech.

Perhaps the major legal issue in *Johnson* and *Eichman* was whether the flag is sufficiently extraordinary to warrant an exception from ordinary free speech principles. In *Marsh v. Chambers*,[56] dealing with paid chaplains and prayers in state legislatures, the Court explicitly abandoned the normal establishment clause test, under which those practices would surely have been condemned, and declared that an exception based on history was appropriate. Here the Court might have emphasized, as did Chief Justice Rehnquist, the unique historical place of the flag and found that unusual protections were appropriate. It might, as in *Marsh*, have declared the usual standards of judgment inapplicable, or it could have found a compelling interest in kinds of considerations that would not usually be sufficient to support a restriction on speech.

Would such an exception be warranted? Some people might answer that such exceptions are never warranted. If a court has sound doctrinal principles for resolving a broad class of cases, if these principles resolve a case one way, and if the case does not lead one to think that the principles themselves stand in need of revision, perhaps a court should simply stick with what the principles indicate should be done. My confidence in the ability of abstract principles to deal with our confused and complex social reality is a bit less than that of many who insist on unwavering adherence to principle. But making exceptions is very risky. How can one be sure an exception is justified? Is it not likely that making warranted exceptions will lead to unwarranted ones? The burden against *ad hoc* exceptions to principles that cover a general class of situations is great, but it can be overcome. Are the reasons for an exception here powerful enough?

Let us think about the right to mistreat flags and the possible damage if we recognize such a right. In terms of the actual ability to express oneself, the right to destroy one's national flag may have some special force and significance, but still it does not rate very high in the general scheme of things. There are other ways to express antigovernment and antinational sentiments. Not many people want to mistreat their national flag. A narrow constitutional exception covering desecration of the national flag would not much affect the degree of free speech in our society. But the right to physically mistreat the flag in a contemptuous way has a broader significance. The right itself reflects the degree of our commitment to free speech. The existence of the right may have an importance for liberty that greatly exceeds the importance of its exercise. In this sense, the Court's claim that its decision in *Johnson* will strengthen the flag by showing its resilience to dramatic protest has force.

What protection against destruction does for the symbolic value of the flag is more complicated. All the opinions talk as if any weakening of that value would be regrettable. The dissenters say *Johnson* will have that effect; the five justices in the majority deny it. Drawing on the distinction between the French fleur-de-lis and the French tricolor, Justice Stevens perceptively observes that our flag represents particular ideas other than nationhood.[57] If our flag represents liberty as a central value, then allowing its mistreatment conceivably will strengthen its representation of liberty. That is what the majority argues. But it seems to me that Justice Stevens has the truer insight about the nature of symbols.[58] They may represent ideas and complex values and forms of life to which we give knowing adherence, but the power of the symbol itself operates at a nonrational level. Through continued usage and honor, we develop feelings of reverence for the symbol itself. If others do not respect the symbol, our own respect for it is likely to decline, and this may happen even if we do not consciously will it. Disrespect by obvious enemies of one's deeper values will not undermine the value of a symbol. If ancient Romans or modern Communists break crosses, that does not shake the power of the cross as a symbol for Christians. But if people with whom one identifies, more or less, show disrespect for a shared symbol, it loses luster and power. For this reason, commercialization and trivialization of the flag, for instance in clothing, may actually have a more insidious effect on its power than overtly hostile actions by dissidents.

The opinions are unanimous in wishing to preserve the flag from weakening as a symbol. Are they right in that aim? I was struck by Justice Kennedy's comment that "the flag holds a lonely place of honor in an age when absolutes are distrusted and simple truths are burdened by unneeded apologetics."[59] If the flag is the best one has to believe in, is something wrong? And if one believes in the flag more than anything else, is one misguided? The meanings that people assign to the flag may vary, but if someone has lost faith in whatever meanings he assigns, why should he continue to believe so strongly in the flag? Rationally, strong belief in the flag should coincide with strong belief in something else, not be a substitute for it.

There are, moreover, negative aspects of "honoring the flag." If we attach a kind of nonrational reverence to the flag, we are subject to manipulation by those who control the flag. Now, of course, no one really controls the flag; it can be used on behalf of dissident causes as well as progovernment ones. But Chief Justice Rehnquist's opinion is remarkably understanding in mentioning wars, burials of soldiers, patriotic occasions, and government buildings as connected to our associations with the flag. Our introduction to the flag as a symbol is largely in these contexts. By its very composition, the flag represents the federal union of the original thirteen states and of the present fifty states. The symbolism of the flag operates in favor of the government as well as the national union. The next to last sentence of the Rehnquist opinion talks of men being conscripted into "the Armed Forces where they must fight and perhaps die for the flag."[60] How easily this phrase evokes our feelings, but people should fight and sometimes die for what the flag represents, not for the flag. Of course, Chief Justice Rehnquist might respond that I am just being picky; that is what he meant. But the argument for protecting the flag is much stronger if one thinks of fighting for the flag itself. This notion involves the strongest form of reification, attributing value to a thing that has no inherent value. Recall Charles Wiggins's lament that flag desecration undermined the morale of American troops in Vietnam. Chief Justice Rehnquist does not delve into the question why. Suppose it were reported that some unrepresentative fringe, say a few citizens of Hungarian origin, had burned American flags because our government did not protest the Austrian government's treatment of its Hungarian minority. Would knowledge of that act have demoralized troops in Vietnam? Presumably what demoralized the troops was knowing an opposition to the war shared by many citizens was so intensely felt by some of them that they engaged in the extreme act of burning the flag. But the intensity of their opposition was precisely what the protesters were trying to express. If demoralizing is taken to mean sapping the will to fight, they *wanted* to demoralize the citizenry generally about the war in Vietnam. In a free society in which soldiers know what is happening back home, a natural effect of weakening the will of the public to fight may be demoralizing soldiers to a degree.

If the flag is venerated, reverence for the flag may become a substitute for critical thought about government policy. Part of the point of a free society is that images of flag-draped coffins should not lull us into easy belief that the government's use of military force was justified. Given the ordinary and major occasions of its use, there is such a thing as too much reverence for the flag as a symbol.

Finally, insofar as the flag can be said to represent particular values, perhaps some of those values are now too highly regarded. Chief Justice Rehnquist reports that Johnson shouted various slogans: "Reagan, Mondale, which will it be? Either one means World War III"; "Ronald Reagan, killer of the hour, Perfect example of U.S. power"; and "red, white and blue, we spit on you, you stand for plunder, you will go under."[61] Certainly one of the ideas that our flag represents is our relatively free and capitalist economic system. It also represents the importance of national interests and, in our times, it is a sign of national power. Johnson was urging crudely that the pursuit of American power and national interests is unjust and promises nuclear destruction. Johnson did not really question that the flag stands for nationhood and that nationhood exists; rather, he challenged the desirability of our concept of nationhood. Perhaps at this stage of history, humankind needs less emphasis on nationhood. Reverence for the flag, the symbol of our nationhood, may impair our sensitivity to this possibility.

My last comments disturb me, partly because of my own feeling for the flag and also from a sense that casting doubt on its place is disloyal. But I have a more developed basis for my disquiet. Any society needs symbols of unity and cohesion as well as perceptive criticisms.[62] One of the dis-

eases of intellectuals is their predominant attention to the latter. Our job
is to provide thoughtful criticism. My temperament and occupation may
disqualify me from giving due weight to the value of symbols. Perhaps so,
but I hope I have pointed out that reverence for symbols can carry costs.
Honor for the flag is not an undiluted good.

Given uncertainty about the overall effect of a constitutional decision,
either way, on the flag as a symbol, and uncertainty even about the desirable degree of honor for the flag, my own conclusion is that the Supreme
Court did well in *Johnson* and *Eichman* not to carve out an exception
from ordinary First Amendment principles.

A Constitutional Amendment?

There are two powerful reasons why no constitutional amendment
should be adopted to eliminate the constitutional right announced by the
Court. The first follows from what I have said about a possible exception
to First Amendment principles. On balance, permitting communicative
destruction of the flag is probably better than forbidding it. The cumber-
some process of formal constitutional amendment is hardly warranted to
deal with what is really a minor problem that may already have been
disposed of in the best way possible.

The second reason has to do with the appropriate function of constitutional amendments. Unless one counts the thirteenth amendment as
overturning language in *Dred Scott*[63] that slaves are property under the
due process clause of the Fifth Amendment, not a single constitutional
amendment is directed at a Supreme Court decision that guarantees liberty under the first eight amendments. The Bill of Rights, like the flag, has
a traditional status not to be tampered with lightly. Some judicial guarantees of rights could warrant being overturned by the amendment process,
but overturning is a very serious matter. The initial rush to undo *Johnson*
had more to do with shallow political desires not to appear deficient in
patriotism than with deep conviction. Using the amendment process as a
quick fix for an unpopular, well-publicized, but minor decision would
have been a most unfortunate course to follow. It would have had an
unhealthy effect on respect for free speech and respect for the Supreme
Court, it would have validated a cynical view of the present state of
American politics, and it would have provided an insidious example for
the future.

After the *Eichman* decision blocked the statutory effort to overturn
Johnson, the possibility of amendment was renewed. However, given the
intervening year, judgments were more balanced and the impetus for
amendment was less. Proponents of amendment were unable to obtain

the necessary votes in either House of Congress. Although Justices Brennan and Marshall have left the Court, *Johnson* has been cited as a settled part of the law.[64] Apparently, it is now solidly established in the Court's jurisprudence, and has receded to something like its true (minimal) importance in the public mind.

As we have seen in chapter 2 and will see in chapters 4 and 6, the Canadian Supreme Court uses very different doctrines to deal with communication aimed at expression. It is from those cases that we must judge how it would regard the status of flag burning under the Charter.

Chapter Four

INSULTS, EPITHETS, AND "HATE SPEECH"

THIS CHAPTER, which deals with strong insults and epithets, including "hate speech," has a number of purposes. After surveying various uses of insulting language, I claim that an important distinction exists between "targeted vilification" and other insults and epithets. I consider reasons that have been thought to justify punishment, or civil recovery, for such speech, and I also address constitutional principles, looking at a number of American cases and important recent constitutional decisions by the Supreme Courts of the United States and Canada. This examination reveals striking differences between the two countries in doctrinal standards and the protection of controversial speech.

STRONG INSULTS AND GROUP EPITHETS

Extremely harsh personal insults and epithets directed against one's race, religion, ethnic origin, gender, or sexual preference pose a serious problem for democratic theory and practice. Should such comments be forbidden because they lead to violence, because they hurt, or because they contribute to domination and hostility? Or should they be part of a person's freedom to speak his or her mind? Any liberal democracy faces this dilemma.

One feature of strong insults and epithets is that they tend to shock those at whom they are directed *and* others who hear. They are not expressions that are used in civil conversation or academic discourse. A setting like this book presents a problem: how much to risk offending readers by repeating upsetting words and phrases; how much to risk failure to come to terms with the real issues by avoiding the words that shock. I shall indicate briefly the sorts of remarks I am considering, and then use them sparingly.

Many strong insults use coarse language in a highly derogatory way: "You are a stupid bastard," "cheating prick," "conniving bitch," "fucking whore." Other insults may be strong without any single shocking word: "Your mother must have discovered your father in a pigpen." Very broadly, epithets are words and phrases that attribute good, bad, or neutral qualities; but usually epithets are thought of as negative. Some epithets denigrate on the basis of race, religion, ethnic origin, gender, or sexual preference. Among these are "wop," "kike," "Spic," "Polack," "nigger," "pansy," "cunt," "Nip," "slant-eyes," "faggot," "dyke," "honkey," and "cracker."

Even this summary account reveals some obvious points. Group epithets frequently strengthen other insulting words. Group epithets and other words of insult often are spoken against someone in a face-to-face encounter, but they are also used before friendly audiences to put down outsiders. The strength of insults and group epithets varies; much depends on tone of voice, context, and prior relationships. Saying just when words and phrases pass beyond the bounds of civil discourse at any moment in history is daunting. If the law is to curb insults and group epithets, the task of categorizing what should be restricted is formidable.

Insults and Group Epithets as Uses of Language

The *meaning* of most insults and epithets amounts to mixed assertions of facts and values. Words like "stupid" and "cheating" have fairly definite content. The significance of group epithets is much more vague, but they call to mind whatever "negative" qualities are associated with a group, qualities such as laziness, greed, dishonesty, stupidity, vulgarity. They also indicate a harsh, unfavorable judgment about members of the group.

If insults and group epithets involve assertions of fact and value, does it follow that they are covered by the reasons for freedom of speech? Even if they are covered, their restriction *might* still be warranted because these comments are too dangerous or too misleading; but should we recognize candidly that restriction is an exception to the privilege speakers usually have to choose their own terms to express their views? When insults and group epithets are spoken about people who are not present, they are indeed an extremely crude way to attribute characteristics and render judgments.[1] Many of the broad reasons for free speech clearly apply.

In contrast, when insults and epithets are employed face-to-face, the analysis of their use becomes more complicated. In such encounters, abusive remarks often approximate "ordinary" action more closely and may even amount to situation-altering utterances. At the extreme, social convention might establish that certain insults invite or even "demand" set responses, i.e., calling a man "chicken" to his face might be understood as a challenge to fight.[2] In that event, uttering the insult would be a different way of saying "I challenge you to fight." As chapter 1 explains, such a statement is situation-altering because it changes the normative environment. It grants the listener a privilege to fight, and in some environments may place him under a kind of duty to fight if he is not to be judged a coward. The phrase, "you are chicken," seems to have some fact and value content, attributing cowardice, but if "you are chicken," just happens to be how one invites a fight, the situation-altering aspect matters more than any message about the qualities of the person who is challenged. No insults function widely with this kind of precision in modern western societies, but conventions among various subgroups may approximate this kind of clarity. In settings where a person utters abusive words that are understood by him and his listener to invite a fight, the communication is dominantly situation-altering.

The circumstance is subtly different when a speaker, without overtly inviting a fight, hopes to provoke the listener to fight by making him furious.[3] If the speaker tries to manipulate the listener into fighting, his own expressive interests remain slim; but for the listener the import of the insult differs now. He is angered by the malicious things that have been said. His reaction is partly to the intense message of facts and values.[4]

Often a speaker consciously sets out to wound and humiliate a listener. He or she aims to make the other feel degraded and hated, and chooses words to achieve that effect.[5] In what they accomplish, insults of this sort are a form of psychic assault; they do not differ much from physical assaults, like slaps or pinches, that cause no serious physical pain. One writer has suggested that this use of words is performative in treating the listener as a moral inferior.[6] Usually, the speaker believes the listener possesses the characteristics that are indicated by his or her humiliating and wounding remarks,[7] but the speaker selects the most abusive form of expression to impose the maximum hurt. The speaker's aim diminishes the expressive importance of the words. The words are not used to inform, nor do they attempt to indicate genuine feelings. The aim is to wound, and the congruence of what is said with actual feelings is almost coincidental.[8]

Many speakers who want to humiliate and wound would also welcome a fight. But in some of the cruelest instances in which abusive words are used, no fight is contemplated: white adults shout epithets at black children walking to an integrated school; strong men intimidate women at a physical disadvantage.[9]

For many persons, serious use of group epithets is regarded as reprehensible and is quite rare; and serious use of strongly insulting words in face-to-face encounters occurs only during moments of high emotion. Out of frustration and anger a person hurls words of intense feeling that are also meant to wound; he or she does not expect responsive physical force but is not careful to avoid it. Abusive words in these situations are a true barometer of feelings, and, as such, have substantial importance as expression.

I have suggested that the circumstances in which people insult each other vary a good deal. The reasons for free speech are much more relevant for some circumstances than for others.

I turn now to the harms that insults and group epithets can do. I review four main bases for suppressing abusive language: (1) the danger of immediate violence; (2) psychological hurt for persons who are the object of abuse; (3) general offense that such language is used; and (4) destructive long-term effects from attitudes reinforced by abusive remarks. I comment about existing law and sensible legislative and constitutional approaches.

THE DANGER OF VIOLENT RESPONSE

Insults and group epithets may cause listeners to react with violence. I focus on the situation in which violence is initially used against the speaker, and the person who is provoked to respond with physical force is the immediate object of abuse or that person's friend.[10] Words highly likely to provoke violence are ordinarily made criminal by breach of the peace or disorderly conduct provisions. Under the Model Penal Code's section on disorderly conduct, adopted in substance by some jurisdictions, one must purposely or recklessly create a risk of "public inconvenience, annoyance or alarm" by making "offensively coarse utterance, gesture or display" or by addressing "abusive language to any person present."[11] The Code also forbids harassment; one commits a violation if, with a purpose to harass, he "insults, taunts or challenges another in a manner likely to provoke violent or disorderly response."[12]

Much is unclear about how the First Amendment applies to abusive remarks, but courts have steadily assumed that restriction is permissible if the danger of responsive violence is great. The leading case was decided half a century ago.[13] Chaplinsky, a Jehovah's Witness, was annoying some people with his proselytizing. A city marshall warned him to "go slow."[14] Chaplinsky replied that the marshall was "a God damned racketeer" and "a damned Fascist," and that the whole government of Rochester was comprised of Fascists.[15] He was convicted under a statute that forbade addressing "any offensive, derisive or annoying word to any other person. . . . [or] call[ing] him by any offensive or derisive name."[16] Despite the political nature of Chaplinsky's remarks and the fact that they were addressed to an official whose job presumably required a measure of self-restraint, the Supreme Court upheld the conviction. It said:

> There are certain well-defined and narrowly limited classes of speech, the prevention and punishment of which have never been thought to raise any Constitutional problem. These include the lewd and obscene, the profane, the libelous, and the insulting or "fighting" words—those which by their

very utterance inflict injury or tend to incite an immediate breach of the peace. . . . [S]uch utterances are no essential part of any exposition of ideas, and are of such slight social value as a step to truth that any benefit that may be derived from them is clearly outweighed by the social interest in order and morality.[17]

Reasoning that the state court had construed the statute only to cover words that "men of common intelligence would understand [to be] likely to cause an average addressee to fight," the Supreme Court decided that the statute was neither too vague nor an undue impairment of liberty.

Two major developments have occurred since *Chaplinsky*. In *Cohen v. California*,[18] the Supreme Court overturned the conviction of a young man who wore a jacket saying "Fuck the Draft." It stressed the emotive elements of communication and their constitutional protection. Given *Cohen*, not all remarks that amount to fighting words could be simply dismissed as lacking any expressive value.[19] The second development was a series of opinions in which the Court invalidated statutes directed at offensive language as overbroad and vague.[20] The Court emphasized the lack of danger of immediate violence.

The prospect of immediate responsive violence is a proper basis for restricting abusive words,[21] but when is such restriction warranted? I shall focus on three aspects: the speaker's aims and understanding, the probability of violence, and the breadth of the circumstances against which that probability is assessed.

I have suggested that when a speaker tries to provoke a fight, his or her expressive interest is slight; his or her remarks represent initial action toward engaging in the fight and may be punished. What if the speaker is not aiming to start a fight, but understands, or should understand, that these words may have that effect? The lowest appropriate standard of culpability would require some understanding of danger by the speaker.[22] A speaker who was actually unaware that the sorts of words used might provoke violence should be protected. If persons are punished for speaking words they do not realize can cause harm, open communication is genuinely threatened. As far as the Constitution is concerned, it should be enough that a speaker know the propensity of words, even if, in a moment of rage, he or she did not consider their likely effect. Ignorance about the effect of words should provide a constitutional defense, but a failure to bring one's understanding to bear should not.

How likely should responsive violence have to be for remarks to be punished on that basis? The state court in *Chaplinsky* wrote of "words likely to cause an average addressee to fight,"[23] and the federal Supreme Court's reliance on this language as limiting the state statute may have given some support to the idea that this standard is formulated to represent the proper constitutional measure. This phrase, however, has ambiguities and is probably not to be taken literally.

The first ambiguity concerns the persons to be counted among potential addressees: are they everybody, only people to whom a phrase really "applies," or all those likely to be angered by having the label applied to them? Someone of French origin may react less strongly to being called a "Polack" than someone of Polish origin. But a man or boy may be very offended by being called a "little girl."[24] Unless an epithet is one to which most people react with great anger, "average addressee" should include only those to whom the epithet might apply or who would otherwise be seriously upset by having it directed at them.

How is the "average addressee" to be conceived? The *Chaplinsky* language reflects the tendency of courts to imagine male actors for most legal problems. Women, as well as children and older people, are potential addressees for most abusive phrases; but outside of quarrels among intimates, abusive words are very often publicly spoken by and to younger men, frequently after drinking alcohol. The average person to whom insulting words are actually addressed may be more ready to fight than the average potential addressee. Even if we focus on those actually addressed,[25] probably no words now cause the average listener to respond with violence. In any event, that is too stringent as a minimum constitutional test for regulation. Suppose a study showed that 20 percent of listeners respond violently to certain abusive words spoken in certain contexts. That should be enough to restrict.[26] The standard should be whether provoking actual violence is a substantial probability.

Against what situations is the likelihood of violence to be gauged? If the danger of actual violence on that occasion is the overriding reason for restraint, the simplest approach is exemplified by the Model Penal Code: make the likelihood of violence an inquiry into particular circumstances. This approach has an obvious logic if the rationale is to prevent violence, but it is, nevertheless, deeply troubling. Imagine that in an area where few blacks live,[27] a twenty-five-year-old white man of average size and strength waits for a bus with a solitary black person, and the white directs a torrent of insults and racial epithets toward the black person. Does it matter if the black listener is (1) a strong twenty-year-old man, (2) a seventy-year-old man on crutches, (3) a small woman of fifty, or (4) a child of nine? Only in the first setting is violence likely. Can the same remark be punishable if directed at the one person able to physically retaliate and be constitutionally protected if directed at people not able to match the speaker physically? Even posing this question suggests two propositions. The first, to which I shall return, is that proper reasons for restraint go beyond preventing immediate violence. The second is that even if preventing such violence is the main reason for restraint, some principle of "equalization of victims" is needed. Despite the flavor of some Supreme Court language,[28] inquiry should not concentrate on the perceived capacity of a particular victim to respond physically. The test should be whether remarks of that sort in that context would cause many listeners to respond forcibly. Neither statutory nor constitutional standards should require that the particular addressee be, or appear, likely to react violently.

Wounding the Listener Who Is Abused

Abusive words can be deeply wounding to their victims, but is that a proper basis for criminal penalties or civil liability? Much harsh language is a natural part of heated personal exchanges and strong intellectual disagreements. Since few of us are able and inclined to modulate our discourse to the magnitude of a subject, the law must tolerate many words that hurt. The Supreme Court has been right to invalidate criminal provisions that reach broadly to offensive or opprobrious language.

If the use of any words can be punished because they wound the listener, it is only a small subcategory of all injurious words; a category narrowed in terms of the speaker's aims, the way language is used, damage to the listener, or some combination of these criteria. Suppose that four men think that humiliating a Hispanic woman who is standing alone would be "fun." They use their harshest words to insult her gender and ethnic origin, and call her a "whore." Their words wound deeply. Remarks whose dominant object is to hurt and humiliate, not to assert facts or values, have very limited expressive value. Their harm can be serious. Writing of racist remarks, Mari Matsuda said, "The negative effects of hate messages are real and immediate for the victims. Victims of vicious hate propaganda have experienced physiological symptoms and emotional distress ranging from fear in the gut, rapid pulse rate and difficulty in breathing, nightmares, post-traumatic stress disorder, hypertension, psychosis, and suicide."[29] Viewed alone, verbal behavior aimed dominantly at humiliation should not be constitutionally protected against punishment.[30]

This conclusion fits the actual language of *Chaplinsky*, which speaks of words "which by their very utterance inflict injury *or* tend to incite an immediate breach of the peace."[31] But line-drawing problems are severe. The speaker's motives may be mixed, and separating an intent to humiliate from an honest but vulgar statement of views is often difficult. A general criminal prohibition of abusive words that are designed to hurt and humiliate probably should be judged unconstitutional.[32] However, penalties are proper when, as in my example, someone has *initiated contact* with a person just to harass him or her. Such behavior resembles making harassing telephone calls, an activity that courts have consistently assumed may be punished despite the absence of a danger of immediate violence. Penalties are also proper when abusive language accompanies a clear intent to intimidate someone from exercising legally protected rights.

My conclusions about remarks that tend to provoke violence have a crucial bearing here. I have recommended a principle of equalization of victims. That principle, which would protect some victims not likely to respond with physical force, implicitly recognizes the legitimacy of protecting against deep hurt. The test whether words would cause many listeners to fight is a good test for whether remarks have passed the boundaries of what innocent citizens should be expected to tolerate. The hurt in a particular instance may not correlate with a willingness to fight; indeed, words may hurt the defenseless more than those who are able to strike back. However, the sorts of comments about which some listeners do fight are the ones that hurt the most. The propensity to generate a violent response is partly a measure of the intensity of hurt. This hurt constitutes a reason why a particular listener's apparent capacity to fight back should not be an element of the speaker's crime.

If the particular victim's fighting capacity should be disregarded, so also should some other features of confrontational situations. The number of people supporting the abusive speaker and the presence of bystanders who might help the victim should be irrelevant, though these affect the likelihood of a physical clash. A more subtle point concerns groups whose members are generally less likely to fight. Suppose women, or members of a particular ethnic group, are much less likely to fight than are men, or members of other ethnic groups. That does not mean the listeners are less hurt when insulted. I have proposed that the difference in likely physical response is irrelevant for words that apply generally, but what of abusive words that apply peculiarly to the group in question? Is equivalent abuse more protected if the broad class of addressees is less likely to fight? The answer should be "no." An ethnic slur should be treated like other ethnic slurs of similar viciousness.[33] In the absence of a persuasive argument that the viciousness is not the same, calling a woman a "cunt" should be treated like calling a man a "prick," even though the latter may be more likely to provoke violence.[34] When the question is asked if words "of this sort" would lead many addressees to fight, the inquiry about the words should abstract from the inclinations to fight of the particular class that is abused.

Words that wound may lead to civil recovery in place of, or in addition to, criminal penalties. A standard for civil damages can be more vague than is acceptable for criminal liability. Presently, the main vehicle for recovery in tort is infliction of emotional distress.[35] That tort requires extremely outrageous conduct and severe emotional distress. When these conditions are met, liability for abusive words is appropriate. However, an absolute privilege is needed for some communications with general public significance, as the Supreme Court has held for parodies of important public figures.[36]

Do some abusive expressions hurt so generally in face-to-face conversations that they should be singled out as creating legal liability? Perhaps the most obvious candidates in our society now are racial and ethnic epithets and slurs;[37] similar remarks directed at religion, gender, and sexual preference might also be reached. Even for race and ethnicity, determining which expressions should be treated as wrongful is worrisome. One problem is that those who are secure in a favored status can accept denigrating terms that apply to their privileged position with less distress than can those who know the terms reflect a wide dislike of their group. For example, in most contexts in our society, "honkey" hurts a lot less than "nigger."[38]

Differences in harm may concern kind as well as amount. Epithets used against members of oppressed groups may reinforce feelings of inferiority and fear of violence in a way not characteristic of epithets used against groups that have been dominant historically. This reality leads some to suppose that racist speech is constitutionally punishable if it is directed at historically oppressed groups, but not otherwise.[39] Even if the constitution is thought to permit an "even-handed" approach, one might believe that a statute should be drawn to distinguish hate speech on the basis of the kind of group attacked.

This is a very complicated issue. Some hate speech is directed by the oppressed at oppressors; some is directed by members of one oppressed group (e.g., African-Americans) at members of another (e.g., Jews); some is between members of groups that have not suffered recent, wide-scale oppression (e.g., in most areas of the country, Irish-Americans v. Italian-Americans or Roman Catholics v. fundamentalist Protestants). Much insulting speech that reinforces personal feelings of inferiority is not cast in terms of group membership at all: e.g., "You are a fat slob"; "You are just incredibly dumb." I will return to this broad problem of categorization when I consider long-term harms. Here I conclude that *if* one is focusing primarily on damage to the direct object of hate speech, it is unjustified to draw an *explicit distinction* based on the historical status of the group whose members are attacked.[40]

Despite vigorous objection, the U.S. Supreme Court in *R.A.V. v. City of St. Paul*[41] has apparently blocked the possibility of any statute that treats hate speech against groups as special, even a statute that is "even-handed" among the groups themselves.[42] This 1992 decision reveals much about the present state of First Amendment adjudication in the United States. The case involved the burning of a cross by white teenagers inside the fenced yard of a black family. R.A.V. (a juvenile) was charged under a city ordinance that provided: "Whoever places on public or private property a symbol, object, appellation, characterization or graffiti, including, but not limited to, a burning cross or Nazi swastika, which one knows or has reasonable grounds to know arouses anger, alarm or resentment in others on the basis of race, color, creed, religion or gender commits disorderly conduct and shall be guilty of a misdemeanor."[43] The Minnesota Supreme Court had earlier recognized that the language of the ordinance "arouses anger, alarm or resentment in others" might be too broad to survive constitutional attack. Since that language could cover some provocative statements that were constitutionally protected, the ordinance risked being invalid for overbreadth, covering too many communications that could not be punished. The state court had responded to this concern by limiting the ordinance to "fighting words," i.e., "conduct that itself inflicts injury or tends to incite immediate violence."

Under American federal principles, the United States Supreme Court accepts a state court's construction of its own statute. But in spite of the narrowing of the ordinance, every member of the Supreme Court found it to be unconstitutional. Four justices concluded that the Minnesota supreme court had not cured the overbreadth problem, because it had failed to identify which injuries would sustain a conviction. Apparently if someone knew or should have known that a display would create anger, alarm, or resentment based on racial, ethnic, gender or religious bias, that would constitute a violation.[44] Such a law was still too broad. The Justices said, "[a]lthough the ordinance reaches conduct that is unprotected, it also makes criminal expressive conduct that causes only hurt feelings, offense, or resentment, and is protected by the First Amendment."[45]

A five member majority took a more interesting and controversial approach. Justice Scalia's opinion for the Court assumed *arguendo* that the Minnesota court had managed to narrow the statute to fighting words, all of which could be subject to punishment. The vice of the statute was in punishing some fighting words and not others, in drawing distinctions that violated the rule against content-based regulation. As a preliminary to the crucial analysis, the Court noted that fighting words are not without expressive content, that despite some dicta indicating that they are wholly outside the First Amendment, the protections of free speech have some relevance to them. Even if all fighting words are punishable, a legislature cannot choose on the basis of content to outlaw some fighting words and permit others.

As an abstract proposition, some of the Court's approach seems undoubtedly correct, and is not really rejected by the other Justices.[46] If a legislature took two similarly situated, antagonistic groups, say Serbian-Americans and Croatian-Americans, and forbade the first group from using fighting words directed at the second, while allowing the second group to use fighting words that denigrated the first, this would constitute an inappropriate way to favor the position of the first group. This is more or less how Justice Scalia's opinion portrays the St. Paul ordinance. Obviously the ordinance does involve content distinction as to *subject*—some kinds of fighting words are prohibited and others are not—and the Court seems to regard this as sufficient to condemn the law.[47] But the Court goes further and argues that in practical operation the ordinance involves viewpoint discrimination as well. Justice Scalia suggests that a sign against "papists" might violate the ordinance, whereas a sign against "anti-Catholic bigots" would not, since only the former would insult on the basis of religion. Justice Scalia writes, "St. Paul has no such authority to license one side of a debate to fight freestyle, while requiring the other to follow Marquis of Queensbury Rules."[48] The example is a bit strained, and it suffers sharp attack by Justice Stevens.[49] A more realistic example might involve a contest between racial bigots and their victims. The racial bigots would be barred their fighting words. The natural fighting words of the victims of bigotry might be things like "Fascist" and "Nazi," which would be permissable. The ordinance would apply asymmetrically. However, when racial, religious, and gender groups square off against each other, the ordinance would apply with an even hand. Although the ordinance could *sometimes* result in viewpoint discrimination, that is far from its main thrust.

All the opinions show more realism about content distinctions than had some language of earlier cases. They recognize that various content distinctions are permissible. The source of disagreement among the Justices is whether this sort of content distinction should be subject to strict scrutiny, and if so, whether it can survive.

Justice Scalia for the Court takes the rule against content distinctions of the kind involved here as categorical, requiring strict scrutiny, despite the low value of the expression involved. Scalia recognizes that some content distinctions are all right: namely (1) when the basis for the content distinction consists entirely of the very reason the entire class of speech is proscribable[50] (as in a law that criminalizes only threats against the President); and (2) when the basis is associated with secondary effects of the speech, so that regulation is justified without reference to the content of the speech.[51] The concurring Justices urge that strict scrutiny is not appropriate for content distinctions among such low value speech; and that the very exceptions of permissible content distinctions Scalia allows apply to the ordinance, given the greater harm that occurs on the basis of the categories of fighting words the ordinance covers. Since threats to persons other than the President do pose some harm and some of those threats could be punished, the analogy of that narrow crime to the narrow crime in *R.A.V.* seems close. A legislature has chosen to punish the instances of speech within a category that cause the greatest harm, although it could also punish other instances within the category. Scalia's response is that the *reason* symbols of racial hate etcetera are worse than other fighting words does not have to do with their propensity to provoke violence. That propensity is the *reason* fighting words, "a particularly intolerable . . . *mode* of expressing" ideas,[52] may be punished. One rebuttal to Scalia is that such symbols of race hate probably do have a greater propensity to cause violence. In any event, even if they are worse than most fighting words for other reasons, such as the humiliation or fear they cause, that should be a sufficient basis to single them out. The concurring Justices have the better of this argument.

The Court's application of the compelling interest test is interesting. It finds compelling interests in ensuring "the basic human rights of members of groups that have historically been subjected to discrimination, including the right of such group members to live in peace where they wish."[53] The Court further acknowledges that the ordinance can be said to promote these interests. But the content distinction is not necessary because a content-neutral alternative is available, i.e., forbidding all fighting words. As the concurring Justices point out, this means that even though the particular government interest is directed at a subclass of all fighting words, the prohibition must reach the whole class to avoid an impermissible content distinction. This is a somewhat odd conclusion, one that evidences the Court's present attachment to a categorical rule against content distinctions.

The concurring Justices regarded the strength of St. Paul's interest as ample in forbidding the words of bias at which the ordinance was aimed, had the city forbidden only unprotected fighting words. Of the concurring Justices, Justice Stevens alone rejected a basic categorical approach to free speech; the other three Justices thought the majority was mistaken in the categories it assigned, but did give overwhelming importance to the category of "fighting words" and its low value speech.

OFFENSIVENESS

A third possible basis for restricting strong insults and group epithets is "general offensiveness." When the words and phrases I have mentioned are seriously used, they shock. They disturb people who are not even the subject of the abuse and they do so regardless of their message. However, determining what words are acceptable depends heavily on social context; and conventional restraints on language have loosened considerably in the last few decades. In the United States, no words or expressions should be illegal simply because they offend those who hear them.[54] People who strongly wish not to be exposed to coarse language should avoid settings where use of that language is likely.

In certain more formal settings, constraints on use of language are appropriate. Lawyers in court may not curse opposing counsel or judges, because curses are destructive of civility in court proceedings. A more debatable situation is a public meeting at which citizens are free to speak. If other citizens need to attend the meeting, flagrantly abusive language is directed toward a kind of captive audience and it may undermine the attempt to maintain reasoned discourse. However, citizens participating in open meetings should probably have the freedom of more informal settings.

Cohen v. California[55] and other cases, including *R.A.V.*, indicate that the Constitution does not permit prohibition based on the offensiveness of language alone. However, the Supreme Court supposes that offense can be the basis for restriction in limited settings. It has upheld discipline of a high school student for offensive remarks at a school assembly[56] and federal restrictions on the broadcast of coarse words on daytime radio.[57] Both decisions are highly questionable. People are free to switch their dials and few children listen to daytime radio; the school remarks were part of a campaign speech that exceeded good taste but were neither shockingly abusive nor extremely crude.[58] Nevertheless, the Court's position that regulation is allowable in some narrow settings is sound.

Long-Term Harms

The fourth reason for suppressing strong insults and group epithets is the avoidance of long-term harms. I shall say a brief word about the quality of public discourse before concentrating on harms that relate to social resentment and inequality. Some have argued that *Cohen v. California* gave insufficient weight to maintaining a civil quality to public discourse.[59] Coarseness and abuse may negatively affect reasoned discourse, but the government should not be in the general business of setting standards for acceptable speech.[60] It is no coincidence that less privileged or overtly radical people often use words and phrases that might be judged to impair civil discourse. Drawing distinctions between what is civil and what is not is difficult, and government control of the terms of discussion should not sanitize expressions of outrage.

The more troubling question involves the long-term effects of insults and epithets that reinforce feelings of prejudice and inferiority and contribute to social patterns of domination. Epithets and more elaborate slurs that reflect stereotypes about race, ethnic group, religion, sexual preference, and gender may cause continuing hostility and psychological damage. They may injure the status and prospects of members of groups that are often abused; they may contribute to structural subordination; they may substantially silence segments of the population; they may undermine the aspiration of equality in diversity.[61]

These broader harms of racist and similar speech need not depend on whether listeners are the objects of the epithets or slurs. Male conversations that demean women can support male prejudices; and women's feelings of resentment and frustration may derive from knowing how they are talked about as well as reacting to how they are addressed. If one focuses on these long-term harms, the particular audience is not of primary importance. Laws in other countries that are specifically directed against racial, ethnic, and religious epithets and slurs[62] do not make the audience critical.

For many years it was uncertain whether a law of this type would be held unconstitutional in the United States. In *Beauharnais v. Illinois*,[63] in 1952, the Supreme Court did sustain a conviction under a law that forbade publications portraying "depravity, criminality, unchastity, or lack of virtue of a class of citizens, of any race, color, creed or religion [in a way that exposes those citizens] to contempt, derision, or obloquy or which is productive of breach of the peace or riots."[64] Beauharnais had organized distribution of a leaflet asking city officials to resist "the invasion of the Negro" and warning that if "the need to prevent the white race from becoming mongrelized by the negro will not unite us, then the aggressions, . . . rapes, robberies, knives, guns and marijuana of the negro, surely will."[65] The Court assimilated this speech to group libel, instances in which something defamatory is said about a small group in such a way that the damaging remark falls on members of the group: for example, "the [fifteen member] firm of Mix and Nix is a bunch of crooks."[66] The Court mentioned the danger of racial riots, which a legislature might reasonably think was made more likely by racist speech.[67] In subsequent years, the Court's protection of civil libel, the *Cohen* case, and invalidations of breach of the peace and disorderly conduct statutes that lacked reference to immediate danger of violence largely undermined the authority of *Beauharnais*. The case was occasionally cited in peripheral contexts, but the prevailing assumption was that a statute so broad would not stand, and that a publication like Beauharnais's would be protected. In cases that arose out of the intense controversy over whether Nazis might march in uniform in Skokie, Illinois, a city inhabited by many Jewish survivors of the Holocaust, appellate judges acted on these premises, striking down ordinances designed to keep the Nazis out and indicating that a Nazi march could not be altogether foreclosed.[68]

During the last two decades the Supreme Court has emphasized that discrimination among communications on the basis of content is constitutionally suspect; and, as *R.A.V.* indicates, a law directed at group epithets and slurs certainly involves content discrimination. Words are made illegal because they place people in certain categories and are critical of members of those categories. It may be said in response that much of the harm of these abusive words derives from nonconscious response to their force, not from conscious consideration of the overall message.[69] Nevertheless, if a law forbids comments made generally about members of groups, and it covers the "ordinary" language of the publication in *Beauharnais* as well as harsh epithets, what is being suppressed really is a message whose content and intensity is judged hurtful and obnoxious. Unlike the fighting words covered in *R.A.V.*, this language cannot be characterized as "low value" speech, except by virtue of a judgment about its substantive message.

Some proponents of laws of this type have argued that if such speech is tolerated, the government implicitly endorses a message that is contrary to our fundamental values.[70] That is not so. The government permits all kinds of speech contrary to our constitutional values. That is an aspect of freedom of speech as we understand it. It is true that in a society where less privileged members of minorities may identify the majority with the government, government passivity may be perceived as approval; but the government can promote equality by its own actions, and by education and advocacy. It can also regulate actions other than speech, such as discriminatory decisions in hiring and renting and "ordinary" crimes like assault that are motivated by bias.[71] Allowing racist rhetoric does not necessarily endorse racism.

Somewhat different arguments rely on the Reconstruction Amendments to support suppression of hate speech. One claim is that the Fourteenth Amendment value of equality is in conflict or tension with the constitutional free speech value.[72] The idea is that Congress and the states have some authority to legislate in favor of political equality, even when that legislation directly restricts private activities. Since hate speech can seriously interfere with equality, restriction of it implements a constitutional value. From this view, a speaker's liberty to engage in hate speech has no evident constitutional priority, and reasonable restrictions should be allowed. Kenneth Karst has pointed out that oppressed and outsider groups may themselves benefit from a broad liberty of speech,[73] one that allows them to reject what are taken to be "reasoned" modes of discourse and to express their sense of anger and injustice in the strongest terms. Thus, some considerations of social equality point toward liberty of hate speech rather than restraint.

Thus far, the courts have not been receptive to the notion that the Fourteenth Amendment authorizes restriction of speech that would otherwise fall within a protected category;[74] they have continued to assume that permitting hostile private speech does not implicate the Fourteenth

Amendment. Akhil Amar has suggested that the strongest constitutional argument for restriction of hate speech is based on the Thirteenth Amendment.[75] Especially when one considers the linkage of much hate speech to acts of physical violence and intimidation against African-Americans, one may regard such speech as imposing a "badge" of slavery or involuntary servitude. If so, legislation against hate speech may be justified by the power to enforce the Thirteenth Amendment. In abolishing slavery and involuntary servitude, the Thirteenth Amendment reaches private individuals directly; the fact that legislation restricts the speech of private individuals does not pose the obstacle here that it does for a Fourteenth Amendment argument. However, under the Thirteenth Amendment alone, it is doubtful (as Amar recognizes) whether a law could reach hate speech about gender and religion; almost certainly it could not reach hate speech against whites.[76] Thus, we can see that whether a law should be "even-handed" or benefit only members of oppressed groups, or members of some oppressed groups, may depend not only upon wise legislative choice but also upon the constitutional source of justification for a law.

R.A.V. seems to foreclose for the near future the possibility of any broad law against hate speech—one that reaches beyond fighting words. Such a law indisputably would involve content discrimination. If strict scrutiny is required for content discrimination among kinds of "fighting words," which are not themselves constitutionally protected, strict scrutiny is also required for content discrimination among speech that includes much that would otherwise be constitutionally protected.

The compelling interest test would certainly apply to a law forbidding hate speech against groups. If Minnesota failed to satisfy the compelling interest test in *R.A.V.*, is it not obvious that a state trying to defend this kind of broader law would also fail? It is not *quite* obvious, the reason is this. A content neutral law was possible in the St. Paul situation because no "fighting words" are constitutionally protected. St. Paul could have covered all kinds of fighting words. A content neutral law that reaches much more broadly than fighting words would not be feasible, because then most of the speech covered by the law would be constitutionally protected.

An argument for a broader law limited to hate speech about race, gender, religion, etcetera could be made in the following way: (1) there is a compelling interest in curtailing racial, ethnic, religious, and gender hatred and humiliation; (2) a prohibitory statute would promote that interest; and (3) since a wider statute would be invalid, a focused content specific statute is required to accomplish the purpose (the point the Court did not accept in regard to the St. Paul ordinance). Despite this somewhat ingenious reasoning, the tone of the Court's opinion in *R.A.V.* and of the concurrences other than that of Justice Stevens is strongly unfavorable to any broader statute that reaches beyond face-to-face vilification. One would expect a statute like that in *Beauharnais* to be struck down.

Many countries have reasonably concluded that suppression of messages of race and ethnic hate is warranted, at some cost to free speech, because values of equality and dignity are so central and so vulnerable.[77] The issue is close, but my own judgment coincides with the prevailing assumption that a law like that in *Beauharnais* should be held unconstitutional in the United States. Part of the reason is the difficulty in seeing how the line of permissible restriction is to be drawn once the harm of messages becomes the main basis for suppression. In any event, direct commitment to positive values of equality and prohibitions of discriminatory behavior other than speech are better ways for a government to show support of equality than silencing speakers.

One conceivable way to meet this objection to restricting messages of fact and value would be to forbid only "false" speech about members of groups.[78] Such speech would lack "full value" because of falsity, and prohibiting it would not open the door for broad prohibitions of speech. Unfortunately, targeting false speech of this kind would either be ineffectual or dangerous. Suppose that the "false" remarks in question purported to be facts about members of groups but were demonstrably false, and were known to be false by those making the assertions: for example, "Every single black person in this country scores lower on standard intelligence tests than the worst scoring white person." Punishing those who make such false assertions would have a modest effect on hate literature. To have substantial bite, the law's coverage of punishable false statements would have to include matters of opinion or much vaguer and ambiguous factual assertions. As far as free speech is concerned, opinions may not be labeled true or false. With respect to vague factual assertions, trials would afford merchants of hate an opportunity to indicate their meanings in full detail, using that public forum to present damaging facts about the group they despise as unsympathetically as possible.[79] Two conclusions emerge. If falsity is an aspect of criminal liability, people should be punishable only for clear assertions of fact, and much vague scurrilous comment about groups would remain unpunishable. Trials about truth, with their publicity for harsh claims about groups, could easily do much more damage than the original communications. Whatever the constitutional status of a law precisely limited to false assertions of fact, adopting such a law would be senseless.

If racial and ethnic slurs are to be made illegal by independent legal standards, the focus should be on face-to-face encounters, targeted vilification aimed at members of a specific audience.[80] With regard to these situations, expressive value is slight because the aim is to wound and humiliate, or to start a fight. Since fighting words are already punishable and the tort of extreme emotional distress is available, what would be the significance of separate provisions for the language of group vilification? They could stand as symbolic statements that such language is peculiarly at odds with our constitutional values; and they could relieve prosecutors, or plaintiffs, from having to establish all the requisites of a more general offense or tort.[81]

Some lesser showing of immediate injury is appropriate for words that historically have inflicted grave humiliations and damage to ideals of equality and continue to do so. Of course, special treatment for class-based insults in face-to-face settings would be an exception to "content neutrality" that is required by *R.A.V.* I believe the majority's view of content distinctions in that case is too rigid, and that this special treatment should, in light of the values involved, be allowed.

Were this conclusion accepted, it would be a troubling question whether hate speech against dominant groups should be covered. I have already suggested that immediate injury to the victims of hate speech does not warrant one-way legislation in favor of oppressed groups. I further believe it damages long-term prospects for equality to enact prohibitions that are on their face uneven. There is also the unfairness of permitting the member of a victimized group to hurl epithets at an "oppressor" but not allow a response in kind.[82] Our existing statutory law and Supreme Court interpretations of the Fourteenth Amendment fit better with criminal laws, and rules for civil recovery, that do not by their terms treat one "race" (whites) differently from others and do not treat men differently from women.

I want to briefly consider the import for strong insults and group epithets of an ideal of civic courage, an ideal eloquently propounded by Justice Brandeis.[83] If a principle of free speech assumes that people are hardy or aims to help them become so, perhaps coarse and even hurtful comments should be protected in the rough and tumble of vigorous dialogue. But group epithets and slurs designed to wound listeners are another matter. It is easier to be impervious to epithets when one is a member of a privileged majority than when one belongs to a marginalized minority; and a general encouragement of civic courage may be more likely if targeted racial and religious abuse is not allowed. Even "courageous citizens" should not be expected to swallow such abuse without deep hurt, and being the victim of such abuse may not contribute to hardiness in ways that count positively for a democratic society.

Canadian Law

The Canadian law on hate speech is the subject of extensive Supreme Court judgments issued in late 1990[84] and in 1992.[85] In each case, a seven member court (two Justices were not sitting) passed on the validity of a statute that had been violated by a defendant. In the 1990 cases, Chief

Justice Dickson wrote the three majority opinions for a four member court. In each case, Justice McLachlin wrote a dissent joined by two other Justices. In the 1992 case, Justice McLachlin wrote for the majority.

In *The Queen v. Keegstra*, a high school teacher in Alberta had described Jews as: "treacherous," "subversive," "sadistic," "money-loving," "power-hungry," and "child killers," responsible for wars and revolutions, and creators of the Holocaust to gain sympathy.[86] He was convicted under Section 319(2) of the Canadian Criminal Code, which prohibits communicating statements, other than in private conversation, that wilfully promote hatred against any identifiable group [distinguished by color, race, religion, or ethnic origin].[87] Among other defenses, a person cannot be convicted if he or she establishes the truth of the statements. One of the cases, *Canada (Human Rights Commission) v. Taylor* involved a civil provision,[88] which makes it a discriminatory practice to communicate via telephone matter likely to expose a person or group to hatred or contempt on the basis of, *inter alia*, race or religion. Taylor and his party, who made recorded messages denigrating the Jewish race and religion, challenged the statute as well as a cease and desist order issued against them. Since the analyses in the three 1990 cases are similar, I shall concentrate on *Keegstra*, making a few comments about *Taylor*.

The first Charter question faced by the Court was whether the guarantee of freedom of expression extends to a public and wilful promotion of hatred against an identifiable group. Drawing from *Irwin Toy*,[89] an earlier decision on commercial speech, Chief Justice Dickson wrote, "Apart from rare cases where expression is communicated in a physically violent form, the Court thus viewed the fundamental nature of the freedom of expression as ensuring that 'if the activity conveys or attempts to convey a meaning, it has expressive content and *prima facie* falls within the scope of the guarantee.'"[90] Keegstra's comments clearly qualified.

Also relevant to the coverage of Section 2(b) was whether the government's purpose was to restrict freedom of expression. Since Section 319(2) of the Criminal Code was designed to prevent particular meanings (those promoting hate against groups) from being conveyed, the aim was to restrict expressive content, thus making Section 2(b) applicable according to the Court's general approach.

The majority opinion then turned to Section (1), which permits such reasonable limits on constitutional freedoms "prescribed by law as can be demonstrably justified in a free and democratic society." The previous case of *Regina v. Oakes*,[91] had established the standard approach to Section 1 analysis. Under that approach, as chapter 2 indicates, the state's objective must be of "pressing and substantial concern in a free and democratic society" and the impugned measure must meet a test of proportionality.[92]

The Court concluded that hate propaganda represents a pressing and substantial concern in a free and democratic society. It supported this judgment by noting Charter provisions supporting equality and multi-culturalism, using them in a manner that somewhat resembles arguments made by certain American commentators that the equal protection clause of the Fourteenth Amendment is a basis for suppressing hate speech. The Court also regarded as significant various international obligations to combat discrimination including advocacy of racial or religious hatred. Relying in part on the findings of the influential 1965 Cohen Commit-tee,[93] Chief Justice Dickson said that hate speech can cause emotional damage of grave psychological and social consequence to members of the target group, and can create serious discord among cultural groups, alter-ing views subtly even when its ideas are consciously rejected.[94]

The proportionality inquiry, sketched in chapter 2, had three parts. Was the law rationally connected to the objective? Did the law impair freedom of expression "as little as possible"? Were the effects of the law proportional to the objective? The Chief Justice indicated that in address-ing proportionality, the Court appropriately took into account how cru-cial the restricted expression was to the principles at the core of Section 2(b).[95] He concluded that "expression intended to promote the hatred of identifiable groups is of limited importance when measured against free expression values,"[96] since it contributes little to truth and tends to frus-trate the autonomy and political expression of members of the targeted groups. The opinion made clear that it did not endorse inflexible "levels of scrutiny," undoubtedly a reference to American constitutional ap-proaches; rather a court is to determine "the manner in which S. 2(b) values are engaged in the circumstances of an appeal."[97]

The Court did not doubt that the aim of the criminal provision was rationally related to reducing hate speech. That, in itself, would satisfy review in the United States when all the government must show is that legislation has a rational basis. But the rationality component under Sec-tion 1 of the Charter is somewhat more demanding. Dickson agreed with the dissenters that if the law *in fact* has no effect or works in opposition to admirable objectives, it fails the test of rationality. In answer to the argument that prosecution gives hate-mongers media attention, the Court responded that prosecutions may reassure those in targeted groups and illustrate society's reprobation of hate speech.[98]

The "minimal impairment" criterion raised issues of vagueness and overbreadth, and the possibility that speech other than hate propaganda would be chilled. The Court noted the statute excepts private speech and allows a conviction only if the accused speaker subjectively desires or foresees as nearly certain the promotion of hatred, the most intense form of dislike. Doubting that a statute must provide a truth defense for those who intentionally promote hatred, the Court deemed acceptable the failure to excuse negligent or innocent error. In answer to a claim that a criminal provision like Section 319(2) was excessive because noncriminal responses could more effectively combat the harm caused by hate propaganda, the opinion approved a combination of diverse measures, declaring that government need not rely upon the kind of intervention that is least intrusive.

Finally, the Court weighed the importance of the state's objective against the effects of the limit on a Charter freedom. Stressing again the "enormous importance" of the objective underlying the code provision, the Court reiterated that the restricted category of expression was "only tenuously connected with the values underlying the guarantee of freedom of speech," and easily concluded that the law's negative effects were not greater than its advantages.[99]

Justice McLachlin's dissenting opinion, supported by two other Justices, agreed with the majority that Keegstra's speech was protected by Section 2(b) and that the federal law was aimed at expression. Justice McLachlin suggested that threats of violence are unprotected, but that Keegstra's words did not fall into that category and that any extension of unprotected speech to cover them would be inappropriate.[100] Like the majority, the dissenters turned to Section 1 to deal with the most difficult issues in the case, and they employed the same formulations in their review. Justice McLachlin quickly concluded that the state's objective was pressing and substantial. Her disagreement with the Court was over the proportionality of the regulation to the harm prevented.

The dissent emphasized that free expression is fundamental to Canadian democracy and that limitations on expression tend to "chill" speech beyond their target.[101] Section 319(2) fails the "rationality" test because it may well discourage defensible expression while dignifying hate speech by its suppression. Noting that pre–Hitler Germany had vigorously prosecuted laws like Canada's anti-hate law, the opinion denied that there is "a strong and evident connection between the criminalization of hate propaganda and its suppression."[102]

On "minimum impairment," the dissent was much more concerned about vagueness and overbreadth than the majority, finding the word "hatred" to be amorphous in content, and worrying that a judge or jury is much more likely to infer a motive to promote hatred when the speech itself is unpopular. Justice McLachlin urged that someone speaking with legitimate objectives may also intend to promote active dislike of a group or foresee that that may happen.[103] For the dissenters, the track record of actions against material that should remain protected was sufficient to show overbreadth.[104] Justice McLachlin suggested that in light of other available responses, including civil human rights legislation, "the very fact of criminalization itself may be argued to represent an excessive response to the problem of hate propagation."[105]

The dissenters also disagreed with the majority about the comparison between the right to expression and the benefit of the legislation. They said that the restriction of individual viewpoints that bear on many subjects of discussion is a serious infringement of expression, and the gains from the law are tenuous. Any questionable benefit is outweighed by the infringement.

In *Taylor*, the Court sustained the provision of the Canadian Human Rights Act that forbids using the telephone to expose a person or a group to hatred or contempt, as the act applies to race and religion. Given the civil nature of the provision, the Court accepted the absence of a requirement of intent to discriminate and the lack of any defense for truth. The Court's easy approval of a cease and desist order, which underlay a contempt judgment, indicated a much more comfortable attitude toward prior restraints than one would find in American courts.

Emphasizing the broad range of communications that might be covered, Justice McLachlin, joined by her two dissenting colleagues in *Keegstra*, found the provision wanting on all three points of the proportionality requirement.

One peculiar aspect of broad application was not noted by either opinion. Religions usually consist of views as well as traditions and practices. If anything *warrants* hatred or contempt, some actual or potential religious views must fit into this category, because religious views *may* support the most contemptible attitudes and practices. Suppose, for example, right-wing members of the South African Dutch Reformed Church move to Canada and preach that people of color, descendants of the cursed Ham, are inferior to whites, and that apartheid should be established in Canada. A citizen telephones neighbors and warns them against this hateful religion being established in their town. Since saying the doctrines are hateful is likely to expose members and the group to hatred or contempt, it seems the citizen has violated the provision, which recognizes no defense of honest religious disagreement (or any other disagreement). Unless Canadian courts are willing to swallow the principle that vigorous religious disagreement is always inappropriate over the telephone, this kind of case seems one in which the impairment of legitimate expression is very great.

Some important features of these cases deserve special mention. The opinions are directed at statutory language, without focused attention to the facts of particular cases. In the actual cases, litigants had no strong claim to protection that other violators would lack. But other cases could be different. I have mentioned the citizen with a conscientious and well-grounded abhorrence of a group's religious beliefs. A problem of more general concern is "hate speech" directed at the dominant white majority. For example, in Great Britain, a substantial percentage of "hate speech" prosecutions have been against members of minorities. Much of what the Court says about the pressing concern to suppress hate speech does not apply to "hate speech" of minorities against socially dominant groups. Presumably, whether such speech can constitutionally be punished remains open.

In contrast to the vast bulk of free speech cases in the United States, the majority and the dissenters agree on the formulation of standards applicable to the problems. The careful and fairly elaborate criteria for Section 1 turn out to be less stringent than the rigorous compelling interest test, under which legislation rarely survives, and more stringent than most other American balancing formulas, under which legislation rarely fails. One may expect a paradoxical effect on stability of doctrine and results. Because the Section 1 approach of *Regina v. Oakes*, and especially its proportionality components, permit so much to be taken into account, it seems unlikely that Justices will find a need to discard it, although nuances of difference in the significance of the approach have emerged.[106] However, since future Justices will probably feel relatively free to treat factors as they regard appropriate, not believing precedent constrains them greatly on the status and weight to be given particular factors, the Court's declaration of the status of some provisions will not be a very sure guide to what a changed court some years later will decide about other provisions. Particular categories like prior restraint and content discrimination carry much less importance in Canada than in the United States. The nuanced, contextualized approach encouraged by Section 1 can yield relative flexibility of result under fairly stable open-ended criteria of evaluation.

The division on the Canadian Supreme Court was illustrated again in the summer of 1992 in *Zundel v. The Queen*.[107] This time a bare majority of four Justices, reviewing the conviction of someone who had published a pamphlet denying the fact of the Holocaust during World War II, declared invalid a modern version of an ancient statute forbidding the wilful publication of false news likely to cause injury to the public interest. Justice McLachlin, who dissented in *Keegstra*, wrote for the majority. A pervasive theme of the opinion was that the statutory requirements that materials be false and known to be so were not sufficiently protective of expression, because of the thin line between fact and opinion and a jury's propensity to infer knowledge of falseness when outrageous propositions are asserted.

Justice McLachlin, in accord with general doctrine, quickly concluded Section 2 of the Charter covered deliberate lies within its absolute protection. She found that the statutory provision failed the Section 1 test for a variety of reasons. She considered some of its terms to be so vague it might not qualify as a "limit prescribed by law," but she assumed that it passed this threshold test. Given the difficulty of assigning any particular objective to the modern reenactment of the ancient statute, she concluded that it lacked the support of a required objective of pressing and substantial concern. Rejecting the dissenters' proposal that the provision could be supported by the need to prevent attacks on religious, racial, or ethnic minorities, she indicated that a new objective could not be substituted for some entirely different original objective. Even assuming some appropriate objective of social harmony and a rational link between it and the statute, Justice McLachlin declared that the statute was much broader than necessary to achieve that aim, suffering the fatal flaw of overbreadth.

In an opinion by Justices Cory and Iacobucci, the three dissenters viewed the section quite differently.[108] They regarded the requirements of falsity of fact and knowledge of falsity as much more significant protections than the majority. They urged that "public interest" should be construed in terms of Charter values and that deliberate lies could seriously injure that interest. Since deliberate lies have little value as expression, such a restriction is warranted under Section (1) and the impairment is not too broad.

The four to three divisions in *Keegstra* and *Zundel* show that adjudication over statutes relating to hate speech is almost certainly not at end. Justices are at odds over how the values of expression bear on laws that allow group vilification to be punished. Their disagreements are not, even in formal appearance, primarily conceptual; they represent plain differential assessments of values.

Given recent American free speech adjudication, these Canadian cases would not lie close to the border. The statutes and their applications would flunk the conceptual barrier against content discrimination and would be declared unconstitutional.

Chapter Five

CAMPUS SPEECH CODES AND
WORKPLACE HARASSMENT

THIS CHAPTER addresses two particular problems concerning abusive speech: campus speech codes and harassment at work. Thus far, American courts have treated these subjects differently. Is this variation in constitutional assessment appropriate? I discuss campus speech codes and then the law of workplace harassment, offering a few final observations about speech codes.

CAMPUS SPEECH CODES

Many members of university and college communities believe there has been a dispiriting increase in hostile speech against minorities, women, and gays over the last decade. Some institutions have responded to incidents on their own campuses by adopting speech codes that set limits of acceptable discourse for academic life. The codes rely substantially on consultation and mediation, but are backed by serious penalties like suspension and expulsion for gross or repeat violations. These codes range widely in what they cover. Some limit themselves to expressions that arguably could be made criminal or tortious by the state more generally. The Stanford University Code of 1990, for example, provides:

Speech or other expression constitutes harassment by personal vilification if it:

a) is intended to insult or stigmatize an individual or a small number of individuals on the basis of their sex, race, color, handicap, religion, sexual orientation, or national and ethnic origin; and

b) is addressed directly to the individual or individuals whom it insults or stigmatizes; and

c) makes use of insulting or "fighting" words or non-verbal symbols.

In the context of discriminatory harassment by personal vilification, insulting or "fighting" words or non-verbal symbols are those "which by their very utterance inflict injury or tend to incite to an immediate breach of the peace," and which are commonly understood to convey direct and visceral hatred or contempt for human beings on the basis of their sex, race, color, handicap, religion, sexual orientation, or national and ethnic origin.[1]

Other codes reach much deeper into what constitutes the expression of ideas in an ordinary manner, prohibiting the expression because the ideas are deemed obnoxious. As originally adopted, the University of Michigan Policy on Discrimination and Discriminatory Harassment made people subject to discipline if, in educational and academic centers, they engaged in:

1. Any behavior, verbal or physical, that stigmatizes or victimizes an individual on the basis of race, ethnicity, religion, sex, sexual orientation, creed, national origin, ancestry, age, marital status, handicap or Vietnam-era veteran status, and that

a) involves an express or implied threat to an individual's academic efforts, employment, participation in University sponsored extra-curricular activities or personal safety; or

b) has the purpose or reasonably foreseeable effect of interfering with an individual's academic efforts, employment, participation in University sponsored extra-curricular activities or personal safety; or

c) creates an intimidating, hostile, or demeaning environment for educational pursuits, employment or participation in University sponsored extra-curricular activities.[2]

Are speech codes for universities and colleges significantly different from criminal provisions for society at large? Or, are the same considerations relevant to more or less the same degree? That, perhaps, is the overarching question in evaluating university speech codes.

Three preliminary observations are in order. First, many universities are run by states; others are private. Thus far in the United States, despite very extensive government involvement in the financing of private university research and teaching, private universities have not been regarded as "state actors." Crucial to our purposes, constitutional limits do not apply to private educational institutions. Unless restricted by federal or state statutes, they may regulate their internal life as they see fit. The situation is different for public colleges and universities. All their actions, including the formulation and application of speech codes, are subject to federal and state constitutions. A student against whom a campus speech code is applied has a possible legal claim that the university has acted in an unconstitutional manner.

This difference in legal status leads to a second preliminary observation. When one asks whether university regulation of student and faculty speech is like state regulation of citizen speech, one is asking a question that is both about constitutionality and wise choice. For private universities, the issue over possible regulation is mainly one of wise choice, though *some* communications may violate statutory rules against discrimination. State universities must also worry about constitutionality. If it is clear that a particular code will be declared invalid by the courts, most state universities will see little point in suffering the upset and bad publicity that accompanies such unsuccessful efforts.[3]

My third observation concerns the way the constitution is regarded. Sensible participants at state universities need to take a substantially predictive approach. They do not want their endeavors to backfire, as is likely to happen if courts tell them they have violated the constitution. They need to look at what the Supreme Court has said as a guide to what it and other American courts will decide. Private universities can look at constitutionality a bit differently. For them the "Constitution" may be one guide to what they as semi-public institutions should do; but they can ask about the Constitution as it *should* be interpreted, rather than the Constitution as it has recently been interpreted by the Justices who happen to be sitting.

Legislators looking at constitutional law may ask themselves yet another question: should they adopt legislation imposing the standards applicable to state universities on private universities? That will depend on whether they have reasonable confidence in the Supreme Court's development of constitutional principles *and* think these principles should be applied to private institutions.

Are universities different in a relevant way from general society? They can hardly be less devoted to the pursuit of understanding and to free discourse. Institutions connected to specific religious ideals may choose to restrict direct challenges to those ideals, but even they encourage free discourse in other domains.[4] The basic reasons for free speech apply powerfully to life at universities. For the typical university, any basis for a less permissive approach to speech would have to lie in a greater need to curb the harm speech can cause. Most universities are self-contained communities, with a more direct concern over the lives of their (mostly young) students than the state has for its citizens. In this respect, the university fits someplace between the general society and a secondary school. It has some responsibility to assure mutual respect among its members and foster conditions in which students may learn and develop. In exercising care for its students, perhaps the university can prohibit speech that would have to be allowed in the general public.

When one sees the issue in this framework, one quickly realizes that "the university" is not a single locus of speech. Criticizing Jews in a classroom discussion or in the middle of campus is not the same as reviling a Jewish student in his room or posting an anti-Semitic sign opposite his door. Jonathan Cole's remark that "free speech is at the heart of university life"[5] is especially true in the classroom and other public settings. A student's room is not a place where others are free to say things that deeply offend him or her.

The fundamental reasons for restricting speech that demeans on the basis of race, gender, national origin, religion, and sexual preference are the same as those we have looked at in the previous chapter. In a particularly influential article, Charles Lawrence has suggested that racism is "both 100% speech and 100% conduct," that "all racist speech constructs the social reality that constrains the liberty of non-whites because of their race."[6] Lawrence writes of the immediate injurious impact of racial insults, of the absence of an opportunity for responsive speech or intermediary reflection on the ideas conveyed. The consequence for those who are the victims of such speech is an instinctive, defensive psychological reaction, leading to silence or flight rather than fight.[7]

Members of university communities have generally been more sensitive to such arguments than the public at large.[8] Part of the reason may be that academics, who tend to be further to the left politically than the general population, are especially concerned with racism, sexism, and related phenomena. As some have pointed out, restriction of speech fits comfortably with attitudes of "political correctness," favoring values of racial and gender equality and respect for alternative lifestyles.[9] One can certainly believe that some hate speech should be forbidden on campuses without thinking that most controversial "right-wing" views should be labelled unacceptable. Nonetheless, those with little tolerance for others they see as insensitive to historical oppression and unjustified inequality often find slight value in speech that they believe continues that oppression.

Lawrence develops the interesting argument that *Brown v. Board of Education*, the decision requiring desegregation of public schools, was based fundamentally on the perception that legally enforced segregation conveyed a demeaning message about blacks.[10] Based on this understanding, segregation itself was a kind of speech. University students who "are forced to live and work in an environment where, at any moment, they may be subjected to denigrating verbal harassment and assault" are not so unlike black children stigmatized by the message of segregation.[11] Given the equal protection value of eliminating messages of racial inferiority, Lawrence argues that the evils of the private deprivations of liberty caused by hate speech should be balanced against the deprivations of liberty that arise out of state regulations that seek to avert the private deprivations.[12] Even if one values free speech, as Lawrence does, this idea of a balance is bound to authorize more regulation of speech than would be possible if one assumes there is a very heavy presumption against regulation—the more standard approach to free speech questions.

People have different visions of the fundamental mission of education; private universities and colleges, and perhaps public ones to a degree, can reasonably define themselves in various ways. Three different concepts of the objectives of public institutions of higher learning have emerged from Robert Post's study of judicial opinions.[13] The most traditional is "civic education." Viewing public education as an instrument of community life, it would permit substantial limitations on speech. The second concept, "democratic education," is much less favorable to restriction. It conceives of education as preparing students to be autonomous citizens, and entails liberties for students similar to those that citizens have, including a right to harsh and obnoxious expression. A third concept, "critical education," sees the university as devoted to the unfettered search for truth. Those who accept this view would not permit any ideas to be suppressed because of their unacceptability, but they might impose requirements of reason and civility, forbidding harassing or personally degrading remarks.

That various private institutions, as a matter of law and sound judgment, may define their missions with different emphases is clear. They may assign civility and a socially unified community more or less importance. As I have mentioned, some may even begin from a commitment to a particular, typically religious, perspective. Universities with great intellectual standing and wide diversity need to be especially generous to free expression; but what is right for Columbia or Stanford may not be right for Brigham Young or Liberty Baptist College. It is arguable that some range of approaches is apt for public institutions as well—that some variations may be desirable or that, at least, the law should leave latitude for different judgments.

In light of different educational missions, we need to identify the genuine points of disagreement between those who want to restrict speech and those who do not. Nadine Strossen, now the President of the American Civil Liberties Union, wrote an article supporting free speech on campus in response to the article by Charles Lawrence mentioned above.[14] Marshalling the arguments against regulation and urging that any viewpoint regulation is unacceptable, Professor Strossen notes that the ACLU accepts bans on assaultive, intimidating, and harassing language,[15] and further indicates agreement with Lawrence that targeted harassment that seriously interferes with the learning environment may be restricted.[16] What mainly divides Strossen's "traditional civil libertarian position" from those who urge more extensive restriction is the status of deeply obnoxious ideas that are not adjuncts of harassment and the degree of danger of code formulations whose precise scope is indeterminate.

The language of the University of Michigan code, a crucial part of which I have quoted, was broad in its scope and seemed to reach into the realm of obnoxious ideas civilly expressed. That coverage was confirmed by an interpretive guide that was later withdrawn. According to the guide, sanctionable conduct included: "A male student makes remarks in class like 'Women just aren't as good in this field as men', thus creating a hostile learning atmosphere for female classmates."[17] The guide further said that someone is a "harasser" who comments "in a derogatory way about a particular person or group's physical appearance or sexual orientation, or their cultural origins, or religious beliefs."[18] A graduate student in the School of Social Work was required to answer in formal disciplinary procedures for his assertions, in and out of class, that homosexuality was a disease and that he intended to develop a counseling plan to change gay clients' sexual orientation to "straight." A divided hearing panel finally determined that he had not harassed students on the basis of sexual orientation.[19]

A federal district court had little difficulty deciding that the Michigan code was both unconstitutionally overbroad—reaching too much protected speech; and unconstitutionally vague—too uncertain in its coverage.[20] In a subsequent case, another court held that the somewhat narrower Wisconsin code was also invalid.[21] Robert Sedler, who litigated the Michigan case, has suggested that any speech code for a public university, or college, is likely to run afoul of recent free speech jurisprudence and to be declared unconstitutional.[22] As Sedler recognizes,[23] *R.A.V.*[24] makes the prospects for state university codes much worse than they were previously. If the Supreme Court sticks to *R.A.V.*'s rigid approach to content discrimination, all the codes that implicitly treat hate speech (focused on categories such as race, religion, and gender) differently from unregulated virulent personal insults are likely to be declared invalid. Even a code that limits itself to fighting words will not be acceptable if it covers only categorical hate speech. Indeed, one concurring Justice in *R.A.V.* hinted that the five member majority may have reached out in the way that it did partly in order to indicate its disapproval of campus speech codes.[25] Apart from possibly persuading some members of that majority to change their minds, the practical hope for state universities that want to regulate rests in formulations that are *narrow*—not reaching too much expression—and *noncategorical*—treating vicious, deeply distressing remarks similarly, independent of whether they demean in relation to categories like race.

R.A.V. does not directly affect private universities; they are not constitutionally bound to behave as are most state agencies. One may well think, as I argued in the last chapter, that *R.A.V.*'s rigid approach to regulations of categorical hate speech is indeed *too rigid* as a matter of constitutional interpretation. A private university may reasonably decide that Justice Scalia's opinion carries no strong moral force for what it should do.

Speech codes certainly should not be embraced with enthusiasm. If a peaceable, respectful, and nonoppressive campus life can be maintained without a code, that is far preferable to introducing a regime of formal regulation. A speech code is a response to some kind of breakdown in civil life. If one seems necessary, the choice whether to cast it in terms of categories of hate speech or to cover all extremely abusive remarks is difficult, subject to considerations raised in the last chapter and to particular experiences in the university involved.

If major diverse universities are to discipline hateful remarks, the compass of those forbidden remarks should be narrow. As I have mentioned, the locus of remarks matters. Even more importantly, expressing ideas is not the same as provoking a fight or seeking to injure. Campus speech codes, if they must exist, should be directed primarily and carefully at the intentionally injurious use of speech.

Should Congress (or a state legislature) enact a law subjecting private colleges and universities to the same standards as apply constitutionally to public colleges and universities? This issue was sharply posed by a bill in Congress, the Collegiate Speech Protection Act,[26] that made for strange bedfellows. Sponsored by Henry Hyde, a conspicuous conservative and a vociferous opponent of "political correctness," it was supported by the American Civil Liberties Union. Even if one favors robust latitude for speech, there are good reasons to oppose this step. One is the appropriate diversity that exists among colleges and universities. If public and major private institutions do not restrict speech much, or at all, beyond what the state may do in respect to ordinary citizens, there should be room for colleges and universities that perceive their functions differently, that seek to create a fairly close community of people with similar outlooks. Further, as Frank Michelman, argues, even if one focuses on the conditions of democracy and the autonomy of citizens, whether regulation of racist speech is helpful or unhelpful is genuinely uncertain.[27] Some universities may reasonably decide, from these perspectives, that more restriction is appropriate than courts will allow for public institutions. Overall, he says, democracy may best be protected if universities have a range of choice, at least if their own internal governance on these matters is fairly democratic[28] (a condition that is certainly not met at many institutions). It does not follow, of course, that private institutions should have carte blanche. Were the conditions of free discourse to be seriously undermined at major private colleges and universities, the government would properly step in to correct things.

WORKPLACE HARASSMENT

In the United States, the law of employment discrimination has been developing outside the mainstream of ordinary free speech jurisprudence. At the workplace, words of supervisors or fellow employees that condemn on the basis of race, gender, or religion may be deemed harassment. Employers that permit an environment in which harassment occurs are guilty of employment discrimination. Courts can impose a range of remedies including injunctions against offensive behavior.

Basic Standards

The law of workplace harassment has grown mainly out of the federal statute, Title VII, which prohibits discrimination in conditions of employment by race, religion, national origin, and sex.[29] Most states have analogous statutes against discrimination, and these have also been a source of decisions on harassment. The simple theory is that various kinds of harassment at work can become bad enough so that an employee suffers discrimination in employment. The employer is directly responsible if upper management engages in harassment; alternatively, and more commonly, the employer is responsible because higher officials learn, or should have learned, about the harassment and have failed to take effective steps to stop it.

The great majority of cases have involved sexual harassment, but harassment based on race, religion, or national origin is also impermissible.[30] I shall concentrate primarily on sexual harassment, assuming that the victim is a woman. Some important forms of sexual harassment have no obvious parallel in the other categories: e.g., "Have sex with me or I will make sure you are never promoted." Other forms do have parallels— "Women are too stupid to handle this job"—and what I say about those forms applies to the other categories of harassment as well as sexual.

The elements of a Title VII violation are: (1) the employee belongs to a protected group; (2) she was subject to unwelcome harassment; (3) the harassment was based on sex (or other relevant category); (4) it affected a condition of employment; (5) the employer knew or should have known of the harassment and failed to take prompt remedial action; and (6) the employee acted reasonably under the circumstances.[31] An example of a case in which the alleged harassment did not fit these requirements involved a woman who asserted that her male supervisor spoke about his homosexuality and tried to draw her into conversations about sexual preference.[32] The court said that since such comments did not single the woman out because of her sex and might be as disturbing to men as to women, they could not constitute harassment forbidden by the statute.

Sexual harassment takes two discrete forms, only one of which generates serious First Amendment questions. One form is called *quid pro quo* harassment; it typically involves conditioning someone's employment position on her sexual involvement. When a supervisor says, "I am going to fire you unless you make love to me," that amounts to *quid pro quo* harassment. As I have explained briefly in chapter 1, this kind of threat alters the situation of the listener. It presents her with a new and potentially disturbing choice—whether to engage in unwelcome sexual relations or lose her job. Such situation-altering utterances[33] are not the sort of speech that warrants protection under a guarantee of free speech. A similar conclusion is warranted if speech is not explicitly *quid pro quo*, but the superior humiliates the employee so she will agree to sexual involvement.

The second form of harassment, the one that concerns us here, is "hostile environment" harassment. It exists when men treat a woman so badly because of her gender that the working environment becomes hostile or abusive. Contrary to what some other federal courts had suggested, the Supreme Court has indicated recently that when conduct is severe or pervasive enough to create an abusive working environment, the conduct violates the statute even if it has not affected the employee's psychological well being.[34] The standard is whether "the environment would reasonably be perceived, and is perceived, as hostile or abusive";[35] a court can make that determination only by looking at all the circumstances.

The Supreme Court did not speak directly to the perspective from which reasonableness should be gauged. In a case involving pathetic but disturbing love letters sent by one employee to another, the Ninth Circuit Court of Appeals said that the standard for what conduct amounts to harassment is that of a reasonable woman (or victim) rather than of a sex-blind reasonable person.[36] Noting that sex-blind standards tend to be male-biased and that Title VII is not a fault-based tort scheme but is designed to prevent abusive conditions of employment, the court defended its decision to classify "conduct as unlawful sexual harassment even when harassers do not realize that their conduct creates a hostile working environment."[37] The Supreme Court has not followed this lead, instead speaking of an environment "reasonably . . . perceived" as hostile or abusive.[38] Probably this language is better understood as avoiding the issue of whether a standard should focus on a "reasonable woman" or a "reasonable (sex-blind) person," rather than resolving the issue in favor of the latter approach.

Free Speech and Harassment

Hostile environment harassment may or may not involve expression. If a boss continually fondles his secretary, that would amount to harassment and would present no free speech issue. In most cases, however, expressions of various sorts make up at least part of the claim that a woman has been harassed. Men may request a sexual relationship or direct sexually explicit or degrading speech at the female employee, or they may engage in sexually explicit or degrading speech that is not directed at the woman but is seen or heard by her.[39] One writer has suggested that such speech conveys either a hostility message—women are not welcome in the workplace or are generally deserving of scorn; or a sexuality message—women, or this woman, are viewed in a sexual light.[40] These two messages are not, of course, always distinct, and some comments may convey both messages. Many expressions are very crude, such as the verbal comment, "You are a dumb ass woman,"[41] or blatantly pornographic calendars in the workplace.

Other expressions fall more nearly within the range of the ordinary, such as a civil comment that, "women are not suited for the kind of work we do." Such civil comments do not figure prominently in cases where courts have found sexual harassment at the workplace, though isolated remarks may fit into this category. In one case, a state court found that the printing of bible verses on paychecks and the inclusion of Christian religious content in the company newspaper constituted religious harassment of an offended Jewish employee.[42]

No one doubts that speech of various sorts can create a working environment that a woman reasonably experiences as hostile. Furthermore, no one doubts that even civil expressions, as in a company newsletter, can contribute to such an environment. Were all workplace speech held irrelevant to harassment, men could make working conditions extremely hostile for women, and drive many of them from their jobs. If women are to be treated equally in the workplace environment, restricting harassing language is very important. On the other hand, expressions of opinion and feeling are normally protected against government restriction by the First Amendment, even when the speech disturbs others. This is the constitutional problem about hostile environment harassment. It is most sharply posed by civil expressions on serious topics that may nonetheless contribute to an abusive work environment. Although such expressions form at most a very small part of claims of harassment that have been pressed thus far, I pay substantial attention to them. If one can arrive at an understanding of how they should be treated, one is in a better position to evaluate the place of the more rude and vulgar fare that composes actual harassment claims.

First, we need to answer a preliminary question: Why does restriction of speech by private employers raise any First Amendment question? After all, private employers are free to restrict what their employees say to one another without constitutional limit; why can't the government require private employers to do what they may do on their own? Especially if the employer claims no interest in expressing itself, where is the constitutional difficulty? The answer is straightforward. The government cannot ordinarily restrict speech. If its law requires someone (the private employer) to restrict the speech of someone else (the employee), it (the government) is restricting the speech indirectly. The law requiring such restriction is, therefore, subject to constitutional limits.[43]

Second, I want briefly to address another preliminary matter: the use of expression in a claim of harassment. Speech may be presented either as constituting or contributing to harassment, or as *evidence* of the significance of independent behavior that may be harassing. As the Supreme Court has recently reaffirmed, no principle of free speech precludes the use of what someone has said in order to understand their actions.[44] Suppose male road construction workers urinate in the gas tank of a female co-worker, and subsequently claim that their "practical joke" had nothing to do with gender, only with the personality of their victim.[45] Proof that the same workers had "incessantly referred to the [victim and others] as 'fucking flag girls' "[46] could amount to significant evidence that the victim's gender was an important basis for the "joke" and was reasonably perceived to be so by her. The use of expression that raises the primary constitutional question is not this evidentiary use to interpret other behavior; it is *counting the expression itself* as part of what amounts to harassment.[47]

Constitutional Factors

Most speech that has contributed to findings of a hostile workplace is constitutionally protected in some sense. The sense is that the government could not treat similar remarks as criminal or tortious if they were uttered in a public place before a general audience. Either the law of workplace harassment is out-of-kilter with general First Amendment doctrine or there is something special about the remarks in context. I will explore various reasons why the First Amendment may not apply, or may not apply with full force, to abusive categorical remarks in the workplace, finding some of these reasons to be markedly stronger than others. I will then draw conclusions about how much workplace speech should be protected and what the significance of that protection should be.

A FORMALIST ARGUMENT FOR A RELAXED STANDARD OF REVIEW

One way to look at the law of workplace harassment is that it is not *really* about speech at all, it is about discrimination. Language in *R.A.V.* suggests the following possibility.[48] Title VII is not directed at expression; it forbids all discrimination according to membership in the named categories. If a law is not directed at speech, but speech is one means by which the law can be violated, the harm of content regulation of expression is avoided. The appropriate mode of analysis becomes the familiar approach of *United States v. O'Brien*,[49] which deals with situations in which speech violates laws not directed at expression. Although *O'Brien* involved symbolic speech (burning draft cards), it should not matter whether the speech actually engaged in is symbolic or ordinary verbal comments. If the government is not aiming at expression, it may prohibit violative speech by satisfying the relatively easy *O'Brien* test.

Whether the Justices who joined the Court's opinion in *R.A.V.* are actually persuaded by this argument, with each of its necessary steps, is unclear. In that opinion, Justice Scalia distinguished the law of workplace harassment from the hate speech ordinance that was being struck down, but his language was too elliptical to clarify a general approach to harassment.[50] It is plain that both the majority and the concurring Justices, who implicitly presented Title VII law as an instance of appropriate classification by content,[51] are favorably disposed to restriction of verbal harassment. This disposition is confirmed by the autumn 1993 case in which the Supreme Court formulated the basic standard for a hostile work environment.[52] The claimed harassment consisted almost entirely of verbal abuse by the company's president directed toward a female manager, yet the Court did not evince any First Amendment worries.

Workplace harassment, nevertheless, is not like the problem the Court formulated for itself in *United States v. O'Brien*. The government's interest in preserving draft cards, or so the Court said, had nothing to do with the message of draft card burning. Comments that harass at work are restricted precisely because they convey a disturbing message. The government is regulating the content of messages because the content of some messages amounts to or promotes discrimination. The regulation of speech is far from incidental; speech is restricted because of its communicative impact. As Eugene Volokh has suggested,[53] the relation between the tort of intentional infliction of emotional distress and instances of distressing speech is a much closer analogue to the relation between a law against discrimination and instances of abusive remarks than is the relation of statute and violation considered in *O'Brien*. The Court has assumed, correctly, that when distressing remarks at the heart of a tort action are claimed to be protected by the First Amendment, *O'Brien* does not dispose of the problem; a court must employ other First Amendment approaches to see if restriction is permissible.[54]

There are various policy arguments why workplace speech is appropriately subject to greater regulation than speech in public. I shall look at a number of these in turn, beginning with the assertion that workplaces are for work, not public discourse.

WORKPLACES ARE FOR WORK

Can it plausibly be said that restrictions on workplace speech are not significant because of the purpose of workplaces, and because people can indicate their views elsewhere? In our society, only a small percentage of people are active in true political spheres. For many people, the workplace is a main locus of discussion about public affairs and matters of personal significance. Free speech has strong relevance for workplace communication, as it does for communication among families and friends. The scope of free speech is not limited to discourse in some public space.

The constitutional status of personal conversation is not entirely settled. Addressing a case in which an off-duty policeman flirted with a local college student and gave her a ride on his motorcycle, Judge Richard Posner wrote for the Seventh Circuit that "[c]asual chit-chat" among two or a few people is not protected by the First Amendment because it is not sufficiently related to the free marketplace of ideas.[55] Earlier the Supreme Court had unanimously concluded that a teacher's criticizing school policies in a private meeting with the principal was constitutionally protected.[56] The "marketplace of ideas" definitely includes private discussions as well as public ones. Discussions within workplaces about whether women are suited for particular jobs are as much within this marketplace as are speeches or letters to newspapers on that topic. What of serious conversations about more personal matters? These matters are of great importance in people's lives. Moreover, one of our primary sources of understanding about general subjects is our conclusions about things that bear directly on our lives. Our belief, for example, about whether people are widely dishonest will be based largely on our distillation of our own personal interactions. Thus, discussions of our personal affairs with others are crucial to our arriving at general opinions. In human life, personal and general subjects are intermingled, and the First Amendment should protect our explorations of both.

One version of the "workplace argument" is that work, as Rodney Smolla has put it, involves "statements of transaction" and that the application of the First Amendment, therefore, is less strict for the workplace.[57] Smolla's core idea of "statements of transaction" is very close to what I have called situation-altering utterances, remarks that do something rather than tell something. Comments such as "Plug that hole" or "Please type this" are situation altering or transactional. Smolla is right that free speech has little to do with these, which are common in settings of work. What does not follow is that other speech that occurs in the workplace should suffer a reduced status. My secretary and I have now known each other for about a decade. We chat about various personal matters and contemporary events. There is no evident reason why those conversations should enjoy lesser protection because we also have transactional conversations and because the basis for our relationship is work. Of course, "ordinary remarks" can sometimes convey subtle messages about how business will be transacted, but these problems are not properly dealt with under some general principle that all speech in "transactional settings" deserves less protection.[58]

SPEECH THAT DISCRIMINATES

A close cousin of the argument about transactional speech is an argument that some speech not only favors discrimination, it directly discriminates. This suggestion, made by Marcy Strauss,[59] has substantial merit; but it does not cover all workplace speech that is regarded as harassment. Suppose a plant manager said to a worker, "You needn't apply for the supervisor's position because we would never promote a woman to that." Whether or not the manager is accurately stating what would be done if the woman went ahead and applied, his speech is already a form of discrimination in employment. It tells the woman that any application would be useless and it would, in fact, discourage most women from bothering to apply. It *is* discrimination not mainly because of any message about the inferiority of women, but because it already treats women differently from men in the promotion process. Although the example is not quite so stark, something similar is involved if a boss says, "I am not going to treat you equally with other workers because you are a woman." The employee is being informed that she should bring different expectations to the job than would a male employee. She is already suffering discrimination. But suppose the boss says, "I think women belong at home and certainly shouldn't be doing this work, but now that you are here, I will do my best to treat you as I would any other employee." Here the woman may be disturbed to be working for such a man, but what disturbs her is her knowledge of his opinions, not an incipient difference in treatment from men.

The significance of what co-workers say will depend on their relation to a woman worker. If they actually work with her *and* they make clear they will not work cooperatively with her, their words amount to differential treatment on the basis of sex. (At least if supervisors have not acted reasonably to stop the behavior, the responsibility for this differential treatment may be placed on employers.) If the male co-workers express opinions but these have no evident bearing on working relations, that kind of differential treatment has not occurred. Again, the woman may be disturbed by having to work with men who find her presence uncongenial, but that is because their expressed opinions distress her.

We now face a crucial question about workplace harassment. If it is true that people are uncomfortable and find work more difficult when they are reminded that fellow employees do not respect them and resent their presence, why shouldn't comments to this effect also be regarded as a form of discrimination? With slightly fuller development, the argument might look like this.[60] Demeaning comments can affect working conditions in a negative way. They put women in the position of having to leave jobs or to accept unfavorable working conditions. This is a "discriminatory" harm that properly concerns the government. Workers can be required to act reasonably to avoid this harm. Acting reasonably may involve not speaking words that cause the harm, even when one's speaking of the words would constitute an honest expression of opinion.

This argument might be proposed as limited to the workplace (and perhaps similar) settings or as a general approach to speech. Acceptance of the argument as a general approach would radically alter First Amendment analysis. Words spoken or written could be treated as discriminatory if they predictably made living in the society significantly more uncomfortable for members of some groups. Speakers would no longer have a nearly absolute freedom to express their honest opinions on sensitive topics in an emotionally powerful way. I shall assume that the argument is not to be taken in this broad way, but rather as claiming that the closeness of relations at work and the cost of a woman's leaving her job make demeaning language discriminatory in that context. In this view, the balance of freedom to speak and power to regulate to avoid harm is quite different for words at workplaces than for words spoken by members of the public in their general relations.

I shall return to this fundamental issue below. Here I conclude that the issue is obscured if all demeaning speech is simply regarded as indistinguishable from active discrimination that involves an actual or prospective difference in treatment. Basic notions of freedom of speech require drawing some line between comments that are fundamentally expressions of opinion and feeling and those that actively discriminate. This effort at classification is by no means simple in workplace settings, but treating all sexist speech as actively discriminating would be a mistake.

TIME, PLACE, AND MANNER

The First Amendment permits regulation of the time, place, and manner of public speech such as demonstrations. But, with limited exceptions,[61] a fundamental principle of acceptable regulation is content neutrality; the government cannot prefer some messages over others. Furthermore, no time, place, and manner discussion has suggested that ordinary conversations can be restricted by the government because people are free to express themselves in other settings. Since restriction of workplace harassment is far from content neutral and much of what is covered is conversational discourse, standard time, place, and manner principles do little to support restriction. Insofar as focus on time, place, and manner draws attention to special features of the workplace setting, these are better considered under different headings.

CAPTIVE AUDIENCES, CAPTIVE SPEAKERS, AND PERSONAL PRIVACY

One of the most fruitful inquiries about workplace speech focuses on the fact that employees are a kind of captive audience. Workers cannot simply walk away from speech they do not like. No doubt, they can quit, but many workers are not assured of finding comparable employment. Also, women recognize that sexism is a pervasive problem and that frequent resignations will not enhance their employability. They have a strong incentive to "stick it out."

Since workers are a "captive audience," can they be protected in ways that would not be appropriate were they free to walk away? Various Supreme Court cases lend some support to this theory. In *Rowan v. United States Post Office*,[62] the Court upheld a statute that allowed householders effectively to stop the unwanted receipt of sexually oriented ads through the mail. A regulation prohibiting the use of highly vulgar language on radio was held permissible in *FCC v. Pacifica Foundation*.[63] In *Frisby* v. *Schultz*, the Court sustained a law that forbade picketing outside residences.[64] These cases protect people in their own houses, but some extension to the workplace may be warranted.

Captive audience arguments need to be understood in two dimensions. One relates to what goes on in the workplace generally: calendars and notices on walls, conversations overheard, and so on. Here the captive audience concern runs up against a countering "captive speaker" concern. *When* people are working, the only place they can express themselves is within the workplace. The speakers are no more free to go elsewhere than the audience. If I spend most of the day in the office *and* I like to look at provocative pictures of nude women, there is no substitute for my hanging such pictures on my office wall or putting them on my desk. Perhaps my claim to be free of government regulation is diminished somewhat by the fact that my employer could insist that I not display pictures, but I am no less a captive at work than other workers who may enter my office and be offended.

A narrower captive audience, or personal privacy, argument concerns remarks directed at a particular person. I would like to approach this argument obliquely by asking whether, more generally, freedom of speech involves the right to address remarks to someone who is your only audience and has let you know that she wants you to stop. This is arguable.

If I hang up on a telephone caller and tell him not to call back, he has no First Amendment right to keep calling. Statutes make it criminal for people to place telephone calls for the purpose of harassing others, and there would be no constitutional difficulty in a law that forbids calling someone who has let you know they definitely do not want you to call. I believe this absence of a right to impose on an unwilling listener should be viewed more extensively. If I am walking on a sidewalk and someone starts talking to me and I say "please stop," and he continues, following me wherever I turn, I probably now have a right to get a police officer to stop him from bothering me. If I do not now have that right, the creation of such a right would not violate principles of free speech and the First Amendment. As the Supreme Court said in *Rowan*, "no one has a right to press even 'good' ideas on an unwilling recipient."[65] I am inclined to think the constitutional principle is the same if I have let someone know at our last meeting that I really do not want to be addressed by him again. He has no constitutionally protected right to speak to me when we next meet each other on the street.

How does this analysis apply to the workplace? The worker cannot go anyplace else, nor can she foreclose communication entirely, because speech with others is essential to work. But suppose she has said she does not want to hear certain kinds of remarks. A legislature may protect her interest in being free of specific communications directed at her that the speaker has been told are deeply offensive to her. That interest may be viewed as canceling any right the speaker would otherwise have to speak the remarks to her.

A problem remains with this analysis. It would be one thing to give all workers a right to be free of remarks (not directly related to work) they have told others are deeply offensive to them. But the law that has developed out of Title VII is not content neutral in this way. It gives people a power to stop harassing and offensive speech only when it fits into particular categories.[66] Whether this kind of content distinction is warranted depends on the reasons that support it, a subject to which I will shortly turn.

LOW VALUE SPEECH

Another argument for restriction is that "low value" speech is mainly involved. Here one must distinguish among kinds of speech. Some photographs on display fit the Supreme Court's definition of obscenity or are sexually explicit enough to fall within a category that is less than obscene but without full value in the Court's jurisprudence. Some comments may amount to fighting words or are so personally abusive they might constitute grounds for a tort action for intentional infliction of emotional distress. These comments also have less than full value. What of a vulgar sexual remark, such as "Hey bitch, your ass is looking sexy today"? This hardly seems a serious expression on any public or personal matter (though, in context, this could represent the beginning of a serious invitation to sexual involvement). The remark does, however, crudely express both the ideas that women are primarily sexual objects and that this woman is sexually attractive. The Supreme Court has rightly suggested that crude speech sometimes expresses intensity of feeling better than polite discourse, and that the First Amendment protects crude, as well as genteel, speech.[67] But in this instance, crudeness may be used to demean the listener. A plausible claim of "low value" speech for comments like this must rest not alone on crudeness and offensiveness but on the purpose to demean.

Some expressions that might contribute to a hostile environment are serious remarks like, "women are not fit to be firefighters." At least if these reflect ideas honestly held, they are not low value speech in the relevant sense. They may be badly misguided and retrogressive, but the constitutional categories of low value speech do not make judgments about the specific ideas asserted. Part of the basic notion of free speech is that the state cannot relegate expressions to a domain of less protection based on a negative judgment about the content of the ideas.

An aspect of the expression of such ideas that the cases reveal, however, can lead to a plausible claim of "low value." Often, the idea of female or racial inferiority is repeated day after day to just the person who will be hurt by it. One feature of the status of the unwilling listener is that ideas are usually of little benefit when they are repeated to listeners who definitely do not want to hear them. Repetition is commonly, though not always, a sign that the speaker is less interested in persuading the listener or indicating his own opinion than he is in putting down the listener. Humiliating people is less deserving of protection as speech than the genuine expression of thoughts and feelings.

As with some previous arguments for lesser protection, the argument about "low value" speech faces the content discrimination problem put by *R.A.V.* Even if the scope for regulation is otherwise expanded because speech has low value, can the law engage in content discrimination?

WORKPLACE ETIQUETTE AND EQUALITY

I have put a very serious argument about workplace speech under the "light" title of "workplace etiquette." The argument is that the law can assure appropriately civil communication among people at the workplace. So far, I have compared the government's power to control speech in the public space with its power to control workplace speech. But this is not the only relevant comparison. One might begin by asking what speech the government can control in its own workplace. Cases establish that the government's power to censor its employees, or to make speech the basis of discharge, is less than that of private employers.[68] The government cannot forbid speech about general ideas or about how the workplace is operating, but it *can* forbid speech that interferes significantly with working relations. No one doubts that the government as employer could discipline or fire employees for continually demeaning subordinates or co-workers. Assuring a modicum of civility and mutual respect is essential for smooth work. Furthermore, since the government may not, constitutionally, discriminate on the basis of race, gender, or religion, it has a basis to forbid comments that demean people in those terms as an aspect of its power to prevent a discriminatory workplace. An I.R.S. supervisor who continually told an employee, "Hey bitch, your ass is looking sexy today," could be fired. Reflection on this example reveals a large gap between what the government can restrict as an employer and what it can restrict for citizens in the public space.

Is there good reason to suppose that the government should possess the same power over private employers that it exercises as an employer, rather than its more limited power in regulating the general behavior of citizens? The government has some interest in effective working conditions; but this concern can largely be left to the judgment of private employers. The government has a greater interest in equality in the workplace, since that equality is so central for genuine equality of citizenship. The government appropriately assures equality in the workplace, and restriction of categorical harassment is an important means of doing that. When one asks how severe an infringement of speech this power involves, it is significant that both the government and private employers will often restrict demeaning speech in their own workplaces. Employees have no *right* in any workplace to demean subordinates and co-workers. A lot of abusive speech does occur, but it could be the basis for discipline or discharge. We might think of showing a minimum of respect for fellow employees as a normal condition of employment. What Title VII does is to enforce this minimum in respect to categories of abuse that are of special concern for federal and state governments.

Standards of Review and Applications

As we have seen in previous chapters and with respect to campus speech codes, it matters what constitutional standard of review a court uses, although one suspects that on some occasions the Supreme Court decides the outcome and then formulates a standard of review accordingly, rather than vice versa. The previous discussion of workplace harassment shows why the task here is not easy, because different kinds of speech may count toward a finding of a hostile work environment.

I shall first consider the standard of review for restricting various kinds of speech that constitute workplace harassment. I have suggested that speech that dominantly *does* something, agreements, threats, etcetera, rather than *says* something is not the sort of speech that the First Amendment protects. I have also suggested that speech *mainly* designed to humiliate has slight expressive value and should be placed in the category of speech that "does" rather than "says." It follows for this chapter that abusive comments directed at an employee and intended to intimidate her, to drive her from her job, or to make her acutely uncomfortable should not enjoy significant protection. If this speech, a high percentage of what figures in actual harassment cases, is viewed in isolation, the government should be able to restrict it upon a modest showing of need.

Other kinds of speech may be deemed of low value. Provocative nude calendars fit into this category; so also does crude sexual innuendo. Low value speech may be regulated on some lesser showing than a compelling interest.

Finally there is speech about ideas and feelings whose content cannot be relegated to a category of low value. An honest remark that "they made a mistake allowing women to be construction workers" would be of this kind. For this speech, does the government need to satisfy a compelling interest? I think the answer is "yes," *if* the speech is uttered occasionally, and in a genuine attempt to convey one's thoughts and feelings, to someone who has not labelled herself an "unwilling listener."

Repetition in the face of complaint is another matter. Suppose a construction worker tells a newly hired female co-worker each day when she arrives at work, "You know, they never should have allowed women in these jobs," and continues to do so after, she complains that the comments disturb her. I have suggested that people have no constitutional right to impose speech on those who have expressed their unwillingness to hear it (when *only* unwilling listeners are involved). Exactly how to conceptualize this conclusion is complicated. One might view preventing such privacy-intrusive speech as itself satisfying a compelling interest or one might view the privacy of the listener as removing the speech from the category that requires any compelling interest for regulation. In either event, the practical point is that the government need not show any independent compelling interest to regulate. Its aim to protect the listener's privacy is enough.

Furthermore, when someone offers opinions day after day to an unwilling listener, as in the construction example, an outsider may often draw the inference that the person is *aiming* to annoy the listener, or, at the least, is grossly indifferent to the listener's feelings. Although the point is debatable, when no genuine communicative purpose is likely to be served in a situation, gross indifference to the previously expressed feelings of the only listener should be sufficient to put speech into the same category as speech that is actually designed to annoy. Sometimes an inference of gross indifference is not warranted. A nonsmoker concerned with a smoking listener's health or a devout religious person concerned with a listener's salvation may continue to pester the listener in the hope of finally "getting through." Most repeated statements to women that women are ill-fitted for a kind of work are not of this type. In context, they do warrant an inference of a purpose to annoy or of gross indifference.

If my analysis so far is sound, some speech that might contribute to workplace harassment should be subject to a compelling interest test, but the vast majority of what is actually spoken should not be subject to such a strict test. *One* possible conclusion would be that so low a percentage of actual speech in the circumstances might qualify for stringent protection that the courts should employ a lower standard for all possibly relevant speech; but that conclusion would be mistaken. If some speech deserves a status of full value under the constitution, it should be given that status. Courts can assess speech in particular cases to judge whether it has that status.

A more principled argument can be made that no speech contributing to unequal working conditions has full value.[69] This argument is a close analogue of the argument, already examined, that all such speech discriminates. Speech honestly expressing opinions and feelings can help make a woman experience her working environment as hostile, because she is told that those around her devalue her. Since women often cannot leave one job for another job that is equally good and is without hostility, society has a serious interest in preventing hostile comments. All hostile comments *do* something as well as *say* something even when they express honest opinions. Supervisors and co-workers have a responsibility to speak reasonably and not to inflict these negative feelings on women. The proper constitutional analysis is to balance expressive interest against likely harm contextually, *not* to assume that some category of speech enjoys nearly absolute protection. A supplementary reason for this approach is that divining whether speakers intend to humiliate or are merely insensitive is too difficult an inquiry for courts.

As I mentioned with respect to the "hostile speech is discrimination" argument, adopting the argument as a general approach to First Amendment problems would significantly reduce constitutional protection. Various forms of speech would be vulnerable to plausible claims that they do more harm than good and that a reasonable speaker would refrain from them.[70] The argument has much greater persuasiveness if limited to the workplace, with all its special features. Nevertheless, the wiser course is for courts to use standard free speech analysis insofar as they can, even for the workplace. Thus, I conclude that focus on whether *the speaker is aiming* to do something or express something should be of importance *and* that when the speaker is mainly aiming to express something (to an audience that is not clearly unwilling), the government should need a compelling interest to regulate.

I have thus far omitted two other major issues. The first involves the relatively straightforward problems of overbreadth and vagueness. Will any actual standard to restrict workplace harassment cover too much protected speech to be acceptable? For this overbreadth question, the critical question is how much covered speech is finally protected. I have argued that relatively little speech in most actual cases is even subject to the compelling interest standard; and the government may have a compelling interest in restricting some speech to which that test applies. Although ordinary workplace harassment standards will pick up some speech that enjoys constitutional protection, that speech is not enough to invalidate the standards on overbreadth grounds. As for the vagueness worry, the standards developed in federal and state regulations and by courts are undoubtedly vague and open-ended; but they may be about as precise as the subject allows. Thus, they should not be held unconstitutionally vague.[71]

The second major issue is more complex and concerns the Court's opinion in *R.A.V.* That opinion declared invalid a content-based distinction among speech of extremely low value—fighting words. It said that to support a content distinction the government must establish that a law is narrowly tailored to serve a compelling interest. If this aspect of *R.A.V.* is applicable to workplace harassment, existing regulation of that is subject to a compelling interest test, even when the speech involved has very low value. As we have seen, the *R.A.V.* opinion suggests that workplace harassment law is not subject to its strictures, but, as we have also seen, its apparent reasons for distinguishing workplace harassment from the St. Paul ordinance are not persuasive.

Four Justices in *R.A.V.* did not think a compelling interest test was appropriate to that ordinance cast in terms of categories of speech, and I concluded in chapter 4 that their position was more sound then the Court's. For similar reasons, I do not think the effective choice to engage in categorical regulation of workplace harassment should be subject to a compelling interest test. Suppose, however, that the opposite conclusion were reached. The government's interest in stopping employment discrimination is a compelling one,[72] and stopping harassing speech contributes significantly to that objective. But is categorical regulation *necessary* (the inquiry that doomed the St. Paul ordinance in the Court's opinion in *R.A.V.*)? It may help here to distinguish the federal from the state government. Perhaps under the Commerce Clause, the federal government *could* legislate against all harassment (including purely personal harassment) that creates a hostile work environment, but that would involve a substantial interference in the domain of state and local government. Furthermore, given the Fourteenth and Thirteenth Amendments, the federal government's interest in stopping categorical harassment (by groups) is much greater than its interest in stopping harassment that is based more personally. For these reasons, a law limited to categorical harassment should be regarded as narrowly tailored to serve a compelling interest. Although states may have more pervasive authority over working conditions within their boundaries, the same conclusion applies to them because of the stronger social interest in combatting categorical discrimination, and the categorical harassment that produces it in many contexts. Thus, I conclude that statutes limiting regulation to categorical harassment should be regarded as constitutionally permissible. The standard of review to be applied for particular speech should depend on the kind of speech involved.

It is time now to turn with a little more precision to contexts of speech. The government's interest in stopping discrimination is great enough to restrict anything that falls outside the genuine concerns of free speech, such as remarks intended to intimidate or humiliate, and also to anything classifiable as low value speech (for reasons other than the content of the ideas expressed). I shall, therefore, concentrate on words, posters, symbols on desks, that would be full value speech in most contexts.

Suppose a male boss thinks women do not belong in his workplace; he is angry and irritated that women are there; and he wants to express his anger to the very people who are misguidedly occupying the positions for which they are not suited because of their gender. He expresses his attitudes to his female subordinates. Some of them are distressed by the remarks, and they wonder whether a boss who expresses such views can possibly deal with them fairly on the job.

An important argument for regulation here focuses on the special relationship of power between boss and subordinate. In this particular case, maybe nothing that a boss says can be treated as pure opinion[73] (unless, perhaps, the boss is very careful to explain that he will not treat the women unequally as workers); female workers are bound to draw implications for how they will be treated. This natural implication about the boss's subsequent behavior is sufficient to curb continued statements of this sort. (*One* initial statement might be viewed as clearing the air and putting the relationship on an honest footing.)

Suppose the speaker is a co-worker. The power rationale does not apply here directly. Does it apply if the boss knows what the co-worker says and fails to stop him? I do not think it can reasonably be said that a failure to reprimand inevitably connotes approval. I argued in chapter 4 that the state's failure to stop hate speech is not an approval of hate speech; similarly, higher management might accept some hostile give and take in the workplace without approving of views expressed or even approving of such active expression of opinions. However, in some circumstances inaction may seem to connote approval; when this occurs, the power rationale kicks in. Moreover, as I have said, co-workers who work directly with the woman do have a kind of power over her. They may fail to work cooperatively with her. If the remarks are reasonably taken as indicating a refusal to cooperate in working relations, they can be restricted on this basis.

The "captive audience—privacy to avoid distressing speech that is directed at you" rationale applies to both bosses and co-workers. One worker's interest in not having someone speak deeply offensive things directly to her, after she has told the speaker that she definitely does not welcome such remarks, is strong enough so that the speaker may be told to stop such remarks. To be clear, I am not suggesting that the listener herself has some constitutional right to be free of such remarks, only that a legislative resolution in her favor does not violate the Constitution. I also am not addressing at all (yet) a multiperson audience; the speaker *may* have a First Amendment right not to be forbidden by the state to say what he thinks to a five person audience, even though aware that one member of the audience does not want to hear such remarks. I have talked only of the situation where *one* listener, or *all* relevant listeners have said they do not want to hear the remarks. Finally, I am not addressing public bodies at all; school board members (at board meetings) cannot say they do not want to hear speech relevant to school.

The most difficult questions about restriction concern "overheard" conversations and remarks made to multimember audiences in which some individuals have not indicated any objections to hearing such remarks. If the point of a male conversation is to be overheard by women workers, all the previous analysis applies. But suppose men on the job, overheard by women, express genuine ideas to each other that are deeply offensive to the women. Bosses have a responsibility to be careful not to continually say offensive things that are overheard, and co-workers can be required to use reasonable discretion; but in principle communications of real ideas not directed at those they offend should be regarded as protected free speech. When remarks are directed at a group, the speaker need not restrict himself to avoid what one member of the group finds offensive; but in the workplace environment co-workers and bosses can be expected to show a reasonable sensitivity to the composition of the groups to which they speak. To take an obvious example, the captain of a firehouse should not indulge his sexist sentiments when he is addressing all the firefighters in the morning.

Relevance and Remedy

I have not endeavored here to apply these general observations to the facts of individual cases. With a few exceptions, the adjudicated cases making a determination of harassment overwhelmingly involved nonverbal behavior and verbal behavior to which something less than the compelling interest test applies. Thus, the inattention of the courts (and lawyers?) to First Amendment aspects is both understandable and not of great practical moment. Closer attention is desirable, however, because future cases are likely to reach deeper into workplace speech, especially after the Supreme Court's clarification that the threshold needed to establish a hostile work environment need not be very high.

Only a small percentage of what might count as harassing speech warrants application of the compelling interest test, and, only a proportion of that speech should be judged to be constitutionally protected. Nevertheless, that constitutionally protected speech might be significant in the conclusion that a hostile environment exists. What should a court and jury do in such a circumstance?

Two conclusions can be stated quickly. First, if the use of protected speech is to cast light on the significance of other behavior, its evidentiary use is appropriate. Second, since the nature of speech (e.g., whether it is mainly designed to intimidate or humiliate) will often be apparent only in context, and further will be disputed by the parties, there cannot be a rule against the introduction of all evidence of protected speech. The status of speech as protected or not will emerge only as the facts are presented and determined. (This problem could conceivably underlie an argument that all possibly protected speech should be excluded from consideration, but I shall pass over that option here.)

How should protected speech affect a determination of a hostile environment? To address this question, we must understand that (1) some protected speech could seriously disturb women, *and* (2) that in some cases everything *but* protected speech might fall short of making the environment sufficiently hostile, while everything including protected speech might make the environment sufficiently hostile. In the extreme case, a string of protected remarks might all by itself make the environment hostile.

If the First Amendment is to be given its proper effect, a finding of a hostile working environment cannot be based exclusively or dominantly on protected remarks. Should that unfortunate combination of protected speech and deeply disturbing effects ever arise, no finding of a violation of Title VII should be made. (I believe this combination is most unlikely when sexual and racial harassment are involved, but I can imagine it occurring with protected religious speech.)

What of the more common situation when most of the incidents claimed to contribute to a hostile environment are not protected speech, but some incidents are protected speech? My initial inclination when thinking about this problem was that no incident of protected speech could count toward a finding of a hostile environment and that a jury should be so instructed. Using this approach, a victim would have to make her case on the basis of incidents other than protected speech. This outcome seems to fit naturally with the idea that liability should not be based even in part on constitutionally protected behavior.

There is an alternative approach, however, that I think makes greater sense. Congress could forbid all unprotected harassing speech, but it has (implicitly) chosen to intervene only when a hostile environment is created. If such an environment does exist, even one produced *partly* by protected speech, imposing consequences for unprotected behavior is appropriate, as is restricting any future unprotected behavior. On this view, incidents of protected speech could count as contributing to a hostile environment.

A conclusion that the First Amendment protects *some* workplace speech that disturbs women has important practical implications for remedies. One obvious consequence is that courts need to be careful in formulating remedial orders. The orders would have to cover only unprotected speech. They could not simply sweep within their ambit all speech that might have a negative effect on the working environment.

Another possible effect concerns situations in which employers directly forbid workers from engaging in speech they think might create a hostile work environment. Some commentors have worried,[74] with good reason, that an employer not very concerned with free expression may forbid much more speech than the government could forbid directly. I have noted that private employers have wide scope deciding what speech to allow. However, *if* a worker can get an employer to acknowledge that its restrictions derived from a fear of a suit for violation of Title VII, then perhaps the worker can succeed in resisting the employer's attempt to restrict. The potentiality of such a suit will rarely, if ever, be realized; but it might offset to some extent the employer's inclination to restrict everything that could conceivably lead to a finding of harassment.

CAMPUS SPEECH CODES REVISITED

How do campus speech codes look in light of the law and analysis of workplace harassment? Should one think of a college campus as a kind of workplace or as at least very similar to a workplace?[75] Of course, for some people, faculty and administrators, a college or university *is* a workplace, but the focus here is on students, the primary intended beneficiaries of speech codes.

Although being a student does not involve gainful employment, it certainly involves work, i.e., the often difficult task of disciplined study. Some kinds of students, medical students and social work students, for example, engage in cooperative efforts that are essentially the same as those done for pay by others. Many students engage in such efforts as part of extra-curricular activities, as writers and editors of student newspapers, say, or players on sports teams. Hierarchical relations of authority exist within colleges and universities. The most common authorities for students are faculty members.

Faculty may or may not control individual success in the manner of supervisors at work; this will depend substantially on whether they make individualized evaluations while aware of the names of the students they are evaluating. Faculty almost always have a significant influence on the conditions of learning. Coaches of athletic teams and student supervisors in activities like newspapers occupy roles that more nearly resemble that of a boss at an ordinary job. Students see the same people day after day, and they live in conditions where it is not easy to avoid others they do not wish to see. Students typically live in shared quarters with common spaces in which no one student can control what is communicated. Although speech that indicates that supervisors will discriminate directly in "work" activities or that "co-workers" will withhold needed cooperation is less frequent on campuses than in workplaces, ample opportunity arises to influence the "working conditions" of students. Students, in general, may change universities more easily than workers can change jobs; but students nonetheless have a large investment in a decent learning environment at the school they currently attend. Women and members of minorities say they are affected by sexist and racist remarks inside and outside of class, and we have reason to believe that such remarks may have some negative influence on learning.

Universities have an interest in assuring decent conditions of learning for all students. Probably at all universities, continuous intense verbal abuse of one student by another would be the basis for discipline. Governments have a special interest in seeing that educational conditions are not unfairly skewed in favor of some groups at the expense of others, given the relevance of educational success for the acquisition and effective performance of many jobs. In short, universities and governments have an interest in equal educational opportunity that encompasses the restriction of categorical verbal harassment. On the other hand, as we have seen in the initial discussion of speech codes, the First Amendment has intense relevance for much campus speech that students might find disturbing.

What conclusion may be drawn from these comparisons of universities and workplaces? Briefly I think the following approaches are warranted, once one recognizes that the conditions of campus life and the reasons for speech codes bear some relation to the notions behind workplace harassment law. First, Congress or state legislatures might put campus speech harassment on a formal footing that is like workplace harassment by adopting laws that forbid categorical discrimination in university education.[76] Second, state universities should be able to forbid *directed* verbal harassment of students, and if they choose to adopt special measures that precisely cover categorical directed verbal harassment, that should be accepted as an appropriate means to combat categorical discrimination in education. Third, in light of the centrality of ideas in educational settings, honest expressions of opinions on various subjects should be protected. This privilege to speak should extend to coarse remarks in informal settings when the speaker is not intentionally trying to humiliate a listener and when the listener has not indicated previously to the speaker that she does not wish to entertain such remarks. The privilege should extend to expressions about personal subjects, such as interracial dating, as well as to more common academic and public subjects. Fourth, courts should look not only to the concept of government as regulator of citizens but also to the concept of government as employer, in order to understand the proper relation of a state university to its students. Fifth, courts must address problems of overbreadth and vagueness in considering campus speech codes; but they should not assume that any speech code is bound to fail these constitutional tests, any more than they assume that workplace harassment standards fail these tests.

Chapter Six

OBSCENITY

PERHAPS NO SUBJECT so quickly reveals similarities and differences between the Canadian and U.S. Supreme Courts as the subject of obscenity. In looking at their treatments of this topic, we need to keep in mind three different perspectives. The first perspective concerns the sorts of material that each court holds not to be protected constitutionally. The second concerns the justifications each accepts as a basis for suppression. The third concerns the extent to which doctrinal approaches about obscenity reflect broader constitutional standards.

In both countries, the nineteenth-century English case of *Regina v. Hicklin*[1] represented the law with respect to obscenity for the first half of this century. Under Chief Judge Cockburn's opinion in that case, material could be determined to be obscene, and suppressed, if "the tendency of the matter charged as obscenity is to deprave and corrupt those whose minds are open to such immoral influences, and into whose hands a publication of this sort may fall."[2] This test permitted a judgment of obscenity based on how isolated passages might affect particularly susceptible people. Under it, serious works of literature, such as D. H. Lawrence's *Lady Chatterly's Lover* and James Joyce's *Ulysses*, were successfully banned.

The most important constitutional developments in the United States took place between 1957 and 1973. In Canada the 1992 case of *Regina v. Butler*[3] is by far the most significant; and it has quickly become the best known Canadian Supreme Court case within the United States.

DEVELOPMENT OF THE LAW IN THE UNITED STATES

The United States Supreme Court first seriously engaged the problem of obscenity in *Roth v. United States* and *Alberts v. California*,[4] companion cases in which the Court considered the constitutionality of federal and state statutes directed against obscenity. The federal law, on which the Court mainly focused, covered the mailing of material that was "obscene, lewd, lascivious, or filthy . . . [or] of an indecent character." The Court, relying partly on inconclusive historical evidence, repeated earlier dicta that the First Amendment did not protect obscenity. At the same time, it transformed the law by indicating that the determination whether or not material was obscene presented a serious constitutional question. The constitutional standard was "whether to the average person, applying contemporary community standards, the dominant theme of the material taken as a whole appeals to prurient interest."[5]

Justice Brennan's opinion for the Court regarded this test as virtually the same as that of the Model Penal Code, which included a requirement that material go "substantially beyond customary limits of candor," and the opinion characterized obscenity as "utterly without redeeming social importance." For some years after *Roth*, the Supreme Court failed to achieve a majority on the appropriate test for obscenity; but in 1966 a crucial plurality in the center adopted the three elements mentioned in *Roth* as an explicit three-part test. For material to count as obscene "it must be established that (a) the dominant theme of the material taken as a whole appeals to a prurient interest in sex; (b) the material is patently offensive because it affronts contemporary community standards relating to the description or representation of sexual matters; and (c) the material is utterly without redeeming social value."[6] This test recognized that the three elements might not always coalesce, that material might, for example, appeal predominantly to the prurient interest and not be beyond customary limits of candor or not be utterly without redeeming social value. Indeed that is what the plurality concluded about John Cleland's *Memoirs of a Woman of Pleasure (Fanny Hill)*.

In a 1973 decision, *Miller* v. *California*, five Justices united behind a variation of this threefold test. To meet difficulties of vagueness and overbreadth, the Court indicated that statutes must be written or construed to be confined to works depicting or describing sexual conduct which is "specifically defined." The works must be ones that "taken as a whole, appeal to the prurient interest in sex, . . . portray sexual conduct in a patently offensive way, and . . . taken as a whole, do not have serious literary, artistic, political, or scientific value."[7] Apart from the specificity requirement, the *Miller* formulation appears somewhat less protective of material than the previous plurality standard; most crucially the requirement that material must be "utterly without redeeming social value" is replaced by the requirement that "taken as a whole," it "not have serious literary, artistic, political, or scientific value." The new test specified what kind of value material must have (giving sexual pleasure or aiding masturbation clearly would not be enough); it also indicated that the value must be serious and that the work as a whole must have this value. If one matched the *Memoirs* plurality test and the *Miller* test, one would conclude that the *Memoirs* test is more protective; but to a large extent the precise language of constitutional standards has been outdistanced by changing social mores. Sexually explicit material has become so widely circulated and accepted in the United States that it is doubtful whether any purely written material may be suppressed under *Miller* (purely written material rarely is suppressed, in any event); and the pictorial material that may be banned probably does not extend beyond "hard-core" pornography: moving pictures, photographs, and cartoons graphically depicting acts of sexual intercourse and lacking any pretense of artistic value. Indeed, the *Miller* majority speaks of its test as directed at hard core pornography. When Justice Stewart had previously provided an account of hard-core pornography (following a now famous quote in an earlier case in which he had said "perhaps I could never succeed in intelligibly [defining hard-core pornography]. . . . [b]ut I know it when I see it"[8]), he assumed that the plurality's test in *Memoirs* v. *Massachusetts* would allow suppression of material other than hard-core pornography.[9] In a sense, more permissive community attitudes have largely eliminated any gap between the *Miller* variation on the *Memoirs* test and a rule that directly protects everything but hard-core pornography.

I shall concentrate on the central issue of what counts as obscene for constitutional purposes, summed up by the *Miller* formulation, omitting such important subsidiary issues as the treatment of child pornography,[10] the breadth of territory for which community standards are to be gauged,[11] the status of material that has a predominant appeal to the prurient interest of its intended audience but not to most people,[12] and a special right to view obscenity in one's home.[13]

A central doctrinal assumption that has survived the law preceding *Roth* is that obscene material, however it is defined, is outside the protection of the First Amendment. This characterization of obscenity resembles what has been said about fighting words and libel, to which it has often been linked in judicial opinions as forms of communication that are not protected speech.

The consequences of this doctrine are striking. If obscenity is not within the protection of the First Amendment (except for the right to use it within one's home), government can suppress it without demonstrating a compelling interest in doing so. All that the government needs to show is some (much weaker) reason for suppression. Furthermore, the normal rule against content discrimination is inapplicable. This is highly important, because criminal laws against obscenity indisputably discriminate on the basis of content. They discriminate on the basis of subject matter; obscene material is forbidden, all other material is permitted. Since obscene material commonly carries an implicit approval of the erotic, and perhaps also an anticonventional message, prohibitions of obscenity, in practice, operate against material with a particular point of view and thus constitute a kind of indirect viewpoint discrimination. (However, the prohibition does not depend directly on viewpoint, *and* nonobscene material with a similar viewpoint favoring the erotic is allowed.)

The majority's approach in *R.A.V.*,[14] discussed in the last chapter, cautions that *some* forms of content discrimination could affect the constitutionality of an obscenity law. If, to take a trivial example, a law forbade only antireligious obscene material, that would be an obvious impermissible form of content discrimination. A much more important issue, to which I shall return, is a ban on material that degrades women, or degrades people. In any event, the crucial point here is that a statute banning obscene material is not itself regarded as an impermissible content discrimination, because obscene material is outside the First Amendment and material left free by the statute is inside the amendment's protection.

OBSCENITY AND FREE SPEECH: JUSTIFICATIONS FOR SUPPRESSION

What, if anything, could justify the assumption that obscenity, as presently defined, is not protected by the First Amendment? One possibility is that obscenity really is not expression in some basic sense; the other possibility is that it is expression, but has such low value that the First Amendment does not protect it. An argument along either line presents difficulty. The "low value" approach is runs into the cardinal principle of freedom of expression that government generally should not decide what expression has value; rather there should be a free marketplace of ideas. Even if one is not unalterably opposed to legislatures and courts making such judgments of value, one may worry that officials who decide that some forms of expression do not have much value may indiscriminately relegate other forms to that status. In addition to this broad "slippery slope" argument against classifying speech by value, many civil libertarians claim that because obscenity has an implicit anticonventional message with political overtones, it is not nearly as valueless as its opponents have assumed.

At least two arguments that obscenity should not count as expression refuse to concede that the crucial question is one of degree of value. Frederick Schauer has suggested that obscenity is more akin to an actual physical device to stimulate the sex organs than to ordinary communication, because its effect is simply to stimulate sexual desire without having ideational content.[15] Most obscenity, however, implicitly portrays sex as very pleasurable and carries a wider message of rejection of conventional attitudes towards sex.[16] Of course, the latter message is usually implicit, not explicit, and the pleasure of sex is portrayed rather than stated; but much fiction and photography show how people feel in situations without rendering any abstract account of what gives pain or pleasure. Obscenity differs significantly from the physical devices to which Schauer compared it, because obscenity initially affects one's emotions and mental states, and whatever physical stimulation occurs is a result of those altered mental states. Sexual stimulation by physical devices, like all sexual stimulation, also involves changes in mental and emotional states, but their role is less primary.

A more subtle distinction differentiates unprotected obscenity from protected aesthetic expression, which may not (as much music does not) involve ordinary ideational content. It is said that aesthetic expression requires distance between the observer and work of art, a psychic distance that allows the observer to grasp a symbolic representation.[17] Obscenity, on the other hand, tends to destroy distance between the viewer and material, instead involving the viewer in immediate experience. Lacking both direct ideational content and aesthetic merit, obscenity, the argument goes, should not qualify as expression. This view of obscenity might reasonably affect a legislature's judgment, particularly when it realizes that the vast majority of producers and consumers of obscenity are not interested in ideas or aesthetic experience; but the principle of detachment hardly seems an appropriate guideline for First Amendment protection. Some rock music and popular literature may succeed best when the consumer loses a sense of distance from the work, and work that seeks to provide intense nonintellectual experience may nonetheless alter one's intellectual understanding over time. Furthermore, it would be very difficult for courts to say exactly when photography, fiction, and music create, or seek to create, detachment, and when they do not. Deciding that "detachment" is a *sine qua non* of First Amendment protection would be a mistake.

A realistic approach to obscenity that places it outside the ambit of ordinary First Amendment protection must claim that it is expression of very low value, as opposed to no expression at all. The conclusion that such speech has very low value may rest on three factors: (1) those who produce and distribute obscene material are overwhelmingly interested in making money by satisfying sexual appetites, not in expressing ideas; (2) the consumers of obscenity want to be titillated, not to receive ideas; (3) the influence of obscenity on beliefs and attitudes is largely on the subconscious level, and the ideas conveyed are therefore not easily answerable by more speech. In such a framework, the doctrinal issues with respect to obscenity resemble those concerning hate speech.

Relying summarily on the historical claim that the Framers did not mean to protect obscenity,[18] the Supreme Court has never explained fully why obscenity falls completely outside of First Amendment protection. That determination, however, has relieved the Court from looking very hard at the justifications for banning obscenity and from worrying about the rule against content discrimination, as it applies to such bans. The most the Court has said about justifications for prohibition appears in *Paris Adult Theatre I v. Slaton*,[19] a companion case to *Miller*. Presenting the question as whether the Constitution embodies something like John

Stuart Mill's principle that government should not prohibit consenting acts among adults (rather than asking if reasons for prohibition are strong enough to override free speech values), the Court talked of protection of the quality of life and community environment against the crass commercial exploitation of sex, and of a reasonable fear that use of obscene material may be correlated to crime.

Paris Adult Theatre, decided more than two decades ago, does not tell us what interests would justify suppressing full value speech or even low value speech that enjoys some First Amendment protection. Even if obscenity remains beyond the threshold of First Amendment protection in the indefinite future, these inquiries take on considerable importance, partly because they illuminate a comparison of the Court's present position with that of the Canadian Supreme Court, and partly because some feminists have urged that material that is not covered by the present American legal definition of obscenity should be suppressed. Before I consider the justifications for suppression in this light, I need to review the Court's approach to low value speech.

As I mentioned in chapter 2, the Court has carved out a few discrete areas of speech that enjoy some First Amendment protection, but less than full protection. Among the most important of these areas is sexually explicit speech that falls short of obscenity as now defined. In two important decisions, the Court allowed regulation of the location of adult movie theaters, on the theory that such theaters tend to be accompanied by prostitution and sexual assaults.[20] Although some Justices protested against the creation of this category of "low value" speech, a majority sustained the regulations, recognizing that the justifications presented would not be sufficient to warrant regulation of full value speech. Thus, the Court has created three categories of speech: full value speech, speech that falls outside the First Amendment altogether (barring some forbidden form of content regulation of the sort involved in *R.A.V.*), and low value speech that enjoys some constitutional protection but substantially less than full value speech. In *Paris Adult Theatre*, we learned why the Court thinks sufficient reasons support banning obscenity, but the Court assumed there that no First Amendment barrier existed to regulation. Some insight into the present Court's views about low value speech is provided by a 1991 case on nude dancing.[21] That case represents important applications of the *O'Brien* test, mentioned in previous chapters; but part of what matters to some of the Justices in the majority seems to be the slight expressive value of nude dancing.

Indiana's public indecency statute forbids public nudity and requires dancers to wear "pasties" and a "g-string"; the case involved an attempt by establishments that provided "go-go" dancing to get injunctions against the enforcement of that law. The Seventh Circuit Court of Appeals, sitting en banc with extensive opinions, had held the application of the statute unconstitutional because its purpose was to prevent the message of eroticism and sexuality that the dancers conveyed.[22] Four Justices on the Supreme Court, only two of whom remain, agreed.[23] They assumed that the statute would not be applied against nude ballets and nudity in theatrical performances, and they relied on the fact that the statute does not reach nudity within homes (even among strangers). They concluded that the statute was not directed against all nudity among strangers. The coverage of the statute against most nudity in public places could be explained by the aim to prevent offense to nonconsenting viewers, but that rationale would not cover go-go dancing within establishments whose patrons know exactly what they will see. The dissenters decided that the "purpose of the proscription in these contexts is to protect the viewers from what the State believes is the harmful message that nude dancing communicates."[24] They thought that the compelling interest test was the appropriate standard against which to measure the statute's application, and determined that the state failed to meet that standard.

The majority upheld application of the statute, splintering into three opinions. At least four Justices believed that the statute was directed against public nudity in general; all five agreed that the law was not aimed at the communicative aspects of the dancing, and that the appropriate test was the one to be applied when laws not directed at expression happen to have an indirect effect on some expressive activity.[25] Justice Scalia wished to extend the logic of *Employment Division v. Smith*, the free exercise case I discussed in chapter 2. He said that if a general law regulating conduct but not directed at expression is valid, its application to expressive activity "is not subject to First-Amendment scrutiny at all."[26]

The three Justices in the plurality were not willing to abandon the *O'Brien* test for such cases. That test, as previous chapters indicate, sets four conditions for the government to enforce a general law, which is directed at nonexpressive conduct, against expressive activity. The condition on which I want to focus here is the condition that the law further "an important or substantial government interest." Chief Justice Rehnquist's opinion for himself and Justices O'Connor and Kennedy says that "the statute's purpose of protecting societal order and morality is clear from its text and history."[27] The Chief Justice cites *Paris Adult Theatre*, which assumed that obscenity was outside the First Amendment's protection, and *Bowers v. Hardwick*,[28] a case upholding a law against consenting homosexual behavior, for the proposition that the interest in order and morality is an appropriate basis for legislation.[29] Speaking of "societal disapproval of nudity in public places and among strangers," Rehnquist says, "The statutory prohibition is not a means to some greater end, but an end in itself."[30] The plurality, in effect, demands no demonstration or even assertion of tangible harm; it is enough that most people disapprove of public nudity. Furthermore, the plurality seems to regard any appropriate interest for legislation as important enough to satisfy *O'Brien*; it seems to give no force to the requirement that the interest be "important or substantial." Rehnquist's opinion may be a fair indication of just how weak the *O'Brien* standard is for most Justices; but the rest of the opinion may be influenced by the initial conclusions that barroom nude dancing "may involve the barest minimum of protected expression" and that it "is expressive conduct within the outer perimeters of the First Amendment, though we view it as only marginally so."[31] Perhaps the almost cavalier attitude the opinion takes to the application of the *O'Brien* test is partly the consequence of the plurality's view that nude dancing is very "low value" speech.[32]

Justice Souter, the remaining majority vote, confronts the value of nude dancing much more directly.[33] He agrees with the plurality that the *O'Brien* test applies, but his reason is not wholly clear. He says that *O'Brien* is the right enquiry "for judging the limits of appropriate state action burdening expressive acts as distinct from pure speech or representation."[34] What is uncertain is whether Justice Souter thinks it matters that the law is against public nudity in general. It sounds as if he would reach the same conclusion if the law forbade public nude dancing and nothing else. The rest of his opinion reinforces this interpretation. The justification for the application of the statute that he finds sufficient is that nude dancing encourages prostitution, increases sexual assaults, and attracts other criminal activity.[35] (Since these reasons would not apply to public nudity in general, perhaps the rest of the statute's coverage drops out in importance.) Souter relies directly on the cases treating sexually explicit but nonobscene material as low value speech, both for the connection of such activities to the feared harms and for the proposition that the interest in protecting these expressive activities is much less than for most speech.

With this brief diversion, I turn to possible arguments for suppressing obscenity. I consider the intrinsic force of these arguments and their possible constitutional relevance were the Supreme Court to decide that obscenity enjoys some First Amendment protection and that the state must come up with arguments more than the minimal ones necessary to support any regulation of liberty.

We can roughly distinguish offensiveness, moral judgment, criminal activity, and undesirable attitudes and practices. One possible reason for banning obscenity is that it disturbs some people to know that other people are consuming it. Standing alone, this would hardly be a sufficient reason to suppress speech. But this reason rarely stands alone.

Offensiveness is usually combined with a notion that what people do when they consume obscenity is immoral. In *Bowers v. Hardwick*, a slender majority of the Court held that a popular view that homosexual behavior was immoral was a sufficient basis to make it criminal; and three justices on the Court think that a similar view about public nudity meets the *O'Brien* requirement of an important or substantial government interest. Nevertheless, a simple notion that viewing obscenity is immoral would almost certainly not suffice to justify suppression of material thought to have value as expression.

Other arguments for suppression look to harms. The most obvious harms are crimes. It is claimed that viewing obscenity, especially obscenity in which violence is a major element, may lead some people to commit violent sexual crimes. *If* it could be shown that a high percentage of those who consume obscene materials commit violent crimes that they would not otherwise commit, that would be an extremely powerful argument for suppression. No such correlation has been suggested.

Exactly what kind of correlation has been claimed? It is helpful here to consider the report of the 1986 Attorney General's Commission on Pornography (popularly known as the Meese Commission).[36] The Commission asserted a connection between sexually explicit violence and the commission of violent crimes. It said that exposure to sexually violent materials increases the chance that men will be aggressive toward women and that this "bears a causal relationship to antisocial acts of sexual violence and, for some subgroups, possibly to unlawful acts of sexual violence."[37] It went on to suggest that similar but less extensive effects may be involved with material that degrades or humiliates women, "but that these effects are likely absent when neither degradation nor violence is present."[38] The Commission, thus, made no claim that nonviolent obscene material that does not degrade women is causally connected to criminal activity.

The Commission's claim of a causal connection between the consumption of material that is sexual and violent (or degrading) and criminal activity has been challenged, even by some of those whose empirical studies were used as support for the Commission's conclusion.[39] Discerning just how much disagreement is over the facts and how much disagreement is over what "causation" means in this context, and what evidence it takes to support a finding of causation, is not simple. Frederick Schauer, a primary author of the Report, has explained carefully just how modest is the claimed causal connection. He characterizes it as based on a "probabilistic" conception of causation.[40] Schauer suggests recasting the question the Commission was trying to answer as, "Is there sufficient evidence for a government advisory commission without regulative powers to assert that there would be more acts of sexual violence committed by a population every member of which had been extensively exposed to favorable depictions of acts of sexual violence than there would be in a population no member of which had been exposed to favorable depictions of acts of sexual violence?"[41] One of the primary bases for the conclusion was experimental evidence that males exposed to depictions of sexual violence have a short term increase in aggressive tendencies toward women and in their toleration of sexual violence toward women.[42] Nonexperimental evidence and common sense fill in the gap between these short term feelings and a conclusion that aggressive feelings lead to the commission of *some* violent crimes.

In evaluating this conclusion and its relevance, we must attend to two important points. The first is the possibility that for some men the consumption of obscenity deflects them over time from committing violent crimes.[43] It may be likely that *some* crimes that would not otherwise have been committed are committed because men have consumed obscenity; but perhaps other crimes are not committed because of such consumption. The relevant consideration would be the effect of consumption on crimes overall.

The second point relates to the precise nature of the Commission's conclusion on this point. It did not draw a distinction between obscene violent materials and sexually violent materials that are not obscene. This apparent absence of relevant difference suggests the obvious point that if only obscene materials are suppressed and men see many other sexually violent materials, the effectiveness of suppression in eliminating this general cause of crime will be sharply limited. Some evidence suggests further that responses to *nonsexual* violent portrayals are similar to responses to sexually violent portrayals.[44] If so, the basic problem is with violent materials in general, and the crime prevention reason for suppression applies to nonobscene materials as much as obscene ones. If so, can this reason plausibly be used to prohibit *only* sexually violent obscene materials? Such a limited attack on the more general problem of violent materials might be justified on the ground that since the Supreme Court (or the Constitution) permits only obscene materials to be forbidden, legislation should deal with the problem to the extent that the Supreme Court allows. This justification, by itself, raises doubts that constitutional law should continue to treat violent obscene materials differently from other sexually violent materials and from nonsexual violent materials. A different justification might claim that obscene violent materials have distinctively "low value" or generate harms not present with other violent materials.

People may reasonably differ about whether existing evidence suggests any plausible causal connection between the consumption of sexually violent materials and an increased overall total of violent crimes. Even if one believes such a connection does exist, one has to recognize that suppression of obscene violent materials leaves in the market a vast amount of sexually violent but not obscene materials whose effects on violent activity are probably not distinguishable. Moreover, the successful suppression of obscene violent materials may well lead to an increase in the currency of nonobscene violent materials. Given the uncertainty of any negative effect (on balance) of obscene violent materials and the low percentage of such an effect (if one exists), the "crime prevention" argument[45] would definitely not be sufficient to support a prohibition of obscenity, were obscenity regarded as having any serious value as speech.

This leaves what I have called undesirable attitudes and practices. There are two dominant themes. The first is that consuming obscenity encourages people to think of sex mainly as a matter of physical pleasure, unrelated to affection and love. It weakens the sense of responsibility needed to maintain family life. It is thus harmful to healthy sexual relationships and family life. The second is that obscenity often portrays some participants (almost always women) as degraded, its consumption creates or reinforces attitudes of dominance (almost always by males), and it leads to dominating behavior within sexual relationships. This pattern of domination helps to "silence" women, making women hesitant to speak and encouraging men not to take their speech seriously.[46] It also contributes to discrimination against women in employment and other areas of life.[47] One quickly recognizes the first claim about undesirable attitudes and practices as a typical conservative challenge to obscenity and the second as a modern feminist challenge.

These claims converge and diverge in important ways. Occasionally it is said that the conservative is concerned with morality and the feminist with consequences, but this mischaracterizes the situation. Both opponents are concerned with what they consider morally appropriate attitudes and behavior. Each may focus on the narrow morality of consuming obscenity; the conservative finding it immoral for people to indulge such gross appetites for sexual material, the feminist finding it immoral for men to indulge a taste for material that degrades women. But the more forceful arguments from both camps focus on harmful consequences from the consumption of obscenity. What differs is the particular consequences they care about.

These two rationales for suppression do not cover precisely the same materials. Although some materials are plainly reached by both arguments, other materials are reached strongly by one but weakly or not at all by the other. Both arguments cover some materials beyond what is now considered obscene in the United States. The worries about healthy attitudes toward sex and family and about degradation and domination extend to much explicit sexual expression, such as the nude dancing in *Barnes v. Glen Theater, Inc.* example, that does not satisfy the *Miller* test of obscenity. On the other hand, some material that is obscene by present definitions is not covered by the argument against domination and degradation.

Conservative and feminist opponents both argue that obscenity operates significantly at a subconscious level, affecting people in a negative way even if they do not accept, and perhaps self-consciously reject, the harmful attitudes obscene materials tend to induce. The value of speech may be greater when attitudes are adopted as a self-conscious reaction to points of view than when attitudes shift by a subconscious process. This may matter both because self-conscious reaction reflects autonomous choice and because expressions that influence such choice are more open to countervailing speech.[48]

Although many conservatives would like to suppress materials that are not within the present boundaries of obscenity, they have not addressed this problem as directly as the leading feminist critics of pornography, who have clearly and consistently claimed that much material that the Supreme Court treats as constitutionally protected is highly damaging to women. One strategy for dealing with this problem is to suggest that the broader range of material does not really count as the kind of expression that deserves protection, and that the government has an ample interest in prohibiting it.[49] Some feminists have emphasized what pornography does. According to Catharine MacKinnon, "What pornography *does* goes beyond its content: it eroticizes hierarchy, it sexualizes inequality. It makes dominance and submission into sex."[50] Another strategy is to suggest that at least one of the government's countervailing reasons to suppress degrading material is itself rooted in a constitutional right of free speech or equal protection. If the silencing of women that obscenity accomplishes impairs women's rights of free speech,[51] restriction of obscenity may help protect free speech values. Alternatively, or additionally, restriction may promote equal rights more generally for women, in accord with the Fourteenth Amendment value of equal protection.[52] As we have seen in previous chapters, if an issue is cast as a conflict of constitutional rights, the right favored by restricting obscenity might be seen as a compelling interest for limiting speech (according to the standard First Amendment formula), or as leading to some comparison of rights that does not involve compelling interest analysis. On the latter possibility, the low value of sexual materials that degrade women would help make suppressive legislation warranted.

The conservative and feminist arguments for suppression are met by contrary arguments. The very influences on sexual attitudes that make conservatives despair are welcomed by others as liberating. In this light, people should freely explore their own sexuality, and obscene materials help them to break puritanical moral constraints. A significant number of feminists think the arguments for freedom outweigh the arguments for suppression. Nadine Strossen, President of the American Civil Liberties Union, discusses ten reasons why women's rights are "disserved by censoring 'pornography'":

1. Any censorship scheme would inevitably encompass many works that are especially valuable to feminists;
2. Any such scheme would be enforced in a way that discriminates against the least popular, least powerful groups in our society, including feminists and lesbians;
3. Censorship perpetuates demeaning stereotypes about women, including that sex is bad for us;
4. Censorship perpetuates the disempowering notion that women are essentially victims;
5. Censorship distracts from constructive approaches to countering anti-female discrimination and violence;
6. Censorship would harm women who voluntarily work in the sex industry;
7. Censorship would harm women's efforts to develop their own sexuality;
8. Censorship would strengthen the power of the religious right, whose patriarchal agenda would curtail women's rights;
9. By undermining free speech, censorship deprives feminists of a powerful tool for advancing women's equality; and
10. Sexual freedom, and freedom for sexually explicit expression, are essential aspects of human freedom; denying these specific freedoms undermines human rights more broadly.[53]

The legal fate of an Indianapolis ordinance reveals a good bit about the coverage of the feminist argument and its treatment by present American constitutional law.[54] The ordinance was framed as an antidiscrimination provision, with civil remedies, rather than a criminal statute. It reached "sexually explicit" works in which "women are presented as sexual objects who enjoy pain or humiliation" or "are presented in scenarios of degradation, injury, abasement" or "are presented as sexual objects for domination, conquest, violation, exploitation, possession, or use." According to a choice made quite self-consciously by Catharine MacKinnon and Andrea Dworkin, the leading proponents and drafters, the ordinance did not refer to prurient interest, patent offensiveness, or literary, artistic, political, or scientific value, and it did not say that what mattered was the work as a whole rather than isolated passages.[55] The highly publicized ordinance, in short, explicitly reached much material that would not qualify as obscene under existing Supreme Court definitions.

The constitutionality of the ordinance was quickly assailed and, after a district judge declared the ordinance to be invalid, the court of appeals reviewed the challenge. Recognizing that the ordinance did not limit itself to materials considered obscene, the court held that it invalidly engaged in viewpoint discrimination, forbidding sexually explicit material that degraded women but allowing otherwise similar material that degraded men or degraded no one. The court treated the feature of viewpoint discrimination as rendering the ordinance invalid, without even inquiring (as the Supreme Court did in *R. A. V.*) whether the statutory formulation was necessary to serve a compelling interest. In answer to the argument that messages of domination are conveyed surreptitiously, the court responded that many messages influence people in subconscious ways. The court treated the case as an easy one in favor of invalidity. The Supreme Court apparently agreed because a majority of six Justices summarily affirmed the decision without hearing argument.[56]

In assigning liability to material that degrades women and in reaching well beyond materials now regarded as obscene, the Indianapolis ordinance challenged two aspects of existing First Amendment law: the particular notion that sexually explicit materials that are not obscene according to the *Miller* test are constitutionally protected and the much more general idea that content distinctions are highly suspect, especially if they constitute viewpoint discrimination.[57] The defeat of the ordinance was not surprising.

Suppose the Court were to relax the rigid approach to content distinctions that *R.A.V.* reflects. How might the constitutional argument that focuses on degradation of women then fare? The free speech claim about "silencing" and the more general equal protection argument track positions advanced in connection with hate speech and other abusive speech. In each instance, these claims contend that prospective speakers should be directly stopped because their speech impairs the equality and effective speech of others. Historically, freedom of speech has been considered mainly to impede government censorship. If the government was broadly permitted to evaluate the effects of speech by individuals on the self-perception of those spoken about, and on the subsequent appraisal others make of the speech of those individuals, the emphasis of free speech law would shift significantly toward a more positive notion of creating appropriate, more equal, conditions of political life. Similarly, allowing the government not only to outlaw acts of discrimination but also to outlaw speech that leads indirectly by some diffuse process to acts of discrimination would significantly shift free speech law.[58]

If the Supreme Court were inclined to adopt such a shift, hate speech seems a more promising beginning than sexual material that is not obscene. The silencing argument seems strongest when people are direct victims of intimidating and disparaging remarks. *Some* hate speech involves such direct victims. The equality argument seems strongest when the speech that is to be suppressed explicitly asserts the inequality of groups, as does most hate speech. Sexually explicit materials degrading women are (generally) seen by willing consumers. The harmful messages are less explicit, and perhaps less directly relevant to most ordinary illegal discrimination, than are the messages of most hate speech.

THE CANADIAN APPROACH

In the 1992 case of *Regina v. Butler* the Canadian Supreme Court approached the problem of obscenity in a way significantly different from existing American law. The Court reviewed federal prosecutions against the owner and employee of a store who were charged with selling, and possessing for sale, items of obscene material.[59] The crucial issues in the case were: (1) what materials counted as obscene under the federal code; and (2) was that coverage appropriate under the Charter? The trial court held that most of the materials were protected under the Charter, and it thus acquitted defendants on some counts. The Manitoba Court of Appeal, reviewing both convictions and acquittals (in the United States, acquittals are typically not subject to appeal), entered convictions on all counts, concluding that obscene materials are not covered by Section 2(b) of the Charter because they convey no message, a startling conclusion in light of the very broad way (described in chapter 2) that the Canadian Supreme Court has defined all that counts as expression under Section 2(b). This set the stage for the decision of the Supreme Court, which responded to questions about the constitutionality of the federal code. With the exception of one issue, the Court was unanimous. Justice Sopinka wrote for himself and six other Justices.

The Statute

The present code provisions were adopted in 1959, successors to earlier 1892 and 1949 statutes that had been interpreted in accord with Chief Judge Cockburn's approach to obscenity in *Regina v. Hicklin*.[60] Unlike its predecessors, the present code, in Section 163(8), defines obscenity: "any publication a dominant characteristic of which is the undue exploitation of sex, or of sex and any one or more of the following subjects, namely, crime, horror, cruelty and violence."[61] According to the Court, this definition replaced the *Hicklin* test; its present scope could be understood only with reference to a series of rules developed by the courts in cases that mostly preceded adoption of the Charter.

The statute provides that exploitation of sex must not only be the dominant characteristic, it must be "undue." The most important test of whether exploitation is undue is community standards of tolerance.[62]

These standards are national ones; they are the standards of the community as a whole, and not some small segment of the community such as a university; the standards are contemporary and change over time. The government need not introduce evidence of the standards as part of its case. The standards are ones of tolerance, not taste. "What matters is what Canadians would not abide other Canadians seeing because it would be beyond the contemporary Canadian standard of tolerance to allow them to see it."[63] In a previous case, the Court had divided over the question whether material might be obscene if shown to one audience but not another, because members of the community might accept its being shown to the second audience but not the first. The *Butler* Court apparently followed the majority view that whether material was obscene did not depend on the constituency to which it was shown.[64]

Justice Sopinka wrote that in recent cases there has been a growing recognition that material said to exploit sex in a "degrading or dehumanizing" manner will necessarily fail the community standards test.[65] Such materials "place women (and sometimes men) in positions of subordination, servile submission or humiliation" and "run against the principles of equality and dignity of all human beings."[66] These materials "apparently" fail community standards not because they offend "against morals" but because they are "perceived by public opinion to be harmful to society, particularly to women." In contrast to the view of Chief Justice Dickson in an earlier case that materials that degrade or dehumanize might involve "undue exploitation" even if tolerated by the community, Justice Sopinka follows the position that Judge Wilson had taken then that the community is the arbiter of what is harmful to itself. Courts, however, can view material to judge the likely harm from exposure; "[t]he stronger the inference of a risk of harm the lesser the likelihood of [community] tolerance."[67]

Material that might otherwise qualify as obscene does not involve undue exploitation if it is required for serious treatment of a theme, as in the movie *Last Tango in Paris*.[68] This "internal necessities" test is not just one factor to be weighed among others; rather, a court asks first whether there is material that by itself would constitute an undue exploitation of sex and if the answer to that question is "yes," it asks whether undue exploitation of sex is "the main object of the work" or "this portrayal of sex [is] essential to a wider artistic, literary, or other similar purpose?"[69]

Finally, on the statutory question, Justice Sopinka said that pornography "can be usefully divided into three categories: (1) explicit sex with violence [including threats of physical violence], (2) explicit sex without violence but which subjects people to treatment that is degrading or dehumanizing, and (3) explicit sex without violence that is neither degrading nor dehumanizing."[70] Material in the first category "will almost always constitute the undue exploitation of sex"; material in the second category "may be undue if the risk of harm is substantial"; material in the third category "will not qualify as the undue exploitation of sex unless it employs children in its production."[71] The major point on which Judges Gontheir and L'Heureux-Dube disagreed with the majority was over the third category; they thought that some material in that category, other than that for which children are employed, should be regarded as covered by the statute.

Interestingly, the court did not conclude that all material left free by the federal statute is constitutionally protected; it assumed that the provinces have some latitude to regulate the availability of other sexually explicit materials. According to Justice Sopinka, "Typically such legislation imposes restrictions on the material available to children."[72] It is uncertain whether the justices think much latitude remains for further regulation in relation to adults.

It is worth pausing here to make some observations about the court's approach to the statute. First, the degree of harm materials cause has little to do with whether they are expressive in some simple sense. An obscene movie in which a participant is portrayed as degraded is every bit as much expression as obscenity in which no one is portrayed as degraded. I have already suggested that obscenity cannot be written off as not involving expression. That approach becomes even more implausible if likely harm becomes the central measure of what counts as obscenity.

Second, Canada's statutory standard bears a significant relationship to the constitutional standard elaborated in the United States. The two standards overlap a great deal but each is more and less protective in certain respects than the other. Both contain a thread that saves material that would otherwise count as obscene. Justice Sopinka asks "is undue exploitation of sex the main object of the work or is this portrayal of sex essential to a wider artistic, literary, or other similar purpose?"[73] The *Miller* test inquires whether material "taken as a whole" has "serious literary, artistic, political, or scientific value."[74] In both countries, courts make this inquiry. One could parse the language at greater length, but I will simply say that my own sense is that the American standard requires a judge to find material constitutionally protected if the work as a whole has some serious point, even if the judge thinks that exploitation of sex is both dominant and unnecessary. The Canadian standard seems to invite a judge to hold material obscene if exploitation of sex is dominant, and this judgment can be affected by whether the judge regards the portrayal of sex as "essential" to a wider purpose.

As presently formulated, the Canadian standard seems to present a kind of gap. An inquiry into the "object" of the work sounds like a question about the author's purpose (or, conceivably, the purpose reasonably to be ascribed to an author who produced those words). It is fairly straightforward to ask (if difficult sometimes to answer) whether the dominant purpose of the work is the exploitation of sex (plainly, it does not matter whether the author thinks this exploitation is "undue"). Suppose the judge concludes that the author's main purpose is something else, but that that main purpose is realized to a very slight degree and that the extensive undue exploitation of sex found in the work is wholly unnecessary to accomplishment of the purpose. This version of the test does not tell the judge what to do with such material. Exploitation of sex is not the main object of the work (therefore the work may not be obscene), but the portrayal of sex is not essential to a wider purpose (therefore the work may be obscene). Other passages in the opinion do not settle this small problem, but they intimate that the author's purpose is most important.[75]

The Canadian standard finally turns the judge back to the community: "The court must determine whether the sexually explicit material when viewed in the context of the whole work would be tolerated by the community as a whole."[76] This approach would seem to treat as obscene some works that might be protected under *Miller*, which does not make the social value strand a matter of community sentiment.

The main Canadian inquiry is whether there is undue exploitation of sex, judged by community tolerance and with special attention to likely harm. The *Miller* standard treats as obscene works that predominantly appeal to the prurient interest and portray sexual conduct in a patently offensive way. One might imagine an exploitation of sex that is undue but which does not involve appeal to prurient interest, or the lust of the viewer. That apparently is protected in the United States, but might be covered by the Canadian statute. Any material that *does* appeal to prurient interest *and* is patently offensive might appear to be an undue exploitation of sex; so on an initial glance the Canadian formulation seems to treat as obscene all that the *Miller* formulation does. But this assumption would be misconceived given Justice Sopinka's gloss on the formulation. American courts have never said that all nonviolent material that does not involve degradation is protected. Imagine a movie showing only explicit scenes of consensual "equal" sexual intercourse, or showing group sex in which no one is particularly degraded.[77] This "hard-core" pornography is unprotected under *Miller*, yet the Canadian Supreme Court says it does not violate community tolerance in that country (with two Justices dissenting on this point and the majority leaving open the possibility of provincial regulation). In this regard, the Canadian statutory standard protects some material left unprotected by the American constitutional standard.

The Canadian Court's emphasis on violence and the harm of degradation, however, suggests that Canada will treat as obscene some material that would not be thought "patently offensive" in the United States, where, so far, application of the patent offensiveness standard has not treated violence and degradation as central elements. In this important aspect, the Canadian formulation protects less than does the *Miller* standard.

This comparison leads to another observation about the nature of the Canadian standard in comparison with that of the United States. In American criminal prosecutions, it is assumed that predominant appeal to prurient interest and patent offensiveness will be determined by juries.[78] Jurors are supposed to assess these matters by something like a statewide standard, but what they are likely to do is mainly to apply their own standards. Judges, including the Supreme Court, stand as a back-up to protect against aberrations unfavorable to defendants (since acquittals are not appealable in the United States, aberrations in favor of defendants go unreviewed). When judges do make these judgments, their responsibility is passive—it is to replicate dominant community reactions and judgments about predominant appeal to prurient interest and patent offensiveness.

If one reads the surface of Justice Sopinka's opinion in *Butler*, one discerns considerable ambivalence about the role of judges. There is language to suggest that it strongly resembles that of American judges in this area. At the least, however, an important practical difference is that in Canada the status of materials is always up to the judge. Furthermore, the opinion emphasizes that likely harm is a critical element for judgment. If community tolerance is the test, how is the Court so confident that likely harm is *now* a crucial element in what the community will tolerate? In application, if not in theory, the judicial standard of community tolerance is bound to be fairly elite; judges are going to be aware mostly of what educated opinion is about various kinds of materials, not of what ordinary working class people feel. Beyond this, one senses strongly that the Court itself is making community standards more than following them. It is educating, even telling, people what should and should not be tolerated; and in cases of any doubt it will exercise its own judgment. Of course, this is bound to occur to some extent in the application of any legal standard, but Justice Sopinka's language explicitly encourages it to a much greater degree than one would normally find when judges are told to apply community standards.

The Charter

I turn now to the Canadian Court's treatment of the Charter issue, namely whether Section 163 of the Criminal Code, which defines obscenity, is in violation of the Charter. The first inquiry is whether the materials are covered by Section 2(b) of the Charter. The Court differed with the majority of the Manitoba Court of Appeal and concluded that obscene materials are expression under Section 2(b), which covers any regulation of materials because of their content and meaning.[79] Even if material simply reproduces physical activity (as in a film of sexual inter-course), it constitutes expression and represents the maker's attempt to convey meaning. Although I suggested in chapter 2 that the Court's ideas about protected expression are now too broad in certain respects, I have no quarrel with its treatment here, since I agree that obscenity constitutes a form of expression.

Having decided that obscenity is expression within Section 2(b) of the Charter, Justice Sopinka turned to the central question whether Section 163 of the Criminal Code can be justified under Section 1 of the Charter. He asked first if the statutory provision is, as required, a limit prescribed by law. A provision can fail to be a "limit prescribed by law" if it is too vague or too imprecise to be a reasonable limit. Given judicial construc-tion of the statute and the need in the law generally for standards such as "undue," Justice Sopinka concluded that the provision was not too vague or unintelligible.[80]

The next question was whether there was an objective underlying the obscenity provision sufficient to warrant infringing on expression cov-ered by Section 2(b). Justice Sopinka said that before 1959 obscenity leg-islation was evidently aimed at prohibiting "immoral influences" of ob-scenity and "safeguarding the morals of individuals into whose hands such works could fall."[81] This "particular objective is no longer defen-sible in view of the Charter. To impose a certain standard of public and sexual morality, solely because it reflects the conventions of a given com-munity, is inimical to the exercise and enjoyment of individual freedoms, which form the basis of our social contract."[82] Although preventing "dirt for dirt's sake" is not a legitimate objective, Parliament can legislate "on the basis of some fundamental conception of morality for the purposes of safeguarding the values which are integral to a free and democratic soci-ety."[83] (Justice Gontheir's separate opinion emphasized the absence of any sharp distinction between protecting morality and preventing harm.)[84] In any event, the overriding objective is not moral disapproba-tion but the avoidance of harm to society, most importantly the reinforce-ment of unhealthy male/female stereotypes that harm both sexes. As a Report on Pornography by the Standing Committee on Justice and Legal Affairs put it: "A society which holds that egalitarianism, non-violence, consensualism, and mutuality are basic to any human interaction, whether sexual or other, is clearly justified in controlling and prohibiting any medium of depiction, description or advocacy which violates these principles."[85]

Justice Sopinka paused to meet an objection based on the "shifting purpose" doctrine. In Canada, as in the United States, people have challenged legislation that requires shops to close on Sunday on the ground that the purpose of such laws is religious. In the United States, the Supreme Court acknowledged that the historical purpose had been religious, but nonetheless sustained the laws on the ground that a secular purpose, a uniform day of rest, now supports them.[86] The Canadian Supreme Court said that a law could not be supported by a "shifting purpose" different from that underlying enactment of the law.[87] Butler argued that the Court should not sustain the obscenity provision on a theory different from that on which it was enacted. Justice Sopinka's response was that harm to society is inextricably linked to moral corruption of a certain kind and that "prohibition of such materials was based on a belief that they had a detrimental impact on individuals exposed to them and consequently on society as a whole."[88] Even if there have been some changes in the kind of harm emphasized, and in how pressing various harms may appear, that does not violate the "shifting purpose" doctrine, particularly since the community standards test builds into the legislation a permissible shift in emphasis.[89]

Having found a legitimate objective, Justice Sopinka turned to whether it is "pressing and substantial," as required under Section 1. He refers to *Keegstra*, the hate speech case, to indicate the importance of combatting messages of inferiority that threaten the dignity of members of target groups. Sopinka wrote, "if true equality between male and female persons is to be achieved, we cannot ignore the threat to equality resulting from exposure to audiences of certain types of violent and degrading material. Materials portraying women as a class as objects for sexual exploitation and abuse have a negative impact on 'the individual's sense of self-worth and acceptance.'"[90] Furthermore, relying in part on the existence of legislation against obscenity in virtually all organized societies, he concluded that the Charter did not deprive Parliament of this historical power. Finally, he noted that the burgeoning pornography industry renders the concern in combatting obscenity more pressing and substantial than it was in 1959.[91]

The third inquiry under Section 1 of the Charter is about proportionality: for a provision to be valid, there must be (1) a rational connection between it and the objective, (2) minimal impairment of the right or freedom, and (3) a proper balance between the effects of a provision and the objective. In this inquiry, the court takes into account the expression that has been infringed. Justice Sopinka said that the expression covered by the statute "does not stand on an equal footing with other kinds of expression which directly engage the 'core' of the freedom of expression values,"[92] a conclusion that is buttressed by the aim of economic profit which motivates the production of the overwhelming majority of these materials. He suggested that the provision does not inhibit "good pornography," which celebrates human sexuality.

Although the social science evidence connecting obscenity to harm is controversial and not conclusive, Justice Sopinka, citing *Paris Adult Theater* and *Keegstra*, said that Parliament had a *reasonable basis* to decide that such harm is caused. That was sufficient to pass the rational basis requirement.

The "minimal impairment" requirement was also satisfied. The provision does not cover sexually explicit erotica that do not create the risk of harm; it does not include material with scientific, artistic, or literary merit; it deals with a problem for which other, more specific, formulations would prove inadequate; it has been interpreted (parallel to a constitutional doctrine in the United States) not to extend to private use or viewing of obscene materials; it could not meet its objective by restrictions on time, place, and manner alone. Thus, the law does not impair expression further than is necessary to meet the objective. Other responses may abate the problem of violence against women, but there is nothing that requires Parliament to choose those responses to the exclusion of a restriction on obscene materials.

Given the importance of the object of the legislation—the enhancement of "respect for all members of society, and non-violence and equality in their relations with each other"[93]—and the relative unimportance of the expression, the Court concluded that the provision comfortably satisfies the third proportionality standard; the importance of the legislative objective is not outweighed by the restriction on freedom of expression.

The Court's disposition was to remand all counts for decision under the standard it had set down. In accord with the questions posed in the appeal, it regarded its task as stating the right standards, not figuring out their application to particular materials.

It is noteworthy that Justice Sopinka's opinion does not accept moral disapprobation of obscenity for its own sake as constituting a sufficient objective. In the nude dancing case, Chief Justice Rehnquist made a point of saying that precluding behavior judged immoral, with no attention to subsequent harmful consequences, was a sufficient purpose to meet the requirement of an important or substantial government objective. As of now, the U.S. Supreme Court is much more accepting of "moralism" for its own sake than the Canadian Supreme Court.

Justice Sopinka's opinion represents virtually full endorsement of the feminist challenge to obscenity. The legislation the Court reviews does not directly embody that theory in the manner of the Indianapolis ordinance. It does not, even as interpreted, prohibit the sale of obscenity un-

less the material violates community standards of tolerance, and lacks
artistic or literary significance; and it does not draw any explicit line in
terms of degradation of women. Material that degrades men will be
treated the same as material that degrades women if both violate community tolerance. As previously noted, the Canadian decision does not
clearly allow much more material to be suppressed than does American
law.[94] Nevertheless, Canada's Court has no strong doctrine against content discrimination, and the theory it adopts might well lead it to uphold
a law cast in the manner of the Indianapolis ordinance.

I think the Court makes things easier for itself by a superficial treatment of the "old" reasons for suppressing obscenity, and this affects
its final conclusion. The conservative condemnation of obscenity has
rarely rested solely on "moralism" regarding the consumption of obscene
materials. Also present has been a notion that such consumption causes
unhealthy attitudes toward sex, and poses some threat to conventional
family life. A legislature might reasonably believe that a conventional
two-parent family is by and large healthy for children, and that high di-
vorce rates are far from ideal for children's emotional stability and
growth. It might conclude that the family stability argument for curbing
obscenity has some force. Justice Sopinka does not pause to explain why
that argument is abandoned completely in favor of the equality argument.
Is Canada so advanced that the average Canadian, man as well as
woman, regards the equality rationale as vastly more important than the
family rationale? Is it because stable family life is not a Charter value?
One would suppose that a healthy environment for children is a basic
good that would rate as high as explicit Charter values. Is the family
rationale obviously flimsy, given all the other influences on sexual behavior and commitment in relationships?

This problem would be less important if it did not apparently affect
what the Court concludes about coverage of the statute. Sexually explicit
material that does not involve violence or degradation of either sex may
encourage members of both sexes to be liberated sexually. Liberated sexual attitudes may encourage people who are married to explore sex outside of marriage. If extramarital sex alone does not threaten a marriage
(and it will threaten some marriages in which the other partner clings to
an ideal of sexual fidelity), sexual involvements often lead to deep affec-
tions, and these extramarital ties of affection can threaten marriages. In
short, a "family rationale" may extend to material in the Court's third
category, the category which it says will not be obscene unless children
are involved in its production. Of course, the Court indicates that Canadians now tolerate all such material, but how it arrives at this conclusion is opaque. The Court seems to assume that most Canadians now

regard the equality rationale as the dominant one for suppression; but it reads that opinion through its own somewhat progressive view of these matters.

Comparisons with the United States

There are various standpoints from which *Butler* can be compared with American law. On the narrow question of what material may be suppressed, the Court's statutory interpretation brings it not too far from the *Miller* test, although some nonviolent, nondegrading material suppressible under *Miller* is not covered as "obscene" by the Canadian provision as now interpreted. More important, the provision probably bans some violent and degrading material that would not be thought to violate contemporary standards of offensiveness in the United States.

In terms of general constitutional doctrine for free speech, *Butler* further illustrates major differences between the United States and Canada. The Canadian Supreme Court does not embrace any principle against content distinctions, and it is willing to countenance as an appropriate basis for prohibition the substantive harms that come from acceptance of a message. It has a very broad idea of what is covered by the Section 2(b) protection of free expression, but it is flexible about what can finally be prohibited under Section 1. The language of Section 1 underpins a balancing approach that is much more favorable to regulation than the compelling interest test in the United States and yet involves considerably more scrutiny than the American "rational basis" standard. The *Butler* Court's consideration of the value of a particular kind of expression as relevant to the proportionality requirement under Section 1 bears some resemblance to the U.S. Supreme Court's treatment of low value speech, but the Canadian Court is much more flexible in considering value and it treats value as relevant in a much broader range of cases.

The theory under which the Canadian Court supports suppression is strikingly in line with the claims of those feminists who regard obscenity as a major evil. Its adoption of that theory to the exclusion of all others is truly remarkable, given how controversial that theory is and continuing public support for more conservative reasons to suppress obscenity. When one puts *Butler* together with *Keegstra*, one realizes that equality, and especially the aspirations to equality of groups victimized in the past, rate very high as constitutional values in Canada. Especially for speech that is at the margins in one respect or another, the Supreme Court is willing to entertain arguments that equality demands its suppression. Closely similar arguments, often cast in terms of a conflict of the Fourteenth Amendment value of equality with the First Amendment value of free speech, have been made in the United States; but they have yet to bear much fruit in judicial decisions.

Can one conclude that the Canadian Court is, in general, more sympathetic to restrictions on free speech? Probably so, and with the warrant of Section 1. Historically, much suppression of speech has taken place in the name of prevention of crime and national security. The first value accompanies the equality argument in favor of suppression of obscenity, and is given weight by the Court. It is hard to see how the second can be disregarded if a plausible claim is made that speech does threaten national security in some way. Some argue that hate speech and obscenity are special cases, but one doubts that the Court's acceptance of regulation in *Keegstra* and *Butler* can be contained, unless the key is that they involved the fringes of expression. I have already suggested that speech covered by the *Taylor* decision (which accompanied *Keegstra*), strong criticism of someone's religious ideas, is hardly at the fringes of expression. More to the point, there are many circumstances in which prohibited expression other than hate speech and obscenity would arguably be at the fringe of the values of free expression.

What lessons might Americans draw from *Butler*, and *Keegstra*, about general principles of First Amendment interpretation? It is hard not to be attracted by the flexible and intelligent evaluation of the Canadian Supreme Court; that seems so much more sensible than the categorical boxes and blindness to nuance of dominant American approaches. However, the cost of following the Canadian path would also certainly be reduced protection for expression. The force of the Canadian approach could not easily be limited to obscenity and hate speech.

Chapter Seven

INDIVIDUALS AND COMMUNITIES

THIS CHAPTER shifts ground. It relates actual and possible constitutional decisions to the theme of individuals and communities, asking what difference it makes if courts pay attention to the place of community in human life. The relevance of community has composed part of the background for previous chapters; here I attend to it explicitly. This chapter reexamines in varying detail the topics of the last four chapters—flag burning, hate speech, campus speech codes, workplace harassment, and obscenity. I will also introduce two new topics about free speech in American law that illustrate the central theme—campaign financing and medical advice about abortions. In addition, I discuss religious liberty and its implications, because aspects of that subject clearly show the complexity of considering the respective places of individual and community.

I begin with some challenges to liberal individualist perspectives. I then try to sort out precisely what it could mean to pay more attention to community in adjudication, before I proceed to the particular examples of free speech and free exercise of religion that help show the importance of various facets of community in constitutional adjudication.

The guarantees of freedom of speech and the press and of religious exercise lie at the very center of liberal democracy. Any country that denies them is not free. Why do we believe these liberties are so important? Because they contribute to a peaceful and just society or because restricting what people say and how they worship is inherently wrong? Since the beginning, some justifications have focused on individuals, while others have focused on the community. The adopters of the Bill of Rights understood that the fruit of religious conflict had been bloody war and cruel oppression. They thought religious liberty and federal nonestablishment of religion would help ensure civil peace. But more than this, John Locke had argued that enforcing religious convictions was not the state's business;[1] sectarian Protestants agreed. In 1791, many people believed they had a natural right to seek religious truth for themselves.

At that time, freedom of the press overshadowed freedom of speech. Both rights were regarded primarily as social protections against government tyranny and corruption. But the idea that people have some fundamental right to say what they believe was also emerging; and it had become more significant by the adoption of the Fourteenth Amendment,[2]

the part of the Constitution that has been judged to make the First
Amendment applicable against states and localities.

The Supreme Court did not develop First Amendment liberties until
this century. The height of expansion was in the 1960s and early 1970s
under the Warren and Burger Courts. The framework of those rulings
remains largely in place. Some decisions invoked wide social effects, but
the Court mainly spoke about protecting individual autonomy and self-
expression. Recognizing creative and emotional elements of self-expression, the Court's conception of personality was more romantic than that
of late eighteenth-century rationalists. Nonetheless, the vision was dis-
tinctly liberal; it stressed personal integrity and self-direction and the restricted authority of government.

During the past two decades the Supreme Court has shifted toward
accepting what other officials decide, justifying its approval with words
of deference and references to the limited aims of those who established
rights. The explanation for the Court's change is not complex. Presidents
Reagan and Bush strongly opposed a liberal activist judiciary. They appointed Justices to rectify that defect, and they largely succeeded. Most
major decisions protecting personal rights have yet to be undone, but
some startling retractions in First Amendment doctrine have occurred.

The main intellectual challenge to a liberal understanding of rights has
come from the left, not the right. The movement called critical legal studies is one manifestation. Some scholars in that movement express extreme
skepticism about reason and about discerning the meaning of texts. They
insist that judicial decisions are essentially subjective, not distinct from
unguided political choice. Many believe that talk about basic rights actually serves to support the status quo.[3] The aim of these theorists, of
course, is to shift opinion and social institutions over time; but we can see
that, in the present, their message is not likely to trouble conservative
judges who are inclined to sustain laws that diminish individual freedom.
If judging is essentially political, why not sustain the actions of politicians
with whom one sympathizes?

Modern civic republicanism and certain feminist approaches are more
encouraging about the potential for shared understanding and dialogue.
They challenge the individualistic, atomistic philosophy they understand
as liberalism. They emphasize the social character of persons and the centrality of communal life in constituting individual identity. They deny
that the personal sphere is separated from the political, and that legal
divisions of private and public domains are natural. They express hope
that under desirable conditions sympathetic mutual understanding and
reasoned discourse can resolve many social problems.

My main effort in this chapter is to assess how greater emphasis on community might bear on free speech and the free exercise of religion. I then measure some judicial decisions against the combined wisdom of approaches that focus on individuals and communities. What I conclude is that:

First, an understanding that human character is social and that communities are vitally significant should definitely not lead to the abandonment of distinctions between public and private in determining rights.

Second, judges should be sensitive to how rights will affect the general polity, but they must also pay attention to individual integrity and the integrity of less inclusive groups.

Third, free exercise rights differ from free speech and free press rights, but comparison reveals strong similarities in how they should be conceived.

Fourth, in some major cases involving speech and religion, the U.S. Supreme Court has not adequately recognized the importance of either individuals or groups.

The Social Character of Human Beings

Communitarian critics often say that liberals assume individuals are rational and autonomous, with interests formed independently of their communities. People combine in organizations to present and protect their shared interests. Government protects people from each other and accommodates conflicts of interests. *If* thoughtful modern liberals accepted this account, bashing liberals would be easy, because human nature is decidedly not atomistic.

People perceive and care about the things they do partly because they find themselves in particular societies and subgroups. Identities are socially formed. Government helps determine them; so do other associations and more amorphous groupings like race and gender. Thoughtful liberals do not deny that community is essential for human life, that much of who we are derives from our communities. Many advocates of community conveniently challenge a liberalism made of straw, but they rightly see that defenses of rights must begin with our social nature.

The Personal Is Political: A Feminist Perspective

When I first heard the feminist slogan: "the personal is political," I felt the resonance of profound insight, but I did not quickly grasp the content. I was reassured to discover that those who espouse and criticize this epigram do not always have the same thing in mind. But I have learned that it embraces related perceptions about the personal and political, the public and private.

Most obviously, political power is pervasive; political structures largely determine personal life. According to Susan Moller Okin, "to the extent that a more private, domestic sphere does exist, its very existence, the limits that define it, and the types of behavior that are acceptable and not acceptable within it all result from political decisions."[4] "The personal is political" also conveys the political importance of "private experience." Catharine MacKinnon wrote: "women's distinctive experience as women occurs within that sphere that has been socially lived as the personal–private, emotional, interiorized, particular, individuated, intimate . . . to *know* the *politics* of woman's situation is to know women's personal lives."[5] Kenneth Karst has emphasized one kind of private experience that is relevant for politics. Those who make law are motivated by personal needs; more particularly, male legislators act upon conceptions of women that serve their own intimate needs.[6] Their political actions create the conditions in which women live. Yet another point is that any group's ability to participate fruitfully in politics will depend on the self-definition of its members.[7]

If any personal event is also political,[8] no sharp natural line demarcates private matters from public ones. Legal distinctions between public and private conceal the political roots of inequality[9] and the state's support of unjust domination in the "private realm."[10]

Those who have explained how "the personal is political" have concentrated on the *most* personal matters, such as family relations, but if these are partly defined by politics and have political importance, so also do other associations. Many activities are not under the state's direct supervision. Character is formed within friendships, working relations, churches, and social clubs. Political structures affect these associations and are affected by them.

CIVIC REPUBLICAN PERSPECTIVES

During the last decade, constitutional scholars have proposed civic republicanism as a communitarian alternative to liberalism. They draw republican attitudes from threads of Federalist and anti-Federalist positions, from Whig writers, and from more ancient history. They explain how their recommended approaches resemble and differ from these older theories.[11] I shall bypass these matters, saying only that modern theorists do a lot of picking and choosing in offering models for contemporary evaluation.

Even in modern dress, civic republican theory is hardly uniform, but the following elements predominate. Individuals are understood as having social characters, grounded in communities. The "animating principle" of civic republicanism has been said to be civic virtue; "the willingness of citizens to subordinate their private interests to the general good."[12] Participation in politics is a primary good. Members of a republic do not just make trade-offs to secure their existing values and interests, they deliberate to choose values that will guide the community in public and private life. Frank Michelman writes of a form of practical reason that is dialogic.[13] Cass Sunstein suggests that under republican approaches, laws must be supported by arguments and reasons, not simply fought for as products of self-interested deals.[14] Republicanism is sustained by a belief that different approaches to politics, or different conceptions of the public good, can be mediated by discussion and dialogue.[15] According to Michelman, the people will constantly redetermine "the terms on which they live together."[16] He says "[r]epublicanism contests with a so-called pluralist vision, which regards the political system as, ideally, designed to serve the self-defined private interests of individuals or groups, fairly represented in political forums, where they compete under fair rules for fair shares of the outputs of public policy."[17] Pluralism involves "the deep mistrust of people's capacities to communicate *persuasively* to one another their diverse normative experiences: of needs and rights, values and interests, and, more broadly, interpretations of the world"; pluralism "doubts or denies our ability to communicate such material in ways that move each other's views on disputed normative issues toward felt (not merely strategic) agreement without deception, coercion, or other manipulation."[18] Republicanism holds onto the hope that such transformation is possible.

Whether a republican believes that collective discourse can arrive at values that are independently worth achieving or that each community settles for itself what is to count as good, skepticism about values, in a sense often attributed to liberalism, is rejected. The government is not to remain neutral among competing conceptions of the good. It is the locus where conceptions should be debated and adopted.[19]

For dialogical politics to work, participants must be equal. Political activity is good for individuals as well as the community. It yields self-development, feelings of social solidarity, and empathy.[20] People realize autonomy by selecting values with others, rather than by implementing prechosen ends.[21]

Where is one to locate republican virtues in complex diverse societies? Republican theorists disagree. Some think we cannot expect widespread active citizen participation in government, even at the local level. Others suggest that citizens may be encouraged to participate actively, or that they do so at transformative historical moments.[22] Whatever the potentialities for ordinary citizens, perhaps legislators may realize a model of deliberative practical reason.[23] Frank Michelman has suggested that courts are the institutions best suited for collective deliberation about values.[24]

The question of where republican virtues are to manifest themselves bears on the reasonable aspirations of civic republicanism. Were legislatures or courts able to accomplish genuine collective deliberation, they might in some manner represent these capacities for ordinary citizens. However, it is not easy to see how ordinary citizens would be enriched much in their own individual lives by sensitive legislative or judicial dialogue.

Under civic republican theory, the public helps define private virtue that is important to public life. Like feminism, that theory challenges existing divisions between public and private.

DEFENSIBLE IMPLICATIONS OF COMMUNITARIAN PERSPECTIVES FOR RIGHTS ADJUDICATION

At present, constitutional distinctions between the public domain and private domains of choice are centrally important. If the personal is political, if public and private virtue are intertwined, if no natural, obvious line exists between public and private activities, what should happen to those distinctions? This is another way of asking what might happen to constitutional principles if a philosophy that strongly emphasized communities over individuals were widely accepted.

The most extreme consequence, one not advocated by theorists I have discussed here, would be a complete collapse of lines between public and private. These would cease to be relevant categories. The government could intervene in all areas and aspects of life for the benefit of the corporate polity.[25]

Alternatively, we might retain some distinctions between public and private, but draw them in terms of benefit to collective political life. Various scholars have suggested that rights should be understood as communal in nature.[26] When citizens and organizations claim rights to private choice, courts might ask what will best contribute to citizens' participation in politics. Do women have a right to terminate pregnancies? That would depend on the significance of the right for women's self-conceptions and their ability to participate in politics. What freedom belongs to nongovernmental organizations? That would depend on their contributions to virtues of good citizenship.

We can see just how *radical* these communitarian implications could be for rights of private choice if we look at their implications for religious activities. In 1791, many people thought churches were vitally important for human life, and mostly for reasons apart from ordinary government.

Within religious communities, organizational structures are public and political in comparison with a member's private understanding and practice.[27] But from the broader perspective of the entire society, religion and religious institutions are potentially in a private domain distinct from public government. General political life undoubtedly affects religious life and, in turn, religious life affects political life. To take one sensitive example, the exclusion of women from the Roman Catholic priesthood has influenced wider perceptions of women's roles and their political ambitions and status. The exclusion carries some implicit message that practical decisions and public life are mainly for men. The religious and political domains infect each other. Does it follow that no private domain for religion should be recognized? Or that the boundaries of such a domain should be drawn solely with reference to collective political life? Of course not.

Distrust of government authority and belief in human freedom are the primary themes of political liberalism. History provides inexhaustible support for distrust of government. Anyone, religious believer or not, must be disturbed by the idea of the government controlling religion to pursue a public good of egalitarian, participatory politics. Since people feel so strongly about religion, government control would produce distress and conflict. Then there is the slight impediment of religious truth. Concluding that human beings have a social character tells us very little about what might be true in the realm of religious belief. Many theologians as well as secular theorists oppose atomistic individual concepts of human character. A wide spectrum of religious beliefs fits with the notions that character is socially formed and truth is socially learned. If some spiritual reality that is more than a figment of human imagination does exist, people chosen for mundane tasks of governing are not especially adept at discerning it. But perhaps politicians would not need to worry about spiritual truth; they could employ the religious myths useful for good government and suppress others. No subject of the human quest for understanding should become simple fodder for the government's promotion of citizenship; and the prospect of government freely manipulating religion for political ends is appalling. Only an extraordinary reversal of cultural values could lead us to think religion belongs entirely in the public political domain.

What of the less extreme alternative—recognizing some division between public and private, but drawing lines in terms of the collective political good? Government intrusions into the lives of citizens might still be very great. And why should we think that wise judgment, fairness, and the elimination of undesirable structures of domination would mark those intrusions more than prejudice and pursuit of self-interest?[28] Courts could protect against the most tyrannical acts, but judges would have trouble identifying many abuses. Courts would effectively cede to the political branches forms of action that could be badly misinformed and destructive.

Seeing all domains of life solely in terms of their relation to collective existence would be disastrously myopic. People care about relationships and organizations for reasons that reach well beyond politics. The point is obvious for religious institutions; it is true also for historical societies and friendships and virtually all other associations. Our law must leave room for the dominant conviction that the significance of human associations transcends politics.

Values of participation and dialogue for individuals are not uniquely realized in public governance. People debate and select values in various nonpublic associations. These experiences are valuable for their own sakes, not just because they affect how people act as citizens. Exposure to other points of view helps individuals reflect upon and transform their own self-conceptions and social roles. These opportunities to develop autonomy arise in many settings.[29] Collective self-determination is a vital part of human life, but it is hardly restricted to government. The point is forcefully made by Terrance Sandalow that "the existence of vital intermediate structures undermines the claim that politics must be pervasive and all-encompassing."[30] Robert Cover suggested the idea of various communities providing their own interpretations of culture. Life within such communities has its own importance, even if the community, like the Amish, is distant from government.[31] The law should regard intermediate associations as having their own intrinsic significance and scope. Rights that affirm community may affirm communities smaller than the entire society.[32]

I conclude that collapsing all distinctions between public and private or drawing such distinctions exclusively with an eye to public citizenship would be a grave error. People are citizens but they are much more. Legislatures and courts need to consider multiple perspectives in evaluating lines between public control and private choice. Collective political good should affect constitutional understanding, but it definitely should not supplant other perspectives.

These reasons why government should treat religion largely as a private domain[33] reveal something about a sensible political liberalism. It does not claim that human beings are individual, rational units unaffected in their deepest beliefs and desires by their society. In this regard, liberalism need hold firm *only* to the claim that declaring some domains as mainly ones of private choice, largely off limits to government, enhances human fulfillment and social harmony.

I have used the phrase "largely off limits to government." Nongovernmental associations may be contexts of unfairness, domination, even coercion. Should not the government be able to intervene to assure that these relationships are carried forward in terms that society judges to be fundamentally decent and fair? Intervention on this basis is often appropriate, but it must be carefully calibrated to the kind of association that is involved. Sometimes the state must tolerate what most of its citizens deem to be unfair because too much coercive intervention would be destructive of the values of the association. This is perhaps clearest about religious organizations. If members of a religious group regard their corporate life as regulated in accord with a transcendent perspective, civil government must be very hesitant to interfere on behalf of its own ideas of what is just. The present exclusion of women from the Roman Catholic priesthood again provides a striking example. Most citizens may now regard that as unfair; but the state should not be in the business of telling people how they must choose their religious leaders.

The family provides a different kind of example. If the value of relationships among spouses depends substantially on spontaneity and the freedom to respond with love to each other's personal needs, individual couples need the liberty to work out for themselves arrangements that outsiders may judge to be unfair. Feminists may well respond that women typically end up giving more than they receive. Although people can reasonably differ over the extent to which the state should lay down rules for families, any sensitive person must worry about the state getting deeply involved in relationships between wives and husbands.[34]

VARIETIES OF COMMUNITY

What might 'attention to community' mean in constitutional adjudication? This question requires careful analysis, so that we are not drawn to oversimplifications that can spoil the discussion of this general subject.

The communities to be considered potentially involve both collective political units and subcommunities within those units. Some disputes may involve whether local political units are to be given substantial authority with respect to a larger political unit. For example, will a local government be able to ban books from its public libraries if that is what *its* citizens want to do?[35] I shall not concentrate on such divisions of government authority but rather on subcommunities, such as churches or minority ethnic groups, that are not themselves political units.

Is any judicial approach that favors the government communitarian? Put more specifically, is the Supreme Court's recent drift toward acceptance of choices of the legislature and executive a reflection of one kind of communitarianism? Stephen Macedo has written, "Contemporary constitutional argument provides an example of a version of communitarianism that has succeeded in gaining a share of political power."[36] Judicial acceptance of legislative choice *may* represent one kind of communitarianism, but it need not. What I count as a communitarian political philosophy is one that (descriptively) emphasizes the threads of community in human life and (normatively) attaches great value to the ties of community. Suppose a Supreme Court Justice believes strongly that the values of the national community should be preserved *and* that what Congress says best reflects those values. His accession to Congressional legislation would reflect a conservative communitarianism. Suppose, on the other hand, a Justice thinks that in a liberal democracy dominant power is assigned to legislative choice, and, further, that judges are ill equipped to say what is good or right for the community or individuals. Such a Justice would also defer to legislative choice, but for reasons independent of any communitarian political philosophy.

How are we to tell whether judicial accession to the political branches is communitarian or not? One way is to read the opinion(s) of those in the majority. Another way is to trace the philosophies of the Justices over time as expressed in their opinions and off the bench. Without performing those exercises here, I shall report my sense that the main impetus during the last two decades behind acceptance of legislative and executive choice has *not* been a thoughtful (or even incipient) communitarianism, but rather other reasons of political and legal philosophy for judicial deference.[37] What I call statism is the acceptance of measures of government that impinge on plausible claims of individual and group rights. We need to recognize that statism *can* reflect a form of communitarianism, or partake of elements of communitarianism, but it may be otherwise grounded.

My next question is: What counts as a community, beyond organized political units? Perhaps the most obvious examples are cultural or religious communities that supply a strong sense of self-identification to members. Thus, we can speak of the Amish as a small community or set of communities, and of the Palestinians as a community within the state of Israel. The former Yugoslavia contained a number of ethnic communities (identified partly in terms of religious differences) whose membership correlated imperfectly with political subdivisions. I have chosen here mainly to employ a wide sense of community that includes families, professional associations, and gender. For some purposes, this usage may be indefensibly broad. Much more might be said about what appropriately is considered to constitute a community for various purposes; but what counts in constitutional law is whether groups have the kinds of characteristics that would entail their receiving the consideration that should be afforded to what is undeniably a community. My fundamental claim is that many of the factors that are relevant to obvious communities also come into play for groups whose title as community is more debatable. So long as the reader understands that I am employing the term in this roughly functional way, this broad sense of "community" is justified for this context. When it becomes critical *whether* an association or source of identity constitutes a community in some narrower sense, I will address that problem explicitly.

A different, more complex, question about how a community is defined relates to the practical question of how respect for a particular community is to be shown. One may think of ordinary practices, or overarching values, or modes of self-government as crucial for a particular community. One may accept a community pretty much as is, or conceive of the essential community as purified of unacceptable elements of dominance. One may emphasize the character of a community at a historical moment or see it as a structure capable of substantial change over time (as the French-Canadians shifted from being a dominantly religious to a dominantly secular culture within a few decades).[38] A conservative communitarian approach tends to understand the community as it is presently constituted.[39] Both feminists and civic republicans tend to see the community, or at least the community that should guide decision, as more ideal in comparison with present attitudes and relations. Civic republicans have a model of community that is purged of unjust dominance and concerns itself with basic values; a Justice aiming to decide in accord with civic republican ideas would be much more than a passive reflector of prevailing sentiments and practices. Similarly, a self-consciously feminist Justice would strive for a community in which women were respected and treated equally, something that has not yet been achieved.

A substantial amount of communitarian writing either supposes that relevant cultural communities now have some coherent agreement among values, or that such agreement is attainable under improved conditions. William Galston has pointed out, "Theorists who seek to situate philosophy within specific social or discursive communities frequently talk as though such communities are spheres within which coherent agreement prevails, and as though the only significant differences of belief lie across community boundaries. . . . But closer inspection always reveals tensions among beliefs held within communities."[40] Given a moderate amount of liberty and modern communication across political boundaries, we have no reason to suppose that this condition will change.

Is emphasis on community in opposition to a liberal point of view? As I have said, advocates of community often speak as if this is true. Galston puts it this way: "Liberalism is said to undermine community, to restrict unduly opportunities for democratic participation, to create inegalitarian hierarchy, and to reinforce egoistic social conflict at the expense of the common good. Community, democracy, equality, virtue—these constitute the mantra of contemporary antiliberalism."[41] According to Macedo, communitarians charge "that liberal political theory is too abstract and universalistic to capture the distinctive traditions and common understandings of particular polities."[42] Kymlicka says that communitarians claim that liberalism is inadequate because it "ignores our embeddedness in communal practices; ignores the necessity for social confirmation of our individual judgements; and . . . pretends to have an impossible universality or objectivity."[43]

On closer examination, liberal political theories can admit a great importance for community, although they are opposed to many versions of communitarian theory. Any plausible liberal theory must acknowledge that the identity of people is embedded in communal practice and that, at least to some degree (and at some stages of life), people need social confirmation of their judgments. Communities matter—a great deal. Although liberals are often criticized for having an artificial idea of free choice, Isaiah Berlin, an undoubted liberal, has said that human beings choose as they do because they are determined by fundamental moral categories and concepts that are a part of their being.[44] What liberalism is opposed to is the idea that any cultural elements are so fully settled they are beyond criticism. As Kymlicka says, "What is central to the liberal view is not that we can *perceive* a self prior to its ends, but that we understand our selves to be prior to our ends, *in the sense that no end or goal is exempt from possible re-examination.*"[45] For the liberal, Macedo writes, autonomy involves "the capacity critically to assess and even actively shape not simply one's actions, but one's character itself, the source of our actions."[46] Kymlicka concludes that "[l]iberal individualism is . . . an insistence on respect for each individual's capacity to understand and evaluate her own actions, to make judgements about the value of the communal and cultural circumstances she finds herself in."[47] Liberalism is, thus, committed to a perspective on autonomy that differs from any communitarianism that sees individuals as fully constituted by existing community practices.[48] Neither feminism nor modern civic republicanism is communitarian in this way.

One important version of liberalism is opposed in a fundamental respect to communitarian theories. Some liberal theorists argue that the state should be neutral between competing conceptions of the good. I shall not pause here to say just what such neutrality means. Obviously policies grounded on some other basis will in practice work in favor of and against realizations of various conceptions of the good. A policy of public racial integration works against a conception of the good life that one should limit one's social contacts to members of one's own race. (In this sense neutrality among religious views is also impossible; a policy of integration will disfavor religious conceptions that God demands racial segregation.) But however exactly the ideal of neutrality is understood,[49] it is opposed to any notion that the state should positively reinforce existing dominant conceptions of the good life (a conservative communitarian approach) or that it should actively promote coalescence around healthier conceptions than now prevail (a more radical, activist communitarian view).

Many communitarians who criticize the idea of liberal neutrality have not recognized that if any general approach to value questions exists in the United States, and perhaps Canada, it is some vague Christian perspective, not some secular political outlook. Some conservative theorists do explicitly embrace the idea of a Christian country; but few communitarians of the left do so.

I need to mention a very important qualification to the notion that the state should not promote controversial ideas of the good life. Advocates of liberal neutrality urge that the state may promote adherence to *basic principles of justice*, including equal respect for members of society. Such principles overlap in content with conceptions of the good life. Someone who accepts liberal neutrality may also believe that communal aspects should count in government decisions. He might think, for example, that the government should be attentive to effects on groups and should promote group equality in order to enhance people's equal prospects to realize their ideas of the good. He might take a communal approach to hate speech and obscenity and favor suppression to support equal justice.

Many liberal theorists do not accept an ideal of neutrality;[50] they assume that governments do and should make judgments about the good life. Although such judgments need to be consonant with liberal values, neutrality is not a requisite (except perhaps in the area of religion).

One way of imagining a liberal democracy is itself as a kind of community with distinctive features. (Of course, any degree of emphasis on individuals and disregard of community *could* be characterized as a kind of community, the kind of community that doesn't pay attention to community, but I mean here to assert a community in a stronger sense.) Galston talks about distinctive liberal goods, principles, purposes, and virtues.[51] A liberal citizen, for example, would be public spirited, thoughtful, self-restrained, independent, and tolerant; she might differ from the civic republican citizen in lacking any duty to participate actively in politics and in not necessarily putting the public above the private. In Macedo's view, "Liberalism embraces individuality, religious and social diversity, and commercial energy, by enshrining toleration and personal liberty as core political values."[52] Macedo emphasizes that "the success and stability of liberal politics depends on people's private beliefs and commitments becoming importantly liberalized—becoming, that is, supportive of liberal politics."[53] He says that "[t]he colouring of liberal values splashes pervasively over the vast canvass of a pluralistic liberal society";[54] "[t]he liberal virtues are at once political and personal, civic and private."[55] On this view, "Communitarian values are implicit in the idea of a pluralistic community governed properly by liberal justice."[56] If liberal democracy is understood as one kind of community, made up of something more than isolated self-determining units, legislators and judges in liberal democracies may properly take into account what the effects of practices and decisions will be on that political community, as well as on subcommunities that constitute it.

A final question concerns the way in which communities are taken into account. Kymlicka has written about decisions affecting Native Americans in Canada that the issue is not so much individuals versus the group but rather whether respect for individuals is to be in terms of their being citizens or Indians.[57] This dichotomy allows us to notice that one might make a decision focused on group life with the aim of preserving that group life (as it is, or with suitably changed conditions) *or* one might make a decision focused on helping individuals in light of their relations to a group. I do not want to make too much of this distinction, since helping individuals within the group may be the means of helping the group, and vice versa; but there is an important difference between focusing directly on individuals and focusing on the health of the group. One can concentrate on individuals while paying attention to their membership in cultural communities. As we proceed to examine community in constitutional analysis, we must remember that the inquiry is definitely not a simple one of community or individual, communitarian or liberal.

FREE SPEECH AND THE FREE EXERCISE OF RELIGION

I now turn to some specific problems involving free speech and the free exercise of religion. What difference does it make if courts, and most especially Supreme Courts, pay attention to the effects on community of proposed constitutional rights? I have chosen six issues among possible areas to discuss. Each is complex, and I settle for summary assertions, backed by a sketch of supporting arguments. I begin with a subject that has been mentioned only in passing and then turn to two new topics, before retracing the subjects of the last four chapters.

Violations of Ordinary Laws

Because the implications seem so clear to me, I first discuss circumstances when someone disobeys a law that the court has determined is not itself directed at expression or religion,[58] in order to express himself or as an exercise of religious ceremony or religious conscience. For example, a person burns a draft card to protest the Gulf War or ingests peyote as part of a religious service. For free speech cases, as I have said in earlier chapters, the Supreme Court has struck an intermediate position between holding that expression is always protected and holding that it is irrelevant to the status of an otherwise illegal act. In *United States v. O'Brien*,[59] the Court said that a draft card burner could be punished only if the government's interest was legitimate and substantial and unrelated to the suppression of free expression, and restriction of First Amendment freedoms was no greater than was essential to further that interest. The test sounds much more protective of speech than it has proved in practice. Probably courts should construe the test somewhat more favorably on behalf of liberty; but the formulation does strike a reasonable accommodation between the need to enforce general laws and liberty of expression.

As I mentioned in passing in chapter 2, the 1990 Supreme Court decision in *Employment Division v. Smith*[60] rendered a complete turnaround for the analogous issue of free exercise. Previously the Court had indicated that someone who violated an ordinary law as part of an exercise of religion could be convicted only if such convictions were justified by a compelling interest that could not be served by less restrictive means. The "compelling interest" language was understood to provide considerably *more* protection to individual liberty than the *O'Brien* test. Most notably, the Supreme Court had exempted the Amish from satisfying compulsory school requirements to send their children to school beyond the eighth grade.[61] Some state courts had held that Native Americans in religious groups were entitled to use peyote ceremonially despite general laws forbidding its use.[62]

In 1986 the Supreme Court accepted the flimsy argument that the Air Force needed to enforce its rule prohibiting officers from wearing head gear indoors against a clinical psychologist who wore a yarmulke.[63] Observers worried about the fate of free exercise rights. But that decision was cast in terms of deference to the military. The axe fell in *Smith*, a case involving religious use of drugs in ceremonies of the traditional Native American Church. The Court announced that those engaging in religious observance have no claim to exemption from ordinary criminal laws, none. Since narrow exceptions to *some* criminal laws need not threaten general enforcement or undermine wider community values, the Court's rigidity could hardly be justified on either of those bases. The Court's rule did put religious observers and others on an equal footing (in a sense); but the aim of the religion clauses was to afford some special protection to forms of religious exercise. In effect, the decision allowed members of dominant religions a happy indifference to practices of members of other faiths. The decision was statist and majoritarian in a virulent form. It was inadequate whether one focuses on individual liberty, church autonomy, or the long-term benefit of the polity.

Religious observers often feel obligated by conscience to engage in particular observances. Their need for accommodation exceeds that of people who wish to express themselves politically by violating some law. For individuals, the originally *greater* protection for religious exercise than for expression made sense; the Court's reversal was close to absurd.[64]

Most religious practices involve group activities, and these help to define the identity of serious members. Religious associations need some latitude to define their ways of life. To deny all constitutional exemptions is to disregard our country's religious pluralism. The framers of the First Amendment and state safeguards meant to afford religious groups some protection against general laws. Nothing in modern conditions warrants lesser protection. The *Smith* decision did not respect the autonomy of religious groups.

More broadly, the polity as a whole benefits if diverse religious perspectives are recognized. Of course, *Smith* simplifies criminal enforcement, and might be said to encourage the civic virtue of being law-abiding. But its crude version of equality before the law is grossly indifferent to the variations in understanding and practice that genuine diversity involves. *Smith* was not a major practical blow to our country's religious diversity, since relatively few religious groups assert claims to violate ordinary laws that would have been sustained under the old standard. But the symbolic endorsement of majoritarian statism was genuinely troubling. The central approach of *Smith* was disturbing from individualistic and from communal perspectives, from the viewpoint of liberals and most of those who reject liberalism in favor of other forms of community.

To a considerable extent, the validity of these harsh judgments is shown by overwhelming majorities of Congress adopting legislation, the Religious Freedom Restoration Act,[65] that sets the standard of review back to the pre-*Smith* situation. The act applies to state laws and practices as well as federal ones; Congress's authority to adopt such legislation derives mainly from its own power to enforce the Fourteenth Amendment.[66] Thus, the present law, a kind of legislative interpretation of constitutional requirements, has shifted the applicable standard back to one that fairly responds to the place of religion in the Constitution and in American social life.

Spending Money to Strengthen One's Voice

During the past two decades the U.S. Supreme Court has considered various limits on spending money in the political process. These limits have been devised to forestall corruption and its appearance and to provide more equal debate over candidates and issues.

The leading case was *Buckley v. Valeo*.[67] The Court reviewed a complicated Congressional plan to restrict expenditures for federal elections.

It upheld limits on what individuals and political committees could do-
nate to campaigns, but it struck down limits on personal spending by
candidates, on overall campaign expenditures, and on what others could
pay for independent messages supporting candidates.

The Court treated all these activities as aspects of political expression
that could be curtailed only upon a compelling state interest. It said that
Congress had a legitimate interest in attacking corruption and its appearance, compelling enough to support the restrictions on donations. The
other practices Congress had prohibited did not bear a sufficient connection to corruption. The Court totally rejected justifications cast in terms
of leveling the playing field. It said, "[T]he concept that government may
restrict the speech of some elements of our society in order to enhance the
relative voice of others is wholly foreign to the First Amendment. . . . The
. . . protection against governmental abridgment of free expression cannot properly be made to depend on a person's financial ability to engage
in public discussion."[68]

Two years after *Buckley v. Valeo*, the Court, with a 5–4 vote, struck
down a Massachusetts law that forbade companies to spend money to
influence votes on referenda issues not directly related to their business;[69]
but in 1990 the Court sustained a Michigan law that prohibits corporations from spending general funds to support candidates.[70] Justice
Marshall's opinion for the Court quoted earlier language that "[p]revent-
ing corruption or the appearance of corruption are the only legitimate
and compelling government interests thus far identified for restricting
campaign finances." Noting that special economic benefits are conferred
by the corporate structure, that shareholders may dissent from expressed
views, and that resources in a corporate treasury do not reflect popular
support for its political ideas, Justice Marshall concluded that corporate
expenditures supporting candidates could distort the political process.
The interest in preventing corruption was sufficient to prevent this distor-
tion. When one surveys the reasons given by the opinion, one quickly sees
they have more to do with a level playing field than fighting corruption.
At least for corporate expenditures on political candidates, the Court has
accepted an unfair playing field argument and baptized it as an anticor-
ruption argument.

With respect to political expenditure arguments, one needs to ask
whether spending money to spread one's message is a significant First
Amendment interest, whether business corporations are crucially different from individuals and other associations, and whether equality is a
legitimate and powerful objective.

An easy solution would be that spending money is different from
speaking, and that any restriction of spending should receive only minimal review from the courts. The Court has rightly rejected that approach.

If we turn briefly to religion, we can see that donating money to religious institutions and spending money to propagate one's beliefs are parts of the exercise of religion, very important parts. Furthermore, the right of churches to spend money to promote their religious beliefs is an institutional right of the churches, not reducible to rights of discrete individual members. In the religious context speaking and spending money to speak are not sharply distinct, either for individuals or religious organizations.

Is free speech different?[71] Writers who cannot find publishers sometimes pay to have their ideas published. Rights of free speech and free press surely include the right to spend money to have one's book printed and distributed. And the rights of free speech of political organizations include the right to spend money to promote ideas. The right to spend money to disseminate ideas is a significant aspect of free speech.[72]

When business corporations wish to spend on candidates and political issues, however, no right can be found in any fundamental liberty of the corporate enterprise to speak, or of its shareholders to speak through the corporation.[73] Business corporations are artificial creations of the state, which receive special privileges in order to promote commerce. Any right of theirs to speak on the wide range of political subjects depends on the public's need to be informed.

In these days of television advertising and sound bites, voters do not rationally sift out competing positions and candidates, independent of the money spent to promote them. In a lecture expressing dismay over inequality in the political process, the late Judge J. Skelly Wright noted referenda on which initial public opinion seems to have been turned around by massive corporate spending.[74] Corporate money can create an unfair imbalance in discourse. Since no individual right to speak is involved, courts should focus on the integrity of the collective political process, and the quality of political discourse; in doing so, they should uphold reasonable restraints on business corporate spending.

What of individuals and associations created to engage in expression? The government probably has no legitimate interest in restricting speech to assure equal opportunity for various religious, scientific, or historical ideas.[75] But the government does have a strong interest in reducing the domination of money in politics to ensure a more equal voice for citizens in electing candidates and making laws. So long as people, as individuals or in groups, are free to spend what they want to promote political ideas, their particular interest in spending money to support candidacies should be subject to regulation. (Of course, drawing the line between general political speech and support of candidates is by no means simple.)

Relative equality of voice in the political process should be taken as a legitimate interest, one that is itself grounded in basic ideas of free speech. Courts should be on the lookout for schemes that mainly support incumbents, but they should be more willing than the U.S. Supreme Court was in *Buckley v. Valeo* to uphold restrictions on election spending.[76] In this domain, a sensible regard for the fairness of a collective electoral process, for the way in which the political community's representatives are elected, should more strongly temper attention to the speakers' rights to express themselves by spending money. It is worth remarking that the flexibility of interpretation of Section 1 of the Charter, and the Canadian Supreme Court's disinclination to straightjacket itself with the compelling interest test would make such a result relatively easy to reach in Canada.

Organizational Speech and Funded Activities

I now want to consider a subject for which concern for speaker's liberty and for associational integrity indicates a conclusion contrary to that reached by the U.S. Supreme Court.

In 1991 the Court inquired whether controversial regulations of the Department of Health to implement federal funding for family-planning services were authorized by Congress and were constitutional.[77] According to those regulations, in a provision retracted under the Clinton Administration,[78] recipients "may not provide counseling concerning the use of abortion as a method of family planning or provide referral for abortion as a method of family planning." Whether the Department had statutory authority to issue such a regulation was highly dubious,[79] but five Justices[80] hurdled the statutory barrier with apparent ease, and reached the free speech question.

For that question, the Court assumed that a woman has a constitutional right to have an abortion, and that the government may fund alternatives to abortion without funding abortions. Of course, many people think one or the other of these principles is wrong. That is, many believe that there should be no constitutional right to abortion, and many others who believe there properly is such a right also believe there should be a constitutional right to have abortions funded like other medical procedures. But the two principles together formed the setting for the free speech question. That can fairly be put as follows: In order to see that its money is spent for family planning other than abortion, can the government bar funded projects and individual doctors from mentioning abortion, one of the patient's constitutionally protected privileges, and from recommending facilities that provide abortions even to patients who ask? The Court says "yes," all in the interest of seeing that the government's money is properly spent. If that rationale is correct, the government could prohibit doctors in funded projects from mentioning any other subjects to patients, and from responding to medical questions not related to approved methods of family planning: "By the way, I haven't seen a doctor recently but I've developed a lump in my breast, should I do something about that and can you recommend someone to see?" "I'm sorry, that's not part of what we discuss here." Of course, the regulations do not forbid such conversations; they only forbid conversations about abortions. But if the aim is really to see that time is not wasted, the government could prohibit discussion of anything other than approved family planning methods.

If, instead, the aim is taken as discouraging abortions, can government foreclose all discussion of them in this natural setting? It is as if in a project funded to teach ballet, no instructor could talk to a student about modern dance.

There are limits to how far the government can silence the speech of those it funds. It could not allow doctors to criticize socialized medicine and forbid them from praising it; in American law, this would be forbidden viewpoint discrimination. The regulations represented an impoverished view both of the profession of being a doctor, a kind of loose intermediate organization, and of the narrower association of doctor and patient. The business of doctors is the health of patients. Accepted, constitutionally protected, forms of treatment should never be beyond mention. The government can see that time is mainly spent on funded activities, but it should not be able to block out other natural conversations about health. The regulations did not respect the individual liberty of doctors or of patients (to receive information), the integrity of the doctor-patient relationship, or the appropriate authority of the medical profession to determine its responsibilities. If we view doctors as a kind of community, the regulations did not threaten that community, but they refused to acknowledge its proper range of responsibility. The community of doctor and patient was more directly threatened, because the regulations undercut the assumption of patients that doctors they consult will inform them broadly about medical possibilities they might regard as needed. The Court's decision was strongly statist, wrong under either a libertarian or a sensible communitarian approach to free speech.

Flag Burning

The Supreme Court's flag burning decisions[81] represented a victory of individual rights against claims of the state and national political communities to uphold the value of an important national symbol. I want first to ask whether any narrower communities are involved. One might conceive of political dissenters who wish to express their outrage by burning the flag as a kind of community, but this would be to embrace too artificial an idea of community. The wish to burn flags is too fleeting and narrow a characteristic to constitute a basis for community, and no community of which I am aware has flag burning as a fundamental mode of self-expression. Of course, groups otherwise constituted might themselves decide occasionally to burn flags together (as happened in Johnson's case), but restricting one particular act that a group wants to perform is hardly to strike at the community the group may constitute. Do those who are distressed by flag burning constitute a community? If distress was randomly distributed over the population, the answer would be "no." They would constitute a community no more than do those who wish to burn flags. However, some groups may feel offense at flag burning especially strongly, those who have served under the flag and lost loved ones in battle. Probably the latter have too little in common to count as a relevant community, but veterans groups (and perhaps veterans in general) do make up a loose community not unlike the professional community of doctors. That community *may* be specially hurt by flag burning. Flag burning, however, is rarely directed specifically at veterans; and any special interest of veterans in not having flags burned should have little constitutional weight.

What does count, then, is the concern of the overall political community in the power of its most important symbol, against the liberty of individuals to express themselves and the value for the community as a whole of a vigorous political principle of free speech. The majority in *Johnson* and *Eichman* comfortably supposed that finding protection for flag burners will reinforce free speech without undermining loyalty to the flag. Although I agreed with the results, attention to the values of community would have required more careful evaluation of the places of symbols in political life and the effect of actions contemptuous of major symbols.[82] For a civic republican or other communitarian Justice, the decisions would have been more difficult than for Justices committed to political liberalism, which assigns such a high value to diversity of life and expression.

Abusive Speech

I turn now to abusive speech, covering the topics of chapters 4 and 5. I first add some thoughts about the law's general approach to hate speech, by which I mean extremely harsh personal insults or epithets, or highly denigrating comments, directed against someone's race, religion, ethnic origin, gender, or sexual preference.[83]

Nearly forty years ago, as chapter 4 recounts, the Supreme Court, in *Beauharnais v. Illinois*,[84] sustained a state law that forbade publications portraying "depravity, . . . or lack of virtue of a class of citizens [in a way that exposes them] to contempt, derision, or obloquy." What the Court has done since then, however, and most explicitly and recently in its decision in *R.A.V.*,[85] is to indicate that no statute explicitly forbidding racial and religious vilification would survive today. The Court has often declared that people may express themselves with intense emotion in ways others find crude and offensive. More generally, the Court's primary guiding principle that the law cannot discriminate on the basis of content apparently bars legislation against hate speech directed at categories of race, religion, gender, etc. Rules that explicitly forbid hate speech do punish speech on the basis of content. Speech approving equality is allowed, so, too, is speech attacking a person as stupid or clumsy; speech pungently asserting group inferiority is not allowed. The Court indicates in *R.A.V.* that such distinctions based on content may not be made by legislatures or judges, with the qualification that a content distinction might conceivably be upheld as required to accomplish a compelling interest.

These American cases and doctrines focus mainly on a speaker's liberty, and on the dangers of abuse once government regulates content. Most English-speaking and European countries have laws against racial vilification, and some widely adopted international treaties require them. Under the Convention on the Elimination of Racial Discrimination, which was signed but not ratified by the United States, parties are to make criminal "all dissemination of ideas based on racial superiority or hatred" and "incitement to racial discrimination."[86] This principle reaches well beyond face-to-face vilification, and covers the expression of obnoxious ideas. The constitutional liberty our Court has suggested for hate speech is much broader than the speech treated as free in many other democracies.

When we think about possible regulation of hate speech, the arguments about individuals and communities do not line up neatly on opposite sides. Against regulation, we have the primary argument that individuals should be free to say what they feel like saying, but we also have arguments that regulation will discourage some speech valuable for society, will lead to undesirable regulation in other spheres, and will actually curb the groups that are struggling for equality. In Great Britain, for example, a high percentage of prosecutions has been brought against members of minority groups. General curbs on hate speech may end up inhibiting the political activity of disadvantaged groups, who are particularly likely to use inflated rhetoric and to be the target of police animosity. Supporting regulation are communal arguments that hate speech damages the aspirations of victimized groups, promotes conflict, and has destructive effects on the society as a whole. A victim's claim to have severe emotional injury redressed in one sense is individualist, similar to the individualist claim of someone who has been libelled or slandered to receive compensation. But the claims for individual victims take on a communal coloring, because their group membership is an aspect of the injury and intensifies its magnitude. If courts paid more attention to communal aspects of hate speech, the arguments in favor of regulation would probably appear stronger than they have in modern American decisions.

We have strong evidence for this in the Canadian Supreme Court's decision of *Keegstra*.[87] Section 1 of the Charter explicitly provides for such exceptions to liberty of speech, and other liberties, as "can be demonstrably justified in a free and democratic society." Other parts of the Charter show attention to the common good. Moreover, Canadian traditions are less individualistic, more communal, than the United States heritage. Perhaps it should not be surprising, therefore, that the *Keegstra* Court emphasizes the significance of group membership, and the damage that may be caused by hate speech directed at disadvantaged groups. The Court also gives much more weight to the quality of discussion within the entire political community than has the U.S. Supreme Court.

I have thus far spoken loosely about the entire political society as one kind of community. It is time now to attend to narrower conceptions of community that may be important for how hate speech is treated. Burt Neuborne has proposed a distinction between close-knit true communities—in which "participants manifest a shared set of values, a strong sense of mutual regard and a collective commitment to the whole and to each other"[88]—and "common enterprises"—"looser groupings, designed primarily to enhance the individual interests of participants."[89] Highly skeptical that coercion can create a true community, Professor Neuborne urges that the political society should be viewed as a common enterprise; he proposes an "idealized pluralist approach to community" that he contrasts to communitarian views such as civic republicanism.

What is the "pay-off" of this distinction for hate speech? *If* one regards the political society (as it is constituted or should be constituted) as a genuine community of shared values, one may feel comfortable about restricting categorical hate speech, which typically rejects (at least implicitly) the core values of equality and respect for all citizens. The question of suppression becomes more difficult if one thinks of the political society more nearly as a common enterprise that does not attempt to impose shared values. Even from that viewpoint, equal opportunity for citizens is an important principle. Speakers who successfully interfere directly with equal opportunity by intimidating members of minorities from exercising rights to vote or work may appropriately be punished, as Neuborne recognizes.[90] Although he argues that hate speech that takes a more indirect path to discourage its victims should be left free,[91] others might believe that even such speech can be restricted in the interests of equality.

The Canadian Supreme Court's disposition in *Keegstra* may be understood in different ways. The Court's refusal to adopt a principle against content distinctions might be seen as a rejection of any notion that government must be neutral about what are a good life and healthy ideas. But *Keegstra* might be viewed, more modestly, as trying to assure that members of different groups have roughly equal chances to develop their lives. From this viewpoint, hate speech can be restricted in the interests of political justice, even if the political society is not a true community. In any event, the flavor of Chief Justice Dickson's opinion is much more attentive to communal relations than are *R.A.V.* and other recent American cases, and the result fits that flavor.

When we turn from general regulation of hate speech to university speech codes and workplace harassment, the topics of chapter 5, similar questions arise about individuals and communities (in the broad, political sense) and about communities (in the narrow sense) and less close-knit associations. The more one emphasizes the shared life of participants under conditions of equal respect, the stronger the arguments for restriction will appear. Whatever may be true of some small colleges and of larger universities that are grounded in particular points of view (as Brigham Young University is a Mormon institution), diverse colleges and universities are not communities in the narrow sense, because faculty and students alike are there to explore a wide range of perspectives. As suggested in chapter 5, the nature of (most) universities is to promote freedom to express views, but speech that is directed at fellow members of the institution and that is designed to hurt and demean them may interfere with equal educational opportunity, a principle that guides most modern educational institutions. The arguments in favor of liberty of speech concern not only individual freedom to speak but also the concept of an association in which freedom of thought and speech are fundamental elements. As with hate speech in general, a focus on the conditions of our social life together enriches understanding of the pros and cons of campus speech codes, but it yields no simple resolution.

What has "community" to do with workplace harassment? Chapter 5 shows that considering life within the working environment is very important. Indeed, on this issue it might be argued that courts have attended to the working environment too exclusively, neglecting possible individual rights within the workplace. In any division between "close-knit communities" and "common enterprises," workplaces fall within the latter, since shared values are not a typical requisite of working relations in liberal democracies. The primarily practical purpose of work may make public regulation more acceptable than it would be in respect to voluntary associations of most kinds. As Neuborne urges, however, the law should not force employers to make their workplaces narrow communities of shared values.[92] Regulation to assure general equality of working conditions is appropriate, but regulation to stamp out unhealthy ideas and their expression is not. As chapter 5 reveals, deciding just what speech should be treated as workplace harassment is not simple, even if one begins with a guiding general principle like this one.

Obscenity

As with abusive speech, attention to communal relations yields no simple resolution for the subject of obscenity. There is a critical feminist view that allowance of obscenity actually *reflects* prevailing community standards, which approve male domination, even though the law ostensibly forbids the sale of obscene materials. However, prohibitions on obscenity certainly indicate views about the impropriety of very crude portrayals of sex. The prohibitions, as I have said in chapter 6, are partly designed to reinforce healthy attitudes toward sex and family, and to have a positive effect on the quality of discourse. These are concerns of the larger community. The feminist challenge to obscenity also focuses on the larger community, emphasizing the importance of gender equality in the life of that community. That challenge pays close attention to the status of women as a group in society; it argues that obscenity reinforces the disadvantage that is attached to being a member of that group.[93] A prohibition of this sort does not act to *preserve* the group (women) as a coherent community or basis of identification, but it does reduce some harmful effects of being a member of the group, and seeks to reduce a source of negative identification deriving from group membership. The critical feminist approach can focus on conditions of equality, without claiming that political society should constitute a close-knit society of shared values. The conservative approach to obscenity depends more directly on shared values, at least in the domains of sex and family.

On the side of freedom is the community interest in free speech.[94] Given the undoubted material aims of most purveyors of obscenity and the attitudes of self-indulgence (shameful or not) of consumers, it is harder to find any narrower *community* that is injured by suppression, though many liberal feminists believe obscenity contributes to the sexual liberation of women. Thus, a perspective that focuses on community life is more likely to entertain suppression of obscenity than is a perspective that is individualist and distrustful of government.

By declaring obscenity to be beyond First Amendment protection, the U.S. Supreme Court has acceded to the broad claim of community interest to restrict material that meets a stringent definition of obscene, but that is not the main theory it has adopted. It has said rather that such material is not really relevant expression. The Canadian Supreme Court in *Butler* addressed both the status of a subgroup in society, women, and the value of banning obscenity for society as a whole. It apparently allows more material to be suppressed and it takes a much more explicitly communal perspective.

These analyses of First Amendment doctrines illustrate how individualist and community approaches can bear on interpretation. A thoughtful approach to the place of community for First Amendment liberty is far removed from the Court's present march toward statism. Understanding the values of communities does not warrant disregard of individualist perspectives; rather communal and individualist perspectives should temper each other in sensitive constitutional adjudication.

Chapter Eight

CONCLUSION: GENERAL LESSONS

WHAT GENERAL LESSONS can be distilled from our examination of these various areas of free speech law in the United States and Canada?

Some have to do with more or less technical aspects of constitutional decision. The U.S. Supreme Court has relied heavily on categorical rules that do not involve deference to legislatures whose statutes trigger the application of those rules. *R.A.V.* is a perfect example. According to the majority's assumption, the city of St. Paul has restricted only fighting words; and the majority does not deny that the city has chosen to restrict the kinds of fighting words most people believe do the most harm, those framed in terms of race, religion, and gender. Yet, the ordinance fails because the city has breached the categorical rule against content discrimination, and it cannot show that this breach is *necessary* to achieve a compelling interest in combatting discrimination. Canada's Supreme Court has no such rule against content discrimination. Although it has interpreted the specific Charter provision protecting free speech in a virtually absolute way, Section 1 of the Charter authorizes the Court to uphold legislation that infringes speech but in a manner that "can be demonstrably justified in a free and democratic society." Using this provision and according significant deference to the judgment of the Parliament, the Supreme Court has upheld laws that would undoubtedly violate the rule against content distinctions in the United States and would therefore be declared unconstitutional.

Even a candid judge who is deciding cases might find it difficult to say whether categorical rules dictate conclusions or follow from conclusions already reached. The outsider is harder put to determine just how important the categorical approaches are in comparison with some more flexible balancing of values. What we can confidently conclude is that in the United States categorical approaches and a general lack of deference in free speech cases *accompany* a willingness to invalidate legislative choices that is greater than that existing in Canada, where balancing approaches and considerable deference predominate under Section 1.

A second lesson applies to both countries, and extends to constitutional law more generally. Even in areas of law where most basic values and substantive protections are fairly well settled, large problems may be unresolved. The simplest way this happens is when regulation reaches a new subject matter. That is the case with workplace harassment. Until relatively recently, workplace harassment was a subject for employers, not legal regulation. As it has been brought under legal control, questions have arisen about the extent to which workplace speech is constitutionally protected. Because the phenomena does not quite fit the old categories, people can disagree radically about what the range of constitutional protection should be. Another basis for uncertainty and change is when doctrines developed for some subjects are perceived to have applications for others. Thirty years ago, even some "liberal" justices assumed laws could forbid flag burning. Yet a (divided) much more conservative court has recently held such laws invalid in light of the rule against content discrimination. A more subtle and complex mode of change involves new theories about the nature of communications and their relation to other aspects of society. Neither hate speech nor obscenity present novel legal problems, but the problems appear different because of critical theories about the effects of abusive communications on members of "oppressed" groups. If these theories take hold, doctrines and results will alter accordingly over time. Perhaps one reason why the Canadian Supreme Court has been so much more receptive to recent theories of this sort is because it is unrestrained by the baggage of much prior adjudication under the Charter that is committed to more traditional theories.

For most of the subjects I have addressed in detail, a substantial tension exists between the value of equality, which the government may promote, and the traditional idea of free speech that dictates the government should not restrict expression. This tension between equality and free speech is complicated by the further claim that unrestricted speech by some can actually inhibit the willingness to speak and the capacity to be heard of others. If we take the luxury of viewing Nazism and similar disasters as aberrations, the major political force of the twentieth century has been equality. Over the globe, people have demanded and received more equal treatment. The success of liberal democracy is, in large part, a victory for equality, and socialism and communism in various versions have been grounded upon a yet more radical vision of equality. Of course, we are a long way from enjoying genuine equality in any comprehensible form; but people in most societies are in most respects more equal than their ancestors of recent centuries.

For much of the history of free speech law, freedom of expression has been positively linked to the movement for equality. Speech by radical union leaders figured importantly in the movement for free speech in the United States near the beginning of the twentieth century; and during the 1960s, a number of Warren Court decisions on behalf of speech benefitted the Civil Rights movement, whose members very effectively engaged in marches and demonstrations. The outsiders, those speaking on behalf of the oppressed, communicated controversial messages in unconventional ways. The "establishment" tried to suppress the speech. One may think of the flag burning decisions as continuing this connection between free speech and equality for dissidents.

The relation between speech and equality is strikingly different for hate speech, campus codes, workplace harassment, and obscenity. There are, to be sure, claims that freedom from restriction does reflect equality, that freedom to say hateful things benefits oppressed groups, that obscenity promotes the sexual liberation of women. But the themes now most urgently pressed are that equality itself calls for restrictions, and that oppressors must be silenced in the pursuit of equality of speech and of equality more generally. Thus far, except in relation to workplace harassment, American courts have been relatively unreceptive to these claims. By contrast, the Canadian Supreme Court has embraced them with enthusiasm in the *Keegstra* and *Butler* cases. Predicting the course of intellectual history is a hazardous (perhaps ridiculous) endeavor; but if this emphasis on how speech undermines equality proves a long-term trend, rather than a fad, we can expect American courts to shift over time in the direction of the Canadian decisions.

A pervasive theme of this book is the difference being *saying* something with words and *doing* something with words. I have stressed the importance of the speaker's aims in deciding how particular speech should be regarded. But many of the subjects we have considered show how much speech importantly *does* something, apart from influencing actions because people are persuaded by the ideas that are communicated. Many of those who claim that speech of various kinds undermines equality emphasize what this speech *does*, and they call on the government to stop the harmful effects. I have not in this book tried to work out those theoretical issues in detail; but we can imagine a possible future in which greater attention is given to the quality of what speech does, and much more latitude is afforded to legislatures to regulate on the basis of harmful effects. Were this day to arrive, speech would enjoy much less protection from government restriction than it does now in the United States.

Typically related to claims of equality and claims about what speech does are claims about community. As we have seen, any sensible approach to free speech must consider the place of individuals in communities and the effect of speech in communities. As we have also seen, rarely does a primary focus on individuals or communities yield some easy resolution of a serious problem of free speech. Usually, various arguments about individuals and communities can be made on each side of the balance. Nevertheless, in the United States and Canada at this time, thoughtful claims about community are not usually invoked to suppress those who assert equality against a dominant hierarchy; claims about community are most frequently joined to claims of equality. The standard form is that focus on community allows us to see how speech of certain kinds produces unacceptable inequality. Thus, community is also linked to what speech *does* to others, rather than to the individual's freedom of self-expression.

These highly contested themes are relatively new in discourse about free speech in the United States and Canada. How they play out over the next decades in our two countries and in the rest of the world will have a profound impact on social and political relations in liberal democracies.

NOTES

Chapter One
Introduction

1. This analysis is much more fully developed, with citations, in Kent Greenawalt, *Speech, Crime, and the Uses of Language* 9–39 (New York: Oxford University Press, 1989); and in Kent Greenawalt, *Free Speech Justifications*, 89 Columbia Law Review 119 (1989).

2. Much of what is sketched in this section is quite complex. The positions I summarize here are explained and defended in *Speech, Crime, and the Uses of Language*, at 40–140.

3. The reasons have much less force for assertions of literal truth that the speaker knows to be false.

Chapter Two
General Principles of Free Speech Adjudication

1. Steven Shiffrin has written: "If the First Amendment is to have an organizing symbol, . . . let it be the image of the dissenter. A major purpose of the first amendment . . . is to protect the romantics—those who would break out of classical forms: the dissenters, the unorthodox, the outcasts." *The First Amendment, Democracy and Romance* 5 (Cambridge, Mass.: Harvard University Press, 1990). According to Akhil Amar, only upon adoption of the Fourteenth Amendment did constitutional protection of free speech take on this emphasis, see Comment, *The Missing Amendments*: R.A.V. v. City of St. Paul, 106 Harvard Law Review 124, 152–53 (1992).

2. However, to a degree, recklessness itself is a balancing concept, because the benefit of action is weighed against the risk of harm.

3. State constitutions typically include their own guarantee of freedom of speech; these constitutions, cast in variant language, provide the basis for invalidating many state practices that impair speech.

4. The Constitution does allow suspension of the writ of habeas corpus "when in Cases of Rebellion or Invasion the public Safety may require it," Article I, Section 9.

5. The Charter also includes freedom of conscience as a part of "freedom of conscience and religion," Section 2(a).

6. I do not, of course, claim that differences in language impel these variations; and I cannot prove that the tendencies I discern are anything but hindsight based on what the courts have in fact done.

7. See A. Wayne MacKay, *Freedom of Expression: Is It All Just Talk?*, 68 Canadian Bar Review 713, 730 (1989).

8. For a skeptical view of the practical significance of the phraseology of judicial "tests," see Shiffrin, note 1 supra, at 31–33.

9. On the never entirely settled status of the 1960 Canadian Bill of Rights, see Peter W. Hogg, *Constitutional Law of Canada* 639–47 (Toronto: Carswell 2d ed. 1985), Walter Surma Tarnopolsky, *The Canadian Bill of Rights* (Toronto: McClelland & Stewart, 2d ed. 1975).

10. Commonality of evaluation is emphasized in Robert Sedler, *The Constitutional Protection of Freedom of Religion, Expression, and Association in Canada and the United States: A Comparative Analysis*, 20 Case Western Journal of International Law 577 (1988).

11. See Cohen v. California, 403 U.S. 15, 25–26 (1971).

12. See Retail, Wholesale and Department Store Union, Local 580 v. Dolphin Delivery Ltd., [1986] 2 S.C.R. 573 (opinion of Justice McIntyre); John A. Manwaring, *Bringing the Common Law to the Bar of Justice: A Comment on the Decision in the Case of* Dolphin Delivery, Ltd., 19 Ottawa Law Review 413 (1987).

13. See New York Times Co. v. Sullivan, 376 U.S. 254 (1964).

14. New York Times Co. v. United States, 403 U.S. 713 (1971).

15. Disciplining lawyers that speak to the press remains a possibility, but even then the government must make a showing of likely harm.

16. See Nebraska Press Ass'n. v. Stuart, 427 U.S. 539 (1976).

17. Perry Education Ass'n. v. Perry Local Educators' Ass'n., 460 U.S. 37 (1983).

18. 249 U.S. 47 (1919).

19. Id. at 52.

20. Frohwerk v. United States, 249 U.S. 204, 208 (1919).

21. One of the problems was contempt of court, with the Supreme Court sharply restricting that common law offense. See Bridges v. California, 314 U.S. 252 (1941). When the Ontario Court of Appeals considered contempt of court by scandalizing the court in 1987 (R. v. Kopyto, 62 O.R. 2d 449), it reached a similar conclusion. For a more recent American case in which a majority softened the standard of *Bridges*, see Gentile v. State Bar of Nevada, 111 S.Ct. 2720 (1991).

22. 341 U.S. 494, 510 (1951).

23. Id. at 525.

24. Brandenburg v. Ohio, 395 U.S. 444, 447 (1969).

25. Hess v. Indiana, 414 U.S. 105 (1973).

26. Id. at 107.

27. Id. at 109.

28. In the context of offers of legal services, the Court has drawn a distinction that is somewhat similar. See Ohralik v. Ohio State Bar Association, 436 U.S. 447 (1978), and *In re* Primus, 436 U.S. 412 (1978).

29. State v. Robertson, 293 Or. 402, 649 P.2d 569 (1982), does have an extensive discussion of threats that neither seek nor threaten actions that are independently criminal, a common situation for blackmail or extortion and for the broader crime of criminal coercion.

30. [1951] S.C.R. 265.

31. Reference re §§ 193 and 195.1(1)(c) of the Criminal Code (Man.), [1990] 1 S.C.R. 1123; R. v. Stagnitta, [1990] 1 S.C.R. 1226; R. v. Skinner, [1990] 1 S.C.R. 1235.

32. [1990] 1 S.C.R. at 1134 (opinion of Chief Justice Dickson in Reference re Criminal Code).

33. Id. at 1205.

34. Id. at 1206.

35. Id. at 1181.

36. R. v. Keegstra, [1990] 3 S.C.R. 697, 731–33. Justice McLachlin, joined by two other justices in dissent, suggested that threats of violence do not count as expression under Section 2(b). Id. at 830–31. On the breadth of the Court's approach to freedom of expression, see Lorraine E. Weinrib, *Hate Promotion in a Free and Democratic Society*: R. v. Keegstra, 36 McGill Law Journal 1416, 1418–25 (1991).

37. These are developed in Greenawalt, *Speech, Crime, and the Uses of Language*, chaps. 3–6, 13–15.

38. It may be said that the acts of other participants are attributed to the instructor by standard criminal law doctrine, but the application of that doctrine in context must also be subject to scrutiny under Section 2(b) and Section 1.

39. What I have in mind is what Justice McLachlin alludes to in rejecting an extremely expansive approach to protected speech on government property in a recent case involving political activities in an airport, R. v. Committee for the Commonwealth of Canada, [1991] 1 S.C.R. 139, 232–33, in which she writes: "The state should not be obliged to defend in the courts its restriction of expression which does not raise the values and interests traditionally associated with the free speech guarantee. Indeed, a failure to invest s.2(b) with meaningful content reflective of those principles threatens to trivialize the Charter guarantee of free expression."

40. 391 U.S. 367 (1968).

41. Id. at 376.

42. Id. at 377.

43. See, e.g., Sherbert v. Verner, 374 U.S. 398 (1963); Wisconsin v. Yoder, 406 U.S. 205 (1972). In the latter case, the Court does not enunciate "compelling interest" language, but the case has generally been taken as standing for that approach.

44. People v. Woody, 61 Cal. 2d 716, 394 P.2d 813 (1964).

45. 494 U.S. 872 (1990).

46. Religious Freedom Restoration Act of 1993, Pub. L. No. 103–141, §2, 107 Stat. 1488 (1993) (codified at 42 U.S.C.A. §2000bb-2000bb-4 (Law Co-op. Supp. 1994)).

47. Barnes v. Glen Theatre, Inc., 111 S. Ct. 2456, 2463 (1991) (Scalia, J., concurring).

48. 393 U.S. 503 (1969).

49. 491 U.S. 397 (1989).

50. United States v. Eichman, 496 U.S. 310 (1990).

51. R. v. Keegstra, [1990] 3 S.C.R. 697.

52. Id. at 730.

53. Hague v. Committee for Industrial Organization, 307 U.S. 496 (1939).

54. Cox v. New Hampshire, 312 U.S. 569, 576 (1941).

55. See Ward v. Rock Against Racism, 491 U.S. 781, 796–802 (1989).

56. See Boos v. Barry, 485 U.S. 312 (1988).

57. See Edwards v. South Carolina, 372 U.S. 229 (1963); Gregory v. City of Chicago, 394 U.S. 111, 113–26 (1969).

58. Feiner v. New York, 340 U.S. 315 (1951).

59. Perry Ed. Ass'n. v. Perry Local Educators' Ass'n., 460 U.S. 37 (1983).

60. Police Dept. of Chicago v. Mosley, 408 U.S. 92 (1972); see Carey v. Brown, 447 U.S. 455 (1980). Perhaps these cases may be regarded as involving "place" restrictions on traditional forums, broadly understood to include public streets, that would be permissible except for the distinctions they draw.

61. United States v. Kokinda, 497 U.S. 720 (1990); see Perry Ed. Ass'n. v. Perry Local Educators' Ass'n., 460 U.S. 37 (1983).

62. See Members of the City Council v. Taxpayers for Vincent, 466 U.S. 789 (1984); Metromedia Inc. v. City of San Diego, 453 U.S. 490 (1981).

63. For example, Ward v. Rock Against Racism, 491 U.S. at 798 (1989); Clark v. Community for Creative Non-Violence, 468 U.S. 288, 298–99 (1984).

64. In *Clark*, it was argued that the act of homeless people sleeping overnight in tents in Lafayette Park and the Mall near the White House was not only "facilitative" in making it possible for homeless people to participate easily, but also itself expressive. Susan H. Williams has suggested that types of content discrimination are involved, even when the government has no purpose to discriminate on bases of content, if regulation forecloses expressive aspects of speech (in which event, she claims, no alternative is adequate) or systematically disadvantages certain content categories of speech. Williams, *Content Discrimination and the First Amendment*, 139 University of Pennsylvania Law Review 615 (1991).

65. See generally Roman Stoykewych, *Street Legal: Constitutional Protection of Public Demonstration in Canada*, 43 University of Toronto Faculty Law Review 43, 57–58 (1985).

66. RWDSU v. Dolphin Delivery Ltd., [1986] 2 S.C.R. 573 (Section 2(b) said not to apply in that case, because regulation of secondary picketing was according to common law principles).

67. [1991] 1 S.C.R. 139.

68. See, for example, the opinion of Justice L'Heureux-Dubé, id. at 201–2, citing, inter alia, Daniel A. Farber and John E. Nowak, *The Misleading Nature of Public Forum Analysis: Content and Context in First Amendment Adjudication*, 70 Virginia Law Review 1219 (1984); Richard J. Moon, *Access to Public and Private Property under Freedom of Expression*, 20 Ottawa Law Review 339 (1988).

69. Some justices believed the relevant regulation did not forbid the political activities involved and that the government policy to stop them was not "prescribed by law"; others thought the regulation did cover the activities but suffered from so much vagueness that it did not create a limit prescribed by law.

CHAPTER THREE
FLAG BURNING

1. 491 U.S. 397 (1989).

2. Id. at 400, n. 1.

3. Id. (quoting Tex. Penal Code Ann. §42.09(b) (Vernon 1974)).

4. 347 U.S. 483 (1954).

5. 410 U.S. 113 (1973).

6. M. Nimmer, *Nimmer on Freedom of Speech*, §3.06[B][1], at 3–42 (New York: Matthew Bender Co., 1984).

7. Someone might successfully claim that a statute applying to him or her was invalid on its face under the First Amendment although his or her own conduct was noncommunicative. And it remains to be seen whether even obviously communicative acts will trigger serious First Amendment scrutiny when they violate common criminal provisions, such as restrictions on speeding, parking, and drug use. According to standard First Amendment law, a claimant's success in establishing that his or her act is communicative assures application of at least the test from *United States v. O'Brien*, 391 U.S. 367 (1968), which nominally requires that the state's interest be substantial if suppression is to be upheld. For any serious crime, the state's interest is substantial and thus it does not matter whether the "level of scrutiny" is the *O'Brien* test or the very weak ordinary due process requirement that legislation have a rational basis. But imagine that someone with a sign explaining that she is breaking the law to communicate a message violates a speed limit arguably set very low to "catch out-of-towners," or violates a tenuously defensible parking limit or an unusual prohibition on use of a drug allowed elsewhere. I am skeptical that in such cases a court will or should examine seriously the strength of a state's interest in having such a law or in prosecuting those with a communicative message (along with other violators). The Court's treatment of nude dancing, discussed in chapter 6, raises but does not resolve this question.

8. Texas v. Johnson, 491 U.S. 397, 403–6 (1989) (citing Spence v. Washington, 418 U.S. 405 (1974)).

9. *Spence*, 418 U.S. at 410–11.

10. M. Nimmer, note 6 supra, §3.06[C], at 3–44.

11. 111 S. Ct. 2456 (1991).

12. *Johnson*, 491 U.S. at 432 (Rehnquist, C.J., dissenting).

13. 391 U.S. 367, 377 (1968).

14. Vincent Blasi, *Six Conservatives in Search of the First Amendment: The Revealing Case of Nude Dancing*, 33 William and Mary Law Review 611, 640 (1992).

15. However, as chapter 2 emphasizes, there are forms of regulation, such as laws against criminal solicitation, that may involve viewpoint discrimination but that may not call for exacting scrutiny. Much of the debate over hate speech and obscenity concerns the appropriateness of viewpoint discrimination in those contexts.

16. Tex. Penal Code Ann. §42.09(b) (Vernon 1974).

17. Texas v. Johnson, 491 U.S. 397, 403, n. 3 (1989).

18. Id. Footnote 3 of the opinion explains why the Court need not resolve Johnson's facial challenge to the Texas statute. The footnote is puzzling because most of the Court's analysis suggests that in the vast majority of instances covered by the statute, conviction would be unconstitutional; if that is so, the provision could not survive a challenge based on overbreadth.

19. This point was brought home to me powerfully by a paper my son Robert

wrote on Foucault and flag burning. Sheldon H. Nahmod aptly calls Johnson a "symbol-breaker." *The Sacred Flag and the First Amendment*, 66 Indiana Law Journal 511, 543 (1991).

20. 491 U.S. at 407.

21. Id. at 407–8, n. 4.

22. Tex. Penal Code Ann. §42.09(a)(2) (Vernon 1974).

23. *Johnson*, 491 U.S. at 410.

24. Id. at 412.

25. 485 U.S. 312 (1988).

26. *Johnson*, 491 U.S. at 438 (Stevens J., dissenting).

27. See id. at 412.

28. Id. at 419.

29. See 135 Cong. Rec. 15004-08 (July 18, 1989) (speech by Sen. Biden); Laurence H. Tribe, *Protect It—And Ideas*, N.Y. Times, July 3, 1989, §1, at 19, col. 1.

30. Flag Protection Act of 1989, Pub. L. No. 101–131, 103 Stat. 777 (Oct. 28, 1989) (amending 18 U.S.C. §700 (1988)).

31. *Johnson*, 491 U.S. at 411.

32. 415 U.S. 566 (1974).

33. See *Johnson*, 491 U.S. at 411, n. 6 (citing Justice Blackmun's dissent in *Smith*, 415 U.S. at 590–91).

34. *Smith*, 415 U.S. at 590 (Blackmun, J., dissenting) (quoting *Commonwealth v. Goguen*, 361 Mass. 846, 846, 279 N.E.2d 666, 667 (1972)).

35. The reservation and footnote in *Johnson* may have been inserted at Justice Blackmun's request, and undoubtedly with his acquiescence; so an observer might have assumed that he had not decided yet that his position in *Smith v. Goguen* was untenable as to flag burning.

36. *Johnson*, 491 U.S. at 429 (Rehnquist, C.J., dissenting) (citing *San Francisco Arts & Athletics, Inc. v. United States Olympic Comm.*, 483 U.S. 522 (1987)).

37. Id. at 432 (citing *Street v. New York*, 394 U.S. 576 (1969) (Fortas, J., dissenting)).

38. See *United States v. Haggerty*, 731 F. Supp. 415 (W.D. Wash. 1990); *United States v. Eichman*, 731 F. Supp. 1123 (D.D.C. 1990).

39. 496 U.S. 310 (1990).

40. George Fletcher has strongly urged that the government should be able to "protect a set of rituals designed to express our loyalty and commitment to the country" and to promote a "flag culture." George P. Fletcher, *Loyalty* 138, 140 (New York: Oxford University Press, 1993). Sheldon Nahmod, note 19 supra, expresses a contrary view.

41. Nimmer, note 6 supra, §3.06[E], at 3–63. John Ely reaches a similar conclusion in the well-known article: *Flag Desecration: A Case Study in the Roles of Categorization and Balancing in First Amendment Analysis*, 88 Harvard Law Review 1482, 1504–6 (1975).

42. Johnson, 491 U.S. at 421 (Kennedy, J., concurring).

43. Id.

44. Id.

45. Id.

46. 408 U.S. 238, 405–14 (1972) (Blackmun, J., dissenting). Finally, in 1994, Justice Blackman did adopt the position that the death penalty is unconstitutional as currently administered. Callins v. Collins, 114 S.Ct. 1127, 1128–38 (dissenting from denial of certiorari). To me, the *Furman* issue (whether the state can execute criminals) dwarfs the importance of whether disrespect for the flag is protected; but this may reflect a special insensitivity to which I shall return.

47. Johnson, 491 U.S. at 426 (Rehnquist, C.J., dissenting) (quoting 113 Cong. Rec. 16459 (daily ed. June 20, 1967) (statement of Rep. Wiggins)).

48. Id. at 429–34.

49. Id. at 431–34.

50. Id. at 435.

51. Id. at 436 (Stevens, J., dissenting).

52. Id.

53. Id. at 437.

54. Id. at 439.

55. Id. at 419.

56. 463 U.S. 783 (1983).

57. *Johnson*, 491 U.S. at 436 (Stevens, J., dissenting).

58. See also Fletcher, note 40 supra, at 125–50.

59. *Johnson*, 491 U.S. at 421 (Kennedy, J., concurring).

60. Id. at 435 (Rehnquist, C.J., dissenting).

61. Id. at 431.

62. See generally Fletcher, note 40 supra.

63. Dred Scott v. Sandford, 60 U.S. (19 How.) 393 (1856).

64. R.A.V. v. City of St. Paul, 112 S. Ct. 2538, 2544 (1992) (Court's opinion); id. at 2559–60 (White, J., concurring).

CHAPTER FOUR
INSULTS, EPITHETS, AND "HATE SPEECH"

1. This is true at least if the speaker's primary aim is not to have the comments relayed to those insulted.

2. "Would you like to step outside" may in some circumstances be clearly understood as a challenge to fight (see Michael J. Mannheimer, *The Fighting Words Doctrine*, 93 Columbia Law Review 1527, 1567, n. 227 (1993)), but it lacks the nature of insult that characterizes the words and phrases I am discussing.

3. For purposes of clarity, I am describing a sharp distinction that is clearly drawn and perceptively analyzed in Joel Feinberg, *Offense to Others* 226–32 (New York: Oxford University Press, 1985). Often the two aspects, conventional challenge and anger provocation, will be mixed in such a way that even a thoughtful speaker aware of his own state of mind might have a hard time saying which he is mainly doing.

4. It has been suggested that "fighting words" trigger an automatic reaction. See J. Nowak, R. Rotunda and J. Young, Constitutional Law, § 16.37, at 942–43 (St. Paul, Minn.: West 3d ed., 1986); Mark C. Rutzick, *Offensive Language and the Evolution of First Amendment Protection*, 9 Harvard Civil Rights–Civil Lib-

erties Law Review 1, 8 (1974). No doubt these words can trigger intense responses that reduce control, but most listeners are still able to use some judgment about their chances in a physical conflict. They are not likely to attack an abuser who is also pointing a gun at them.

5. See generally Richard Delgado, *Words That Wound: A Tort Action for Racial Insults, Epithets, and Name-Calling*, 17 Harvard Civil Rights–Civil Liberties Law Review 133 (1982); Donald Downs, *Skokie Revisited: Hate Group Speech and the First Amendment*, 60 Notre Dame Law Review 629 (1985). See also Feinberg, note 3 supra, at 30, 89–91.

6. See Andrew Altman, *Liberalism and Campus Hate Speech: A Philosophical Examination*, 103 Ethics 302, 309–10 (1993). Drawing from the work of J. L. Austin, Altman regards the use of a racial or other slur as inflicting a wrong as an aspect of its illocutionary act, not just its perlocutionary effect. Compare Rae Langton, *Speech Acts and Unspeakable Acts*, 22 Philosophy and Public Affairs 293 (1993).

7. A speaker might conceivably not carry the attitudes the words imply. For example, a woman with no prejudice against Italian-Americans who wished to hurt a particular Italian-American man who annoyed her might say "You wop," hoping that expression would wound him.

8. On this point, Downs writes, note 5 supra, at 651, "[W]hen the *primary* purpose of speech is not communication, but rather the infliction of harm, the law can no longer construe any resulting harm as a secondary result."

9. See generally Ashley Montagu, *The Anatomy of Swearing* (New York: Macmillan, 1967).

10. Thus, I am putting aside circumstances in which abusive remarks lead others to act violently against the victim of abuse.

11. Model Penal Code §250.2(1)(b) (1985).

12. Id. §250.4(2).

13. Chaplinsky v. New Hampshire, 315 U.S. 568 (1942).

14. State v. Chaplinsky, 91 N.H. 310, 313 (1941).

15. Chaplinsky v. New Hampshire, 315 U.S., at 569.

16. Id.

17. Id. at 571–72.

18. 403 U.S. 15 (1971).

19. See R.A.V. v. City of St. Paul, 112 S.Ct. 2538, 2544 (1992).

20. See, e.g., Gooding v. Wilson, 405 U.S. 518 (1972); Lewis v. City of New Orleans, 415 U.S. 130 (1974). See also Rosenfeld v. New Jersey, 408 U.S. 901 (1972).

21. Even this judgment is not uncontroversial. See Stephen W. Gard, *Fighting Words as Free Speech*, 58 Washington University Law Quarterly 531 (1980). Under existing law, the fact that *A* is responding to *B*'s abusive words would not, by itself, either justify or excuse *A*'s use of physical force against *B*. One *might* think that the use of abusive words should not be punishable because of any propensity to induce a violent response. One might believe that people should learn not to respond to such words physically. One might also believe that the present law gives too many opportunities for arbitrary enforcement against speakers who are unpopular or who annoy the police. (As Gard points out, many

cases involve prosecution for words aimed at the police.) I believe that some words evoke such powerful upset and anger that the speaker should be punishable because of the likelihood of violence.

22. Mannheimer argues for a much stricter requirement that the speaker intend to cause violence, note 2 supra, at 1565–70.

23. State v. Chaplinsky, 91 N.H. 310, 320 (1941).

24. Sometimes placing a person in a category that both speaker and listener know is literally inappropriate can be insulting. Calling a boy or man "a little girl" imputes cowardice or other "weakness."

25. To quantify crudely why it matters which group counts: if 80 percent of young men respond by fighting and only 20 percent of the much larger remaining pool of potential addressees respond in that way, and if the abusive words are addressed to young men more than the remaining pool together, then the average potential addressee (the whole pool) would not fight, but the average actual addressee would fight.

26. I am not saying the right standard is 20 percent. I use this figure only to suggest that something less than a 50 percent probability of violence should be sufficient to punish.

27. I add this fact to reduce the possibility that a defenseless black might call on the aid of other blacks who are on, or waiting for, the next bus.

28. In Gooding v. Wilson, 405 U.S. 518, 528 (1972), the Court criticized Georgia appellate decisions for applying a breach of the peace statute "to utterances where there was no likelihood the person addressed would make an immediate violent response." Similar language emphasizing violence by the person to whom, individually, a remark is addressed is at id. at 524.

29. Mari Matsuda, *Public Response to Racist Speech: Considering the Victim's Story*, 87 Michigan Law Review 2320, 2336 (1989).

30. See, e.g., Downs, note 5 supra; Delgado, note 5 supra (on civil liability).

31. Chaplinsky v. New Hampshire, 315 U.S. 568, 572 (1942) (emphasis added).

32. See State v. Harrington, 67 Or. App. 608, 680 P.2d 666 (1984).

33. I do not underestimate how difficult it may be to decide what slurs are similarly vicious.

34. Although these two words may be roughly comparable in harshness and negative force, they have, as Kingsley Browne has pointed out, rather different connotations. Browne, *Title VII as Censorship: Hostile-Environment Harassment and the First Amendment*, 52 Ohio State Law Journal 481, 536, n. 335 (1991).

An argument that hostile words by members of a "dominating group" should be punishable even if hostile words by members of a "dominated group" are not is discussed below in connection with civil recovery.

35. See generally Note, *First Amendment Limits on Tort Liability for Words Intended to Inflict Severe Emotional Distress*, 85 Columbia Law Review 1749 (1985). Jean C. Love, in *Discriminatory Speech and the Tort of Intentional Infliction of Emotional Distress*, 47 Washington and Lee Law Review 123 (1990), describes cases in which liability for hate speech has been recognized. She indicates that the Model Communicative Torts Act §6–103 (1989), which provides

liability for group epithets (but only when there is "a pattern of communication evincing a continuity of purpose"), would actually restrict existing possibilities for victims to recover.

36. See Hustler Magazine v. Falwell, 485 U.S. 46 (1988).

37. See Delgado, note 5 supra; Shawna H. Yen, *Redressing the Victim of Racist Speech After* R.A.V. v. St. Paul: *A Proposal to Permit Recovery in Tort*, 26 Columbia Journal of Law and Social Problems 589 (1993).

38. See Delgado, note 5 supra, at 180.

39. See, e.g., Matsuda, note 29, at 2357–66. Professor Matsuda actually includes as part of the definition of racist speech that it be directed against a historically oppressed group. Whatever virtue that approach may have for legal categorization, common usage, which I follow, assumes that blacks may make racist remarks about whites and that women may make sexist remarks about men. Given the heavy condemnatory tones of the words "racist" and "sexist" in our culture, it strikes me as unfair to stipulate by definition that racism and sexism are a "one-way street." The argument over what the law should do should be carried on in terms different from a one-way definition of racism.

40. The status of the group may indirectly be relevant in affecting the viciousness of epithets, as Delgado has suggested, note 5 supra.

41. 112 S. Ct. 2538 (1992).

42. Yen suggests that a tort of racist speech would not violate the principle of *R.A.V*, partly because others are able to recover for similarly abusive speech under the tort of intentional infliction of emotional distress and because among fighting words, racist speech is particularly abusive (note 37 supra).

43. *R.A.V.*, 112 S. Ct. at 2541.

44. Id. at 2559 (concurring opinion of White, J.).

45. Id. at 2560.

46. According to Justice White's concurring opinion, the First Amendment "does not apply to categories of unprotected speech, such as fighting words," but the Equal Protection Clause limits the distinctions that may be drawn. Id. at 2555.

47. Id. at 2547.

48. Id. at 2548.

49. Id. at 2571 (concurring opinion of Stevens, J.). He claims that the two kinds of signs Scalia has in mind are not responsive to each other, and points out that the expressions Scalia has chosen are probably not fighting words in any event.

50. Id. at 2545.

51. Id. at 2546. Moreover, "a particular content-based subcategory of a proscribable class of speech can be swept up incidentally within the reach of a statute directed at conduct rather than speech." Id.

52. Id. at 2549.

53. Id. at 2549.

54. See, e.g., Nimmer, *Nimmer on Freedom of Speech* 2–30 (New York: Matthew Bender Co., 1984); Rutzick, note 4 supra, at 27. For an elaborate and sophisticated account of varieties of offensiveness and the circumstances in which offensive behavior may properly be punished in a liberal society, see Feinberg, note 3 supra, at 1–96.

55. 403 U.S. 15 (1971).

56. Bethel School Dist. v. Fraser, 478 U.S. 675 (1986).

57. FCC v. Pacifica Found., 438 U.S. 726 (1978).

58. The student gave the following speech at a high school assembly in support of a candidate for student government office:

> I know a man who is firm—he's firm in his pants, he's firm in his shirt, his character is firm—but most . . . of all, his belief in you, the students of Bethel, is firm.
>
> Jeff Kuhlman is a man who takes his point and pounds it in. If necessary, he'll take an issue and nail it to the wall. He doesn't attack things in spurts—he drives hard, pushing and pushing until finally—he succeeds.
>
> Jeff is a man who will go to the very end—even the climax, for each and every one of you.
>
> So vote for Jeff for A.S.B. vice-president—he'll never come between you and the best our high school can be.

Bethel School Dist., 478 U.S. at 687 (Brennan, J., concurring).

59. See, e.g., Alexander M. Bickel, *The Morality of Consent* 72–73 (New Haven: Yale University Press, 1975).

60. See, e.g., Daniel Farber, *Civilizing Public Discourse: An Essay on Professor Bickel, Justice Harlan, and the Enduring Significance of* Cohen v. California, 1980 Duke Law Journal 283.

61. See Robert C. Post, *Racist Speech, Democracy, and the First Amendment,* 32 William and Mary Law Review 267, 273–76 (1991); Matsuda, note 29 supra; Charles R. Lawrence III, *If He Hollers Let Him Go: Regulating Racist Speech on Campus,* 1990 Duke Law Journal 431.

62. See generally E. Barendt, *Freedom of Speech* 163–65 (Oxford: Clarendon Press, 1985); Lee Bollinger, *The Tolerant Society* 38–39 (New York: Oxford University Press, 1986); Hadley Arkes, *Civility and the Restriction of Speech: Rediscovering the Defamation of Groups,* 1974 Supreme Court Review 281, 283–84; Note, *A Communitarian Defense of Group Libel Laws,* 101 Harvard Law Review 682, 689–94 (1988). In a Public Order Act of 1986, the British Parliament amended previous enactments to provide that "[a] person who uses threatening, abusive or insulting words or behavior, or displays any written material which is threatening, abusive or insulting is guilty . . . if (a) he intends thereby to stir up racial hatred, or (b) having regard to all the circumstances racial hatred is likely to be stirred up thereby." Public Order Act, 1986, ch. 64, 18. A similar standard governs publication or distribution of material, public performance or recording of plays, and radio and television broadcasts. Id. 19–22. For the Federal Republic of Germany, relevant statutes and interpretations, as well as recent legislative reform, are carefully described in Stein, *History Against Free Speech: The New German Law Against the "Auschwitz"—and Other—"Lies,"* 85 Michigan Law Review 277 (1986). Although some foreign legislation seems very broad to American eyes, Bollinger has observed that other countries are able to distinguish racist rhetoric from other speech: "It seems a significant piece of corroborating evidence that virtually every other western democracy does draw such a distinction in their law; the United States stands virtually alone in the degree to which it has decided legally to tolerate racist rhetoric." See Bollinger, supra, at 38.

63. 343 U.S. 250 (1952).

64. Id. at 251.

65. Id. at 252.

66. See generally Note, *Group Defamation: Five Guiding Factors*, 64 Texas Law Review 591 (1985).

67. *Beauharnais*, 343 U.S. at 259. The Court sustained the refusal of the Illinois courts to entertain truth as a defense, on the ground that a state might, and did, require "good motives" and "justifiable ends" as well as truth, and if these requisites could not be satisfied the court did not need to consider evidence of truth. Id. at 265–66. This aspect of the Court's opinion is unsatisfying, because the trial court did not indicate that it would consider truth if Beauharnais also made a showing of "good motives" and "justifiable ends." I assume that courts cannot reject motives and ends as unjustifiable because they disapprove of the political program that is urged.

68. See Collin v. Smith, 578 F.2d 1197 (7th Cir. 1978), cert. denied, 439 U.S. 916 (1978); see also David Richards, *Toleration and the Constitution* 191–92 (New York: Oxford University Press, 1986). After extensive litigation, the Nazis finally decided to march elsewhere.

69. Also, people are left free to express any facts or values about members of the group in less obnoxious words.

70. See, e.g., Matsuda, note 29, at 2374–78; Note, note 62 supra, at 690–91.

71. Almost no one has supposed that prohibitions on discrimination in employment, real estate transactions, and service in restaurants offend the First Amendment. The appropriateness of punishing "hate" crimes has been more controversial. The way such crimes work is the following. Someone who commits what would be a crime in any event because of racial (or other) bias is either guilty of a more serious or additional crime, or may be sentenced more severely. Some authors, most notably Susan Gellman, *Sticks and Stones Can Put You in Jail, But Can Words Increase Your Sentence? Constitutional and Policy Dilemmas of Ethnic Intimidation Laws*, 39 University of California at Los Angeles Law Review 333 (1991), and some courts have concluded that such laws violate the First Amendment, because they make one's penalty depend on one's ideas. The Supreme Court has rejected this view in Wisconsin v. Mitchell, 113 S. Ct. 2194 (1993). Since criminal penalties often depend on one's purposes in performing an act, and ordinary antidiscrimination laws are similar in this respect (one's reason for denying someone a job is crucial to whether one has violated the law), I believe the Supreme Court's disposition of this issue is correct. See generally Kent Greenawalt, *Reflections on Justifications for Defining Crimes by the Category of Victim*, 1992/1993 Annual Survey of American Law 617. See also Eric J. Grannis, *Fighting Words and Fighting Freestyle: The Constitutionality of Penalty Enhancement for Bias Crimes*, 93 Columbia Law Review 178 (1993).

72. See Mary Ellen Gale, *Reimagining the First Amendment: Racist Speech and Equal Liberty*, 65 St. John's Law Review 119, 163 (1991). See also Lawrence, note 61 supra. A variation on this approach is to emphasize the First Amendment value of equality of political participation.

73. Kenneth L. Karst, *Boundaries and Reasons: Freedom of Expression and the Subordination of Groups*, 1990 University of Illinois Law Review 95.

74. However, one might argue that the courts' acceptance of restrictions on workplace harassment, see chapter 5, infra, implicitly reflects a view that the equal protection clause of the Fourteenth Amendment allows limitations on speech that would otherwise not be justified.

75. Akhil R. Amar, Comment, *The Case of the Missing Amendments*: R.A.V. v. City of St. Paul, 106 Harvard Law Review 124, 155–60 (1992).

76. Interestingly, if a law was not even-handed and benefitted only oppressed groups, much of the basis for Karst's objections to restricting hate speech (see note 73 supra), would be removed.

77. See note 62 supra.

78. See, e.g., Note, note 62 supra.

79. *Beauharnais* is instructive as to these difficulties. The leaflet in question asserted, among other things, that if the need to prevent being "mongrelized by the negro" did not unite white people, "the rapes, robberies, knives, guns and marijuana of the negro, surely will." 343 U.S. 250, 252 (1952). The *desirability* of white people uniting is a matter of opinion; the likelihood that that will happen is a prediction of vague and uncertain future facts that cannot be punished. Exactly what "negroes" are said to be doing to bring about "mongrelization" is much too unclear to amount to a punishable assertion of facts. That leaves the statement about the "rapes, robberies," etcetera. What exactly is being claimed here: that all "negroes" engage in these bad acts, that most do, that a higher proportion of "negroes" than whites do? The first proposition is absurd and the second is probably demonstrably false, but Beauharnais might say at his trial: "Well, all I meant factually is that the percentages are a lot higher among negroes and that for this reason, the safety of neighborhoods will deteriorate if negroes move in." I do not know what was true in Chicago around 1950, but we do know that Beauharnais offered to prove truth, and that around 1993, the percentage of blacks convicted of many serious crimes is higher than the percentage of whites convicted.

80. See Delgado, note 5 supra; Downs, note 5 supra.

81. See Delgado, note 5 supra, at 151–57. For criminal liability, I am inclined to think that (unless fighting words are involved) either a purpose to initiate contact in order to humiliate or an attempt to intimidate should be constitutionally required. That is, punishment should not be allowed if during a heated conversation a person decides to wound another with such remarks (unless the remarks are of a sort that often lead to violence).

82. This particular difficulty might be met by privileging any hate speech that responds to hate speech.

83. See Whitney v. California, 274 U.S. 357, 372 (1927) (Brandeis, J., concurring). See Vincent Blasi, *The First Amendment and the Ideal of Civic Courage: The Brandeis Opinion in* Whitney v. California, 29 William and Mary Law Review 653 (1988).

84. R. v. Keegstra, [1990] 3 S.C.R. 697; R. v. Andrews, [1990] 3 S.C.R. 870; Canada (Human Rights Commission) v. Taylor, [1990] 3 S.C.R. 892.

85. R. v. Zundel, [1992] 2 S.C.R. 731.

86. [1990] 3 S.C.R. at 714.

87. In *R. v. Andrews*, note 84 supra, leaders of the Nationalist Party of Can-

ada, a white nationalist organization, were punished under the same provisions for publishing the *Nationalist Reporter*, which stated that "coloureds" were responsible for increases in violent crime, do not believe in democracy, and "harbour a hatred for white people" and that Zionists "fabricated the 'Holocaust Hoax.'"

88. Section 13(1) of the Canadian Human Rights Act.

89. Irwin Toy Ltd. v. Quebec (Attorney General), [1989] 1 S.C.R. 927.

90. *Keegstra*, [1990] 3 S.C.R. at 729 (quoting *Irwin Toy*, [1989] 1 S.C.R. at 969).

91. [1986] 1 S.C.R. 103. Lorraine E. Weinrib discusses the *Oakes* standard in *The Supreme Court of Canada and Section One of the Charter*, 10 Supreme Court Law Review 469 (1988). She compares the approaches of the majority and dissenters in *Keegstra* in *Hate Promotion in a Free and Democratic Society*: R. v. Keegstra, 36 McGill Law Journal 1416, 1425–32, 1440–48 (1991).

92. See *Keegstra*, [1990] 3 S.C.R. at 734–35.

93. Report to the Minister of Justice of the Special Committee on Hate Propaganda in Canada (Queen's Printer, 1966).

94. *Keegstra*, [1990] 3 S.C.R. at 745–49 (Dickson, C.J.).

95. Id. at 760.

96. Id. at 762.

97. Id. at 767.

98. Id. at 769.

99. Id. at 787.

100. Id. at 829–30 (McLachlin, J.).

101. Id. at 850.

102. Id. at 854.

103. Id. at 856–57.

104. Id. at 859. The majority noted that some of these actions were under other provisions, but that does not eliminate altogether the evidence they provide that authorities may reach beyond what is covered by a narrow reading of 319(2).

105. Id. at 860.

106. These are notable in the opinions of R. v. Committee for the Commonwealth of Canada, [1991] 1 S.C.R. 139. See also the two articles by Weinrib, note 91 supra.

107. [1992] 2 S.C.R. 731.

108. Id. at 778.

Chapter Five
Campus Speech Codes and Workplace Harassment

1. See Stanford University, *Fundamental Standard Interpretation: Free Expression and Discriminatory Harassment* (June 1990). Thomas Grey, the primary draftsman of the code, explains its provisions and rationale in Grey, *Civil Rights versus Civil Liberties: The Case of Discriminatory Harassment*, 8 Society, Philosophy & Politics §1 (1991). Nadine Strossen argues that the Stanford Code reaches significantly beyond fighting words, according to prevailing Supreme Court doc-

trine, in *Regulating Racist Speech on Campus: A Modest Proposal?* 1990 Duke Law Journal 484, 524–25. Columbia University's Committee for the Promotion of Mutual Understanding issued *Guidelines for Civil Speech and Conduct* in Spring, 1993, which helped define "civility" and emphasized nondisciplinary responses to "incivility," stating expressly that no disciplinary response is appropriate for any remarks that are constitutionally protected.

2. Doe v. University of Michigan, 721 F. Supp. 852, 856 (E.D. Mich. 1989).

3. I do not, however, rule out the possibility of actors doing what "they think is right" or yielding to pressure, expecting the courts to take a different view or bail them out.

4. Various matters concerning these universities that are connected to specific ideals are more complicated than the sentence in text indicates. A university *could* be related to some secular ideal, such as agrarian socialism, just as religious universities are related to religious ideals; but I am not familiar with any such universities in the United States. How far a religious university will allow discourse that challenges its religious foundation at the core is likely to be a troublesome question. For *some* religious universities, the not-to-be-challenged religious premises may be very broad, including such matters as the truth of interspecies evolution and the morality of abortion.

5. Jonathan Cole, Columbia University Convocation Address, September 4, 1991.

6. Charles R. Lawrence, *If He Hollers Let Him Go: Regulating Racist Speech on Campus*, 1990 Duke Law Journal 431, 444. See also Mari J. Matsuda, *Public Response to Racist Speech: Considering the Victim's Story*, 87 Michigan Law Review 2320 (1989).

7. Lawrence, note 6 supra, at 452.

8. A more cynical explanation for the responsiveness within universities to such arguments is that such communities are relatively fragile, that some victims of obnoxious speech are willing to disrupt peaceful academic life if their concerns remain unresolved, that administrators make concessions to keep life on an even keel. Without having studied the politics that have led to the adoption of speech codes, I suspect that this cynical explanation accounts for what has occurred to only a small degree.

9. Robert A. Sedler, *The Unconstitutionality of Campus Bans on "Racist Speech": The View from Without and Within*, 53 University of Pittsburgh Law Review 631, 637 (1992).

10. Lawrence, note 6 supra, at 439.

11. Id. at 465.

12. Id. at 446. See also Recent Cases, *First Amendment—Racist and Sexist Expression on Campus—Court Strikes Down University Limits on Hate Speech*, 103 Harvard Law Review 1397 (1990) (criticizing the court for not taking a contextual approach).

13. Robert Post, *Racist Speech, Democracy, and the First Amendment*, 32 William and Mary Law Review 267, 318–25 (1991).

14. Strossen, note 1 supra, at 484.

15. Id. at 490.

16. Id. at 498.

17. Doe v. University of Michigan, 721 F. Supp. 852, 857–58 (E.D. Mich. 1989).

18. Id. at 858.

19. Id. at 865.

20. Id. at 865–67.

21. UWM Post v. Board of Regents of the University of Wisconsin System, 774 F. Supp. 1163 (E.D. Wis. 1991).

22. See Sedler, note 9 supra.

23. Id. at 683.

24. R.A.V. v. City of St. Paul, 112 S. Ct. 2538 (1992).

25. Id. at 2561 (Blackmun, J., concurring).

26. See Henry J. Hyde and George M. Fishman, *The Collegiate Speech Protection Act of 1991: A Response to the New Intolerance in the Academy*, 37 Wayne Law Review 1469 (1991).

27. Frank Michelman, *Universities, Racist Speech and Democracy in America: An Essay for the ACLU*, 27 Harvard Civil Rights–Civil Liberties Law Review 339, 345–53 (1992).

28. Id. at 367–68.

29. Civil Rights Act of 1964, Title VII, 42 U.S.C. §2000e (1988). The Civil Rights Act of 1991, Pub. L. No. 102–166, 105 Stat. 1071 (1991), makes 42 U.S.C. §1981 (1988) also relevant to harassment at work.

30. The Equal Employment Opportunities Commission, the central enforcement agency for Title VII, has specific regulations for sexual harassment, 29 C.F.R. 1604.11 (1991), and national origin harassment, 29 C.F.R. 1606.8 (1991); but, as courts have recognized, the underlying statutory provision does not distinguish among kinds of discrimination.

31. See, e.g., Moffett v. Gene B. Glick Co., 621 F. Supp. 244 (D. Ind. 1985).

32. Fair v. Guiding Eyes for the Blind, Inc., 742 F. Supp. 151 (S.D.N.Y. 1990). The court also doubted that the comments were disturbing enough to amount to harassment, but was unwilling to resolve that definitively in a motion for summary judgment.

33. The analysis is similar even if the supervisor offers an unexpected opportunity—"I will promote you if you make love to me"—rather than threatening a harmful consequence.

34. Harris v. Forklift Systems, Inc., 114 S. Ct. 367 (1993).

35. Id. at 371. Justice Ginsburg, concurring, suggested that the "inquiry should center, dominantly, on whether the discriminatory conduct has unreasonably interfered with the plaintiff's work performance." Id. at 372. It is enough that the job be made more difficult to do. Ginsburg considered the Court's opinion to be "in harmony" with her view.

36. Ellison v. Brady, 924 F.2d 872 (9th Cir. 1991).

37. Id. at 880. Apparently a "reasonable man" standard would control if a man were the victim, although the court's worry that a "sex-blind" standard tends to be male-biased indicates that men who may be victims do not have the same need for a sex-specific standard as women who may be victims.

38. Harris v. Forklift Systems, Inc., 114 S. Ct. 367, 371 (1993).

39. See Marcy Strauss, *Sexist Speech in the Workplace*, 25 Harvard Civil Rights–Civil Liberties Law Review, 1, 6–10 (1990).

40. Kingsley R. Browne, *Title VII as Censorship: Hostile Environment Harassment and the First Amendment*, 52 Ohio State Law Journal 481, 491–98 (1991).

41. Harris v. Forklift Systems, Inc., 114 S. Ct. at 369 (1993).

42. Brown Transport Corporation v. Commonwealth of Pennsylvania, Pennsylvania Human Relations Commission, 133 Pa. Cmwlth. 545, 578 A.2d 555 (1990).

43. A related question is whether the employer is in a position to make the First Amendment argument if the employer has no interest in expression. So long as the employer is required to be the agent of government restriction, the employer can claim that the restriction is unconstitutional.

44. In Wisconsin v. Mitchell, 113 S.Ct. 2194, 2201 (1993), the Court said, "The First Amendment . . . does not prohibit the evidentiary use of speech to establish the elements of a crime or to prove motive or intent."

45. See Hall v. Gus Construction Co., 842 F.2d 1010, 1013–14 (8th Cir. 1988).

46. Id. at 1012.

47. Were some speech to be constitutionally protected against government restriction, and further, were that speech not "countable" as contributing directly to conditions of harassment, an argument would exist for not allowing the speech to be used as evidence of the significance of other behavior. The argument would be that the prejudicial effect of evidence of the speech would outweigh its probative value for ascertaining the significance of the other behavior. See Browne, note 40 supra, at 545.

48. R.A.V. v. City of St. Paul, 112 S.Ct. 2538, 2546–47 (1992).

49. 391 U.S. 367 (1968).

50. The language is analyzed in more detail by Eugene Volokh in *Freedom of Speech and Workplace Harassment*, 39 University of California at Los Angeles Law Review 1791, 1829–32 (1992).

51. 112 S. Ct. at 2557 (White, J., concurring).

52. Harris v. Forklift Systems, Inc., 114 S. Ct. 367 (1993).

53. Volokh, note 50 supra, at 1830.

54. Hustler Magazine v. Falwell, 485 U.S. 46 (1988).

55. Swank v. Smart, 898 F.2d 1247 (7th Cir. 1990). The court does not purport to settle the status of serious conversation on general topics. Although I am disturbed about the breadth of the court's language in relegating personal chit-chat to the (weaker) protection of Fourteenth Amendment liberty rather than First Amendment free speech, I have no doubt about the correctness of its conclusion that what the officer did, most notably his offering and giving of a motorcycle ride, was not constitutionally protected.

56. Givhan v. Board of Education of Western Line Cons. School Dist., 439 U.S. 410 (1979).

57. Rodney A. Smolla, *Rethinking First Amendment Assumptions About Racist and Sexist Speech*, 47 Washington and Lee Law Review 171, 186–87, 197 (1990).

58. In id., Smolla shifts from discussion of "statements of transaction" to "transactional settings" and "transactional relationships," but he does not indicate any fully developed position for how statements that are not "of transaction" but arise in "transactional settings" should be treated.

59. Strauss, note 39 supra, at 14–15. See also Robinson v. Jacksonville Shipyards, Inc., 760 F. Supp. 1486, 1535 (M.D. Fla. 1991). Neither Professor Strauss nor Judge Melton appear to accept the limitations I outline.

60. This argument, or something very close to it, was illuminated by a conversation with my colleague, Mark Barenberg.

61. The Supreme Court has allowed regulation of the location of "adult" movie theaters whose presentations fall short of being obscene, largely on the assumption that certain negative activities, such as prostitution and other crimes, are connected to the presence of such theaters. Young v. American Mini Theatres, Inc., 427 U.S. 50 (1976); City of Renton v. Playtime Theatres, Inc., 475 U.S. 41 (1986).

62. 397 U.S. 728 (1970).

63. 438 U.S. 726 (1978).

64. 487 U.S. 474 (1988).

65. 397 U.S. at 738.

66. In *Rowan*, 397 U.S. 728 (1970) a content distinction was also involved. Householders could stop only sexually explicit mail from being sent to them. The Court's opinion, written before the principle of "no content distinctions" had become so central, did not deal seriously with this aspect.

67. Cohen v. California, 403 U.S. 15 (1971). See the text accompanying notes 55 and 56, supra, on the status of personal chit-chat. See also Browne, note 40 supra, at 540–44, arguing for First Amendment protection for workplace speech that is offensive. Here, Browne takes occasion to criticize some of what I said in the lecture from which chapter 4 is drawn. Browne reads my lecture comments as indicating that the constitutional status of epithets relating to the race of minorities is radically different from that of epithets relating to "whites" and that of personal epithets. As I have explained more fully in chapter 4, I do not believe that.

68. See, e.g., Connick v. Myers, 461 U.S. 138 (1983); Rankin v. McPherson, 483 U.S. 378 (1987).

69. This argument is even closer to that formulated by Mark Barenberg than the version mentioned in note 60 supra.

70. The problem of dramatic portrayals that lead to harmful imitative acts is perceptively analyzed from this perspective by Laura W. Brill, Note, *The First Amendment and the Power of Suggestion: Protecting "Negligent" Speakers in Cases of Imitative Harm*, 94 Columbia Law Review 984 (1994).

71. Justice Scalia's concurrence in Harris v. Forklift Systems, Inc., 114 S. Ct. 367, 371–72 (1993), noted the lack of precision in the Court's own approach, but did not mention any constitutional difficulty.

72. Compare Roberts v. United States Jaycees, 468 U.S. 609 (1984).

73. An area of law that is relevant here involves limits on employer speech connected to union elections. The Supreme Court has treated as threatening, and proscribable, predictions about likely consequences of unionization that are not

formulated as *quid pro quo* threats. For example, see N.L.R.B. v. Gissel Packing Co., 395 U.S. 575 (1969).

74. See Volokh, note 50 supra, at 1809–14.

75. See generally, Ellen Lange, Note, *Racist Speech on Campus: A Title VII Solution to a First Amendment Problem*, 64 Southern California Law Review 105 (1990).

76. I have not considered the extent to which Title IX of the Education Amendments of 1972, 20 U.S.C. §1681–1683, might be interpreted to have this effect. See generally, Note, *Students Versus Professors: Combatting Sexual Harassment Under Title IX of the Education Amendments of 1972*, 23 Connecticut Law Review 355 (1991).

Chapter Six
Obscenity

1. [1868] L.R. 3Q.B. 360.

2. Id. at 371.

3. [1992] 1 S.C.R. 452.

4. 354 U.S. 476 (1957).

5. Id. at 489.

6. Memoirs v. Massachusetts, 383 U.S. 413, 418 (1966) (opinion of Brennan, J.).

7. 413 U.S. 15, 24 (1973).

8. Jacobellis v. Ohio, 378 U.S. 184, 197 (1964) (Stewart, J., concurring).

9. Ginzburg v. United States, 383 U.S. 463, 476 (1966) (opinion of Stewart, J.).

10. See Ginsberg v. New York, 390 U.S. 629 (1968); New York v. Ferber, 458 U.S. 747 (1982).

11. See Miller v. California, 413 U.S. 15 (1973); Jenkins v. Georgia, 418 U.S. 153 (1974).

12. Mishkin v. New York, 383 U.S. 502 (1966).

13. See Stanley v. Georgia, 394 U.S. 557 (1969).

14. R.A.V. v. City of St. Paul, 112 S. Ct. 2538 (1992).

15. Frederick Schauer, *Free Speech: A Philosophical Enquiry* 181–89 (Cambridge: Cambridge University Press, 1982).

16. See, e.g., David Richards, *Free Speech and Obscenity Law: Toward a Moral Theory of the First Amendment*, 123 University of Pennsylvania Law Review 45, 81 (1974).

17. See, e.g., John Finnis, *"Reason and Passion": The Constitutional Dialectic of Free Speech and Obscenity*, 116 University of Pennsylvania Law Review 222, 232, 235–36 (1967).

18. History alone could hardly dispose of the problem since the Supreme Court has determined that other forms of speech the Framers did not intend to protect are in fact protected.

19. 413 U.S. 49 (1973).

20. Young v. American Mini Theatres, Inc., 427 U.S. 50 (1976); Renton v. Playtime Theatres, Inc., 475 U.S. 41 (1986).

21. Barnes v. Glen Theatre, Inc., 111 S. Ct. 2456 (1991).

22. Id. at 2460.

23. See id. at 2471–76 (dissenting opinion of White, J.).

24. Id. at 2473.

25. On these points, Justice Souter's opinion leaves room for argument as to exactly how his opinion should be understood.

26. 111 S. Ct. at 2463 (concurring opinion of Scalia, J.).

27. Id. at 2461.

28. 478 U.S. 186 (1986).

29. 111 S. Ct. at 2462.

30. Id. at 2463.

31. Id. at 2460.

32. See Vincent Blasi, *Six Conservatives in Search of the First Amendment: The Revealing Case of Nude Dancing*, 33 William and Mary Law Review 611, 639–44 (1992).

33. 111 S. Ct. at 2468–71.

34. Id. at 2468.

35. Id. at 2469.

36. United States Department of Justice, Attorney General's Commission on Pornography: Final Report (Washington: United States Government Printing Office, 1986).

37. Id., §5.2.1, at 326.

38. Id., §5.2.2, at 330–31.

39. See, e.g., Edward I. Donnerstein and Daniel G. Linz, "The Question of Pornography: It Is Not Sex, but Violence, that Is an Obscenity in Our Society," *Psychology Today*, Dec. 1986, at 56–59.

40. Frederick Schauer, *Causation Theory and the Causes of Sexual Violence*, 1987 American Bar Foundation Research Journal 737, 752.

41. Id. at 763.

42. Id. at 764.

43. See Patricia Gillian, "Therapeutic Uses of Obscenity," in Rajeev Dhavan and Christie Davies, eds., *Censorship and Obscenity* (Totowa, N.J.: Rowman and Littlefield, 1978). For an evaluation of many relevant studies, see Marcia Pally, *Sense and Censorship: The Vanity of the Bonfires* (New York: Americans for Constitutional Freedom, 1991).

44. Edward Donnerstein, Daniel Linz, and Steven Penrod, *The Question of Pornography: Research Findings and Policy Implications* 39 (New York: Free Press, 1987).

45. Another crime prevention argument is that the pornography industry often involves illegal coercion against women who are forced to participate in making movies etc. See, e.g., Catharine A. MacKinnon, *Feminism Unmodified* 179–83 (Cambridge, Mass.: Harvard University Press, 1987). I assume that were this coercion the primary concern, some regulation other than a prohibition of obscenity would be the best response.

46. Id. at 193.

47. See Catherine A. MacKinnon, *Only Words* 71–110 (Cambridge, Mass.: Harvard University Press, 1993).

48. The influence of obscenity is not immune to countervailing speech. Here is Nadine Strossen's summary of some relevant experimental evidence:

> Extensive and widely cited experiments by Edward Donnerstein and other researchers involved intensively exposing male college students to violent, misogynistic, sexually oriented films, depicting women as welcoming rape. Shortly after this concentrated exposure, the experimental subjects temporarily revealed attitudinal changes that made them more receptive to adverse stereotyping of women, including the "rape myth" that women really want to be raped. However, when the researchers followed the massive exposure to these violent, misogynistic films with debriefing sessions in which the college men were exposed to materials dispelling the rape myth, the net impact of their exposure to the full range of expression (both the violent, misogynistic films and the pro-feminist material) was striking—the college men had more positive, less discriminatory, and less stereotyped attitudes toward women than they had before the experiment. Moreover, the combined exposure to misogynistic and feminist materials reduced negative attitudes even more effectively than exposure to the latter alone.

Nadine Strossen, *A Feminist Critique of "The" Feminist Critique of Pornography*, 79 Virginia Law Review 1099, 1167–68 (1993) (footnotes omitted). In the controlled experimental setting, the original responses of subjects are revealed and their significance is discussed. Ordinary adult consumers of obscenity are probably less aware of how their attitudes are affected and they may be uninterested in reading literature on the subject. Thus, the controlled experiments provide a less than reliable guide to what happens to most men who consume violent sexual materials.

49. See generally MacKinnon, note 47 supra; Andrea Dworkin, *Pornography: Men Possessing Women* (New York: Dutton, 1989).

50. See MacKinnon, note 45 supra, at 172. In an article that draws upon J. L. Austin's account of illocutionary acts of speech, Rae Langton defends the idea that pornography subordinates women. Rae Langton, *Speech Acts and Unspeakable Acts*, 22 Philosophy and Public Affairs 293, 293–314 (Fall 1993).

51. MacKinnon, note 45 supra, at 156, 193. See Langton, note 50 supra, at 314–28, defending the idea that pornography silences women.

52. MacKinnon, note 45 supra, at 178, 192.

53. Strossen, note 48 supra, at 1111–12.

54. American Booksellers Ass'n. v. Hudnut, 771 F.2d 323 (7th Cir. 1985), summarily aff'd., 475 U.S. 1001 (1986) (with three justices dissenting in favor of full argument).

55. See MacKinnon, note 45 supra, at 174–79. James Lindgren, using law students to evaluate written materials against standards of obscenity or pornography, concludes that substantial disagreement exists over application of the MacKinnon-Dworkin standard, but that it proved somewhat less vague than the Supreme Court's *Miller* standard. *Defining Pornography*, 141 University of Pennsylvania Law Review 1153 (1993).

56. A summary affirmance, unlike the more usual denial of certiorari, is, in theory, a determination that the decision below is correct, but occasionally the

Supreme Court summarily affirms without carefully considering whether or not it agrees with the result.

57. Given what the Court subsequently said in *R.A.V.*, a statute might well be unconstitutional if it were *limited* to material that was obscene, but among all obscene material forbade only material that presented women in a degrading way. *R.A.V.* stands for the proposition that the government cannot engage in viewpoint discrimination, even when it deals with expression that is not otherwise protected by the First Amendment.

58. See generally Ronald Dworkin, *Women and Pornography*, The New York Review, October 21, 1993, pp. 36–42. Professor Dworkin also advances an argument that a kind of right of equality to influence our shared moral environment requires that pornography not be suppressed. This argument, as I understand it, involves a right to live one's preferred lifestyle, so long as one does not interfere with others. Thus far, and most particularly in its decision to sustain criminal prohibitions of homosexual behavior, the Supreme Court has not embraced such a view. Adoption of Professor Dworkin's approach to the First Amendment would make sense only within a context in which other aspects of constitutional law altered.

59. Regina v. Butler, [1992] 1 S.C.R. 452.

60. Id. at 471–73.

61. Id. at 474.

62. Id. at 476.

63. Id. at 477.

64. Id. at 485. Justice Sopinka's opinion is clear that material cannot be deemed obscene because it is shown to a particularly susceptible audience. The opinion is less definite about whether material could be not obscene because it is shown to a particularly "tough" audience.

65. [1992] 1 S.C.R. at 478.

66. Id. at 479.

67. Id. at 485.

68. Id. at 482.

69. Id. at 486.

70. Id. at 484.

71. Id. at 485.

72. Id.

73. Id. at 486.

74. 413 U.S. 15, 24 (1973).

75. See especially [1992] 1 S.C.R., at 505.

76. Id. at 486.

77. This raises the question whether some activities may not themselves be so degrading that *all* human participants are degraded although all are equal and there is no hint of coercion—one thinks, particularly, of human intercourse with animals.

78. That, of course, will not be the situation in injunctive proceedings, in which no jury sits, or in cases where defendants opt for a nonjury trial.

79. [1992] 1 S.C.R., at 489–90.

80. Id. at 491.

81. Id. at 492.

82. Id.

83. Id. at 493.

84. Id. at 522–25.

85. Id. at 493–94.

86. McGowan v. Maryland, 366 U.S. 420 (1961).

87. Regina v. Big M Drug Mart Ltd., [1985] 1 S.C.R. 295. This doctrine was of some importance in the *Zundel* case, discussed in chapter 4.

88. [1992] 1 S.C.R. at 494.

89. Id. at 496.

90. Id. at 497.

91. Id. at 498.

92. Id. at 500.

93. Id. at 509.

94. See Daniel O. Conkle, *Harm, Morality and Feminist Religion: Canada's New—But Not So New—Approach to Obscenity*, 10 Constitutional Commentary 105 (1993).

CHAPTER SEVEN
INDIVIDUALS AND COMMUNITIES

1. Locke did think the state could act against atheists and Roman Catholics, but his reasons were that the former could not be trusted to keep commitments and the latter were agents of a foreign power.

2. See Akhil R. Amar, *The Bill of Rights as a Constitution*, 100 Yale Law Journal 1131, 1147–52 (1991).

3. See, e.g., Mark Tushnet, *An Essay on Rights*, 62 Texas Law Review 1363 (1984).

4. Susan Moller Okin, *Justice, Gender, and the Family* 129 (New York: Basic Books, 1989). Frank Michelman has written of the "ubiquity of 'political' power . . . created and underwritten by social practice and acculturation—even or especially in so-called private spheres such as home and family life." Michelman, *Private Personal But Not Split: Radin Versus Rorty*, 63 Southern California Law Review 1783, 1786, n. 13 (1990).

5. Catharine MacKinnon, *Feminism, Marxism, Method, and the State: An Agenda for Theory*, in *Feminist Theory: A Critique of Ideology* 1, 21, Nannerl O. Keohane et al. eds., (Chicago: University of Chicago Press, 1982); see Catharine MacKinnon, *Feminism, Marxism, Method, and the State: Toward Feminist Jurisprudence*, 8 Signs: Journal of Women in Culture and Society 635 (1983).

6. Karst has said that law is a projection on a social screen of lawmakers' privately defined views of reality, and that "the chief mechanisms by which the personal becomes political lie in the deepest recesses of the psyche." Karst, *Woman's Constitution*, 1984 Duke Law Journal 447, 468, 470–71. See also id. at 460.

7. Kenneth Karst, *Boundaries and Reasons: Freedom of Expression and the Subordination of Groups*, 1990 University of Illinois Law Review 95, 116.

8. See Michelman, note 4 supra, at 1786. See also Margaret Radin, *The Pragmatist and the Feminist*, 63 Southern California Law Review 1699 (1990).

9. See Diane Polan, *Toward A Theory of Law and Patriarchy*, in David Kairys,

ed., *The Politics of Law, A Progressive Critique* 297–98 (New York: Pantheon Books, 1982).

10. See id. at 298–99.

11. In *A Skeptical Look at Contemporary Republicanism*, 41 Florida Law Review 523, 524 (1989), Terrance Sandalow has written:

Despite the importance of republicanism in the history of Western political thought, the effort to find within it resources for addressing issues of contemporary life seems a bit odd—or, to be more precise, anachronistic. Republicanism was rooted in an intellectual and social milieu vastly different from our own. It was premised upon a moral epistemology and an organic conception of society that few moderns can accept. Its expositors assumed— indeed, often insisted—that it was suited only to small, homogenous populations occupying a limited territory. Republican thought was generally anticommercial, often hierarchical, and in some versions depended upon a martial citizenry as well. Its intellectual and social presuppositions were, in brief, precisely the conditions of life and thought that separate modern and premodern times.

See also Sandalow, at 540.

12. Frank Michelman, *The Supreme Court 1985 Term—Foreword: Traces of Self-Government*, 100 Harvard Law Review 4, 18 (1986) (internal quotations omitted).

13. Id. at 22, 40.

14. Cass Sunstein, *Beyond the Republican Revival*, 97 Yale Law Journal 1539, 1544 (1988).

15. Id. at 1554.

16. Frank Michelman, *Law's Republic*, 97 Yale Law Journal 1493, 1518 (1988).

17. Michelman, note 12 supra, at 21.

18. Michelman, note 16 supra, at 1507.

19. A challenge to the central tenets of modern republicanism is made in Sandalow, note 11 supra. Worries about its relation to free speech are voiced by Martin H. Redish and Gary Lippman, *Freedom of Expression and the Civic Republican Revival in Constitutional Theory: The Ominous Implications*, 79 California Law Review 267 (1991).

20. Sunstein, note 14 supra, at 1547.

21. Sunstein, note 14 supra, at 1548. Just what amounts to autonomy once the social construction of individual identity is recognized is not easy to say. Michelman says, note 12 supra, at 26, "we are free only insofar as we are self-governing, directing our actions in accordance with law-like reasons that we adopt for ourselves, as proper to ourselves, upon conscious, critical reflection on our identities (or natures) and social situations." See generally, Jennifer Nedelsky, *Reconceiving Autonomy: Sources, Thoughts and Possibilities*, 1 Yale Journal of Law and Feminism 7 (1989).

22. See Bruce Ackerman, *We The People: Foundations* (Cambridge, Mass.: Harvard University Press, 1991).

23. Studies of modern legislative behavior are not too encouraging on this score, but one might believe present behavior can be significantly altered.

24. See Michelman, note 12 supra, at 66–76.

25. An approach such as this *might* mark the end of First Amendment rights and other constitutional rights, the political branches being allowed to work their will for the general good. But perhaps rights would not end. Courts might review the actions of other branches of government to decide if they offend principles of wise government. Actions deemed unwise enough might be said to violate constitutional rights. Even in this form, however, the collapse of the public-private distinction has very strong statist implications.

26. See Jean B. Elshtain, *Public Man, Private Woman: Women in Social and Political Thought* 246 (Princeton: Princeton University Press, 1981); Nedelsky, note 21 supra, at 13–15; Staughton Lynd, *Communal Rights*, 62 Texas Law Review 1417 (1984). I do not mean to suggest that any of these theorists would reduce rights to the status discussed in the rest of the paragraph in the text.

27. Within religious communities, structures affect private conceptions of religious truth and of self, and those private conceptions influence the development of religious government.

28. See Sunstein, note 14 supra, at 1540.

29. One may think, as did John Stuart Mill, that the progress of humankind depends on eccentricity and diversity. One may also think, as Mill apparently did, that some voyage of self-discovery ennobles individual human beings. Jennifer Nedelsky challenges an atomistic view of human nature, but places a high value on self-determination, being "governed by one's own law." Nedelsky, note 21 supra, at 9–11.

30. Sandalow, note 11 supra, at 535.

31. Robert Cover, *The Supreme Court, 1982 Term—Foreword*: Nomos *and Narrative*, 97 Harvard Law Review 4 (1983).

32. See Deborah Rhode, *Feminist Critical Theories*, 42 Stanford Law Review 616, 632–35 (1990).

33. See Sunstein, note 14 supra, at 1555.

34. Some of the family relationships that strike outsiders as most unfair may be tied directly to the religious beliefs of members. In that event, the worries about state involvement in religious affairs reach the family.

35. See Board of Education v. Pico, 457 U.S. 853 (1982).

36. Stephen Macedo, *Liberal Virtues* 163 (Oxford: Clarendon Press, 1991).

37. Of course, a careful evaluation of my sense would require attention to differences among opinions and among justices.

38. Will Kymlicka, *Liberalism, Community, and Culture* 166–68 (Oxford: Clarendon Press, 1989).

39. This approach would not necessarily lead to judicial restraint; judges might think they should protect community values from destruction by the political branches.

40. William Galston, *Liberal Purposes* 25 (Cambridge: Cambridge University Press, 1991).

41. Id. at 42.

42. Macedo, note 36 supra, at 131.

43. Kymlicka, note 38 supra, at 47. See also id. at 9.

44. In Galston, note 40 supra, at 75.

45. Kymlicka, at 52. See also his observation that earlier liberals (some influ-

enced by Hegel) paid more attention to membership in cultural communities. Id. at 207.

46. Macedo, note 36 supra, at 216. See also id. at 212, 225.

47. Kymlicka, note 38 supra, at 254.

48. Macedo, note 36 supra, at 241, 247.

49. Galston, note 40 supra, at 100, mentions neutrality of opportunity, outcome, aim, and procedure.

50. See, e.g., Galston, note 40 supra, at 100; Macedo, note 36 supra; Joseph Raz, *The Morality of Freedom* (Oxford: Clarendon Press, 1986). My own views on this are sketched in *Private Consciences and Public Reasons* (New York: Oxford University Press, forthcoming).

51. Galston, note 40 supra, at 173–77, 295, 216–24.

52. Macedo, note 36 supra, at 9.

53. Id. at 54.

54. Id. at 259.

55. Id. at 276.

56. Id. at 203.

57. Kymlicka, note 38 supra, at 150–51.

58. As earlier chapters indicate, the court initially asks if the restriction was adopted as a restraint on speech or religion. That is what the court did conclude in 1989 and 1990 when it held invalid statutes that forbade destroying flags. Once a court decides that a statute is actually aimed at expression or the exercise of religion, it will almost invariably decide that the statute is unconstitutional.

59. 391 U.S. 367 (1968). The Court artfully managed to disregard Congress's actual purpose (to suppress radical hostile expression during the Vietnam War) in adopting a statute that punished destruction of draft cards. It said that Congress's aim was to preserve draft cards in order to assure effective administration of the draft system.

60. 494 U.S. 872 (1990).

61. Wisconsin v. Yoder, 406 U.S. 205 (1972).

62. People v. Woody, 61 Cal. 2d 716, 40 Cal. Rptr. 69, 394 P.2d 813 (1964); State v. Whittingham, 19 Ariz. App. 27, 504 P.2d 950 (1964).

63. Goldman v. Weinberger, 475 U.S. 503 (1986).

64. There is an argument that the courts should not delve into religious motivation and intensity, whereas expression is typically identifiable on the "surface" of action, thus permitting more even-handed application when expression is involved. My sentence in the text reflects a belief that this is far from an adequate basis for the constitutional difference wrought by *Employment Division v. Smith*.

One may argue that religious exercises are a form of expression and that worshippers should, therefore, at least have the benefit of the *O'Brien* standard. The Court in *Smith* supposes otherwise.

65. Religious Freedom Restoration Act of 1993, Pub. L. No. 103–141, §2, 107 Stat. 1488, codified at 42 U.S.C.A. §2000bb-2000bb-4 (Law. Co-op. Supp. 1994).

66. Although I strongly believe Congress's power to enact the law has ample basis in prior constitutional decisions, there are some complex issues about that power that I disregard here.

67. 424 U.S. (1976).

68. Id. at 48–49. For radical recommendations in favor of a level playing field, see Edward B. Foley, *Equal-Dollars-Per-Voter: A Constitutional Principle of Campaign Finance*, 94 Columbia Law Review 1204 (1994), and Jamin Raskin and John Bonifaz, *The Constitutional Imperative and Practical Superiority of Democratically Financed Elections*, 94 Columbia Law Review 1160 (1994).

69. First National Bank of Boston v. Bellotti, 435 U.S. 765 (1978).

70. Austin v. Michigan Chamber of Commerce, 494 U.S. 652 (1990).

71. It might be said that "free exercise" includes matters such as acts of worship that are not speech, and that spending money to spread a religious message is an aspect of "religious exercise" that goes beyond speech.

72. However, as Vincent Blasi points out in *Free Speech and the Widening Gyre of Fund-Raising: Why Campaign Spending Limits May Not Violate the First Amendment After All*, 94 Columbia Law Review 1281, 1289 (1994), much campaign money is not spent on speech activities.

73. A kind of "equality" argument might be made that if shareholders *are given* the right to pursue most other objectives by corporate means, they should not be denied the right to engage in political speech. That argument strikes me as rather weak, since no good reason exists why shareholders should be able to pursue all objectives via the corporate form.

74. J. Skelly Wright, *Money and the Pollution of Politics: Is the First Amendment an Obstacle to Political Equality?*, 82 Columbia Law Review 609, 623–24 (1982). Among more recent indictments is Fred Wertheimer and Susan W. Mones, *Campaign Finance Return: A Key to Restoring the Health of Our Democracy*, 94 Columbia Law Review 1126 (1994).

75. Perhaps religion is special here. The government could not even spend to alter a perceived imbalance there. It might spend to alter a perceived imbalance in some other areas.

76. Cass Sunstein notes problems of unintended consequences in *Political Equality and Unintended Consequences*, 94 Columbia Law Review 1390 (1994).

77. Rust v. Sullivan, 500 U.S. 173 (1991).

78. Remarks on Signing Memorandums on Medical Research and Reproductive Health and an Exchange with Reporters, 29 Weekly Comp. Pres. Docs. 85 (Jan. 22, 1993).

79. The act of Congress said, and still says as of the summer of 1994, that none of the funds "shall be used in programs where abortion is a method of family planning." The limitations in the regulations were considerably more severe than the statutory language. This discrepancy raised the question whether the regulations were appropriate under the statute. In support of the conclusion that they were not is the Court's ordinary principle that in cases of serious doubt, statutes will be interpreted not to present substantial constitutional issues.

80. This majority included Justice Brennan's replacement, Justice Souter. This case is one that would have come out differently but for that change.

81. Texas v. Johnson, 491 U.S. 397 (1989); United States v. Eichman, 496 U.S. 310 (1990).

82. See chapter 3, supra; George Fletcher, *Loyalty* (New York: Oxford University Press, 1993).

83. Some vilification involves an especially forceful, indeed outrageous, rejection of some ideas in favor of others. If one denigrates Roman Catholics, one is usually denigrating a system of beliefs and institutional structures. Commonly, religious vilification is a crude expression of religious ideas. What is true about religion is also true about political beliefs and associations; denigrating people because they are Communists, or segregationists, or liberals, or feminists is criticizing their ideology.

Serious expression of ideas is less involved in simple racial, sexual, or ethnic vilification. People then are not being attacked for what they believe or for their voluntary associations. (In this light, anti-Semitic remarks are typically ethnic because they include people as Jewish who do not accept traditional Jewish religious ideas and institutions.) The speaker, no doubt, may be expressing something about the worth of a whole group of people; but often what is expressed is an attitude or feeling that lacks any coherent content. Usually, epithets attached to sexual or racial categories are far removed from the stream of ideas others can consider. Despite this significant difference, I believe the underlying basis for a speaker's contemptuous remarks probably has relevance only in identifying the speaker's main objective. As I explain in chapter 4, a seriously meant claim that all men or all women are liars warrants protection, whereas epithets meant to wound Catholics or Baptists do not.

84. 343 U.S. 250 (1952).

85. R.A.V. v. City of St. Paul, 112 S.Ct. 2538 (1992).

86. See Mari Matsuda, *Public Response to Racist Speech: Considering the Victim's Story*, 87 Michigan Law Review 2320, 2341 (1989).

87. R. v. Keegstra, [1990] 3 S.C.R. 697.

88. Neuborne, *Ghosts in the Attic: Idealized Pluralism, Community and Hate Speech*, 27 Harvard Civil Rights–Civil Liberties Law Review 371, 377 (1992).

89. Id. at 376.

90. Id. at 393–95.

91. Id. at 394.

92. Id. at 401.

93. Parallel to what I have said about hate speech, the egalitarian challenge to obscenity *might* be based on the need to suppress obscenity in order to assure the justice of equal opportunity. Thus a liberal *might* say that although the state should not directly resolve controversial questions about the good life, it should seek the justice of equal citizenship. In this approach, a position on the good life in favor of obscenity would be effectively rejected, *but* the justification for the rejection would be to achieve basic requisites of justice, not to advance some competing idea of the good.

94. One willing to defend male dominance might defend obscenity as contributing to that end; but that is an improper objective in our modern constitutional scheme.

INDEX

abortion: recommendation for, as speech, 142

abusive speech. *See* campus speech codes; insults and epithets; workplace harassment

Ackerman, B., 178n.22

aesthetic expression: contrast of, to obscenity, 103

Alberts v. California, 99

Altman, A., 162n.6

Amar, A., 62, 155n.1 (chap. 2), 177n.2

American Booksellers Ass'n. v. Hudnut, 175n.54

Andrews and Smith v. The Queen. See *Regina v. Andrews*

Arkes, H., 165n.62

Attorney General's Commission on Pornography. *See* Meese Commission

Austin v. Michigan Chamber of Commerce, 181n.70

Barenberg, M., 172nn. 60 and 69

Barendt, E., 165n.62

Barnes v. Glen Theatre, Inc., 30, 110, 157n.47

Beauharnais v. Illinois, 60, 144, 167n.69

Berlin, I., 135

Bethel School District v. Fraser, 165nn. 56 and 58

bias crimes. *See* hate crimes

Bickel, A., 165n.59

Bill of Rights, 11

Blackmun, H., 37

Blasi, V., 158n.14, 167n.83, 174n.32, 181n.72

Board of Education v. Pico, 179n.35

Bollinger, L., 165n.62

Boos v. Barry, 35, 157n.56

Boucher v. The King, 19

Bowers v. Hardwick, 105, 107

Brandeis, L., 64

Brandenburg v. Ohio, 18–19, 156n.24

Bridges v. California, 156n.21

Brill, L., 172n.70

Browne, K., 163n.34, 171nn. 40 and 47, 172n.67

Brown Transport Corporation v. Commonwealth of Pennsylvania, 171n.42

Brown v. Board of Education, 28, 74

Buckley v. Valeo, 139–42

Bush, G., 28, 125

Callins v. Collins, 161n.46

campaign spending: and communitarianism, 139–40; and corporations, 141–42

campus speech codes, 71; as affecting private vs. public institutions, 72–73; and congressional action, 77; similarity of, to workplace harassment regulation, 96–98

Canada (Human Rights Commission) v. Taylor, 65–70, 167n.84

Canadian Charter of Rights and Freedoms, 11, 13–14, 19–21, 25, 27, 65, 155n.5; and hate speech adjudication, 69; and obscenity, 117–22; and rationality inquiry under, 66

Canadian Criminal Code: and obscenity jurisprudence, 117–22; and *Regina v. Keegstra*, 65

Carey v. Brown, 158n.60

categories of speech (United States), 14–15, 104

Chaplinsky v. New Hampshire, 50–51, 53

City of Renton v. Playtime Theatres, Inc., 172n.61

civic courage: and insults and epithets, 64. *See also* republicanism, civic

civic republicanism. *See* republicanism, civic

Clark v. Community for Creative Nonviolence, 158nn. 63 and 64

classified materials, 16

clear and present danger test, 18–20

Cleland, J., 100

Cohen Committee, 66

Cohen v. California, 51, 59, 156n.11

Cole, J., 73

collective self-determination. *See* communitarianism

Collegiate Speech Protection Act, 77

Collin v. Smith, 166n.68

Columbia University's Committee for the

About the Author

Kent Greenawalt is University Professor at Columbia University and a member of the faculty of the School of Law. A former clerk for Supreme Court Justice John Marshall Harlan, he was Deputy Solicitor General of the United States from 1971 through 1972. He is a member of the American Academy of Arts and Sciences and the American Philosophical Society, and the author of numerous works including *Speech, Crime, and the Uses of Language* and *Religious Convictions and Political Choice*.